AMERICA
in the
GLOBAL
'90s

AMERICA
in the
GLOBAL
'90s

The Shape of the Future—
How You Can Profit from It

by Austin H. Kiplinger
& Knight A. Kiplinger

with the staff of The Kiplinger Washington Letter

KIPLINGER BOOKS, Washington, D.C.

Published by
The Kiplinger Washington Editors, Inc.
1729 H Street, NW
Washington, D.C. 20006

Library of Congress Cataloging-in-Publication Data

Kiplinger, Austin H., 1918-
   America in the global '90s.

   Includes index.
   1. Economic forecasting--United States. 2. United
States--Economic conditions--1981-   . 3. Invest-
ments--United States. I. Kiplinger, Knight A.
II. Kiplinger Washington Letter. III. Title.
HC106.8.K54 1989   330.973'001'12   89-8187
ISBN 0-938721-07-0

First printing. Printed in the United States of America.

ACKNOWLEDGEMENTS

Readers of *The Kiplinger Washington Letter* often ask us how we manage to stay ahead of so many issues–business, financial, tax, regulatory and political–week after week. Well, the Letter is short and to the point, but it takes a lot of planning, reporting, writing and rewriting. We set the course and edit each Letter, but it takes a lot of staff work, too.

The same was true of this book. It reflects the contributions of many people. Our deepest thanks go to project manager Jack Kiesner, editorial director of the *Kiplinger Letters,* who spent months coordinating staff reporting, doing legwork of his own, preparing countless memos on every subject and keeping us on track through many drafts of each chapter.

We had the support of the entire editorial staff of The Kiplinger Washington Editors, who gave us their best judgments on subjects in their areas of coverage: editorial manager William Senior and associate editors Peter Blank, Melissa Bristow, Martyn Chase, Lee Cohn, Martha Craver, Kenneth Dalecki, Todd Eastham, John Fogarty, Richard Golden, Gene Goldenberg, Steven Ivins, Gary Matthews, James Mayo, Mark Sfiligoj and Charles Snyder. The editorial staff of our *Changing Times* magazine made major contributions to several chapters, especially "Investing for the '90s."

Fact checking was done by our chief of research, Annemarie Albaugh, and by research associate Gerry Moore. Jennifer Lorenzo, copy editor of *Changing Times,* was a keen reader of the manuscript. The index was provided by Kim McClung. The task of getting the book published fell to the director of Kiplinger Books, David Harrison, *Changing Times* production manager Donald Fragale and their assistants, Dianne Olsufka and Millie Thompson.

Every author feels a debt of gratitude to fellow authors who have struggled through similar material and helped point the way to good troves of data while offering new insights into old topics. Our judgments about the future are influenced by many thinkers, some of whom we agree with and others whose dissenting conclusions have challenged us to refine our own. This long list includes authors with such widely differing views as Herman Kahn, Paul Kennedy, Thomas Sowell, Ben Wattenberg, George Gilder, James Fallows, Robert Reich, Milton Friedman, and Martin and Susan Tolchin.

We particularly want to recognize Robert Hamrin, a Washington economist and consultant, for a masterly, objective presentation and analysis of economic statistics in his book *America's New Economy: The Basic Guide* (Franklin Watts, 1988); it's an invaluable resource.

Accurate information is essential to forecasting, so we are grateful to Gregory K. Spencer, Signe I. Wetrogan, Peter Johnson, Robert Grymes, Marshall Turner, Arthur J. Norton and Martin O'Connell of the Bureau of the Census; Stephanie J. Ventura of the National Center for Health Statistics; Dr. Andrew Cherlin of Johns Hopkins University; and Dr. Roger Avery of Brown University. Also, Dr. Nestor F. Terleckyj of NPA Data Services; Kimball Brace of Election Data Services; Robert E. Warren of the Immigration and Naturalization Service; Dr. Fred C. Bergsten, Institute for International Economics; and the staffs of the Population Reference Bureau and Urban Land Institute.

Special thanks also go to Michael Baum, Dr. John Simpson, Dr. Stephen Hsu and Dr. Leslie E. Smith, all of the National Institute of Standards and Technology; Dr. Roger C. Herdman, Clyde J. Behney, Jane Sisk, Nancy Carson and Gretchen S. Kolsrud of the Office of Technology Assessment; Dr. Seymour Perry of Georgetown University School of Medicine; Dr. Diane Rekow at the University of Minnesota School of Dentistry; Graham Molitor of Public Policy Forecasting; Robert Lesemann at Resource Strategies; Walter Carter of DRI/McGraw-Hill; and Gordon Moore of Intel.

We also tip our hats to Fabian Linden and Audrey Freedman of The Conference Board; Patrick Jackman and Howard Fullerton of the Department of Labor; Dr. Erich Bloch and many specialists at the National Science Foundation; Dr. Bruce Merrifield and the Department of Commerce; and dozens of highly competent country specialists at the International Trade Administration.

Also, Dr. Marvin Kosters at the American Enterprise Institute; William C. Rolland of the National Electrical Manufacturers Association; Richard R. MacNabb at Machinery and Allied Products Institute; Dr. Jerry Jasinowski at the National Association of Manufacturers; Richard L. Breault and William T. Archey of the U.S. Chamber of Commerce; and market specialists at Ameritech, AT&T and Bell Atlantic.

We also appreciate the help of Joel Popkin of Popkin & Associates; Thomas J. Yost of Corning Glass Works; Richard H. Hartke of the Aerospace Industries Association; Dr. Jeffrey Frey at the University of Maryland; J. Tracy O'Rourke of Allen-Bradley Company; and the staffs of the AFL-CIO, Electronics Industries Association, American Electronics Association, Computer and Business Equipment Manufacturers Association, Administrative Management Society, Council on Competitiveness, Employee Benefit Research Institute, Office of Management and Budget, Central Intelligence Agency and World Future Society.

Austin H. Kiplinger
Knight A. Kiplinger

Washington, D.C.
May 1, 1989

CONTENTS

AMERICA in the GLOBAL '90s

1 Meeting the Global Challenge

World economic growth will strengthen in the 1990s.

Democracy and free markets are on the upswing.

U.S. will retain its lead in technology and world trade.

Openness to foreign capital, goods, immigrants is key.

Budget and trade deficits will continue downward.

America is a strong nation getting stronger.

The thesis of this book is clear: The 1990s will be a decade of solid economic growth, broadly shared in an increasingly interdependent world, and the U.S. will continue to be the most influential nation in technology, trade and political leadership.

America will lead because, quite simply, it is the most *international* nation and will become even more so. The U.S. is already benefiting in countless ways from its openness to the rest of the world, by welcoming immigrants, foreign competition and capital. And while most of the industrialized world seems afraid of population growth, both by natural increase and immigration, the U.S. is proudly growing—not as rapidly as in the past, but faster than its competitors.

The engine driving the world toward higher growth will be the same force that has improved the human condition since the beginning of time: technology. But in the decade ahead, the pace of technological change and productivity growth will accelerate. The United States—far from losing its lead in basic research, as some fear—will maintain its supremacy, in fields ranging from molecular biology to physics. And America will do better in transforming basic research into applied technologies and marketable products, something at which it hasn't excelled in recent years.

Weighing the odds

We arrived at these judgments and many others after more than a year of study and discussions with people all over America and in other nations—business managers, economists, educators, public officials, union leaders, financiers and others.

Many of the authorities that we and our colleagues at *The Kiplinger Washington Letter* have surveyed harbor some doubts or nagging worries about one or another American shortcoming. But our sources, when pressed for a hard final judgment, concluded that the strengths of the U.S.—though often uneven and haphazard—far outweigh the weaknesses.

What MIGHT happen to America—forces that could combine to bring down the massive giant of world affairs—can be an almost endless litany of worries. Catastrophe is always possible, whether natural disaster, war or other calamities born of bad decisions. Mishaps must always be weighed as possibilities. But in human affairs, the law of random averages applies across the board to pluses and minuses alike. Sure, there will be plenty of problems. But when the outlook is measured realistically, the probability that emerges is a rising tide of energy and ingenuity in the United States from now until the 21st century. America will be faster on its feet, in even better shape to compete than it is now.

In the chapters that follow, we will examine what is happening now, where these trends will lead, and how you can turn change to your advantage. We will carefully appraise the prospects for the coming years, the changes that are under way and what the results will be. We will identify the areas where America is doing well and where it needs major improvement. While you read, we urge you to make your own notes and observations—and challenges to our judgments—because in many ways you and your fellow Americans are going to be determining the future through your own attitudes and actions. Pessimism about the future can be a self-fulfilling prophecy, because it leads to a lower level of entrepreneurial risk-taking.

Assumptions about today

The credibility of a forecast requires a high degree of agreement on where things stand right now . . . current conditions. Those of us in the forecasting business know that a prediction that diverges too far from your perceptions of a present situation just won't be plausible—and that you won't take it seriously.

For example, if you believe that the U.S. is well down the road toward "deindustrialization," then you will have a hard time believing that America will play a major role in world manufacturing in the 21st century. If you believe that America's export strength is limited to Coca-Cola and Michael Jackson records, then you'll find it implausible that the U.S. trade deficit will continue to trend downward. If you believe that America is drowning in the "twin deficits" of budget and trade, then you might find it hard to believe that these are both manageable and in the process of correction. If you believe that American education is terrible and getting worse, you'll have a hard time believing our labor force can meet the challenge of the Global '90s. If you think American research has lost its edge, then you'll have trouble understanding why we believe U.S. technology will continue to lead the world in the decade ahead.

If you haven't guessed by now, we think all of these popular impressions—and many others we'll explore later—are erroneous. What's worse, they are dangerous. If America bases policies for the future—whether in trade, taxes or education—on faulty information about the present, there's a strong risk of prescribing the wrong medicine, making a healthy patient sick.

In 1982, during America's worst economic downturn since the Great Depression, Herman Kahn of the Hudson Institute had the temerity to bring out a very optimistic book about America's future. In the preface, he acknowledged the implausibility of his thesis: "It does not seem like a good time to publish a book called *The Coming Boom.*" But he argued that the problems of the moment, while real and certainly painful, were already abating.

"Unless my prognostications are disastrously wrong, a revitalized America—revitalized in terms of traditional values, of worldwide status and influence, and of citizenship and morale, as well as of economic improvement—seems to me very probable, and with sensible social and economic policies, a near certainty."

Kahn's economic forecasts proved uncannily correct over the following few years, but skepticism about a rejuvenated America did not abate. In 1986, we encountered similar resistance to the thesis of *The New American Boom,* our first forecast of strong, stable economic growth in the 1990s, with a surge in productivity from emerging technologies. In the minds of many people, apparently, the prosperity of the mid '80s was just a house of cards. (A best-seller the following year was Ravi Batra's *The Great Depression of 1990,* a mystical piece of historical determinism predicting a worldwide depression as severe as that of the 1930s.)

Our judgment about the coming decade has not changed since 1986. We still believe that the American economy is fundamentally sound, that it has great adaptability, and that the U.S. will continue to be the world's most influential society—technologically, economically and diplomatically—during the decade ahead.

Confidence in the future

We know that the willingness to accept this judgment varies widely among different individuals and groups in American society. We often find the greatest pessimism among people who are somewhat removed from the action—professional observers, analysts and dissectors of society, whether journalists, economics professors, Wall Street financiers or members of Congress who don't get out of Washington enough. Author George Gilder, an astute chronicler of America's role in the world economy, says those people suffer from the peculiarly American malady of "economic hypochondria." We agree. Mesmerized by theories and statistics, many of the "hypoconomists" have lost touch with the grass-roots vitality of America.

Conversely, we find the greatest confidence among the people on the firing line—the men and women who are creating America's future. Many of them have their own money on the line—or their company's money—and they're too busy to sit around wringing their hands over every problem, real or imagined. They are small-business owners, engineers, research scientists, local-government leaders, volunteers and millions of other resourceful Americans, both native-born and immigrants.

It's puzzling to us that the people of *other* nations seem to think better of the U.S. than many Americans do and that world leaders are more confident of America's future than some of our own leaders are. It must have something to do with our relentless self-criticism and self-examination, which is both a strength and a weakness. It means that we Americans are never smugly satisfied with our progress, always striving to do better, to keep moving ahead. But it also means that we often fail to savor our successes.

America as world role model

The U.S. today is still the country the rest of the world emulates—usually for better, occasionally for worse. In the years since World War II, the emulation too often focused on superficial traits of American prosperity, for example, pop culture and a craving for consumer goods. Paradoxically, there was widespread rejection of the economic and governmental systems—free markets and democracy—that make American prosperity possible. Until the 1980s, central economic planning—whether in democratic or totalitarian settings—held a strange appeal for both Europe and the developing countries of Asia, Africa and Latin America.

Now this is changing, and this shift is the single most important—and largely unappreciated—harbinger of economic progress the world has seen in the years since World War II. Many more nations are trying to emulate not just the superficial characteristics of American life, but also the models of political and economic freedom that are the essence of America. From Great Britain to the Soviet Union, from China to Mexico, and even in a few of the struggling nations of Africa, the fresh breeze of economic choice is beginning to blow. For the first time in decades, there is a broad consensus that free markets, which are characterized by private ownership, smaller public sectors and openness to foreign capital and products, simply *work better* to raise living standards than any other system.

The major agent of this change is *information*, which is flowing more rapidly around the world, through more diverse and decentralized modes of transmission than anyone ever dreamed of. Repressive governments rely on information control, and their power is rooted in the ignorance of their people. Two or three decades ago, governments could easily control information by their sole ownership of expensive radio, television and telecommunications systems, and by jamming broadcasts from the free world. Today—in a world of cheap radios and tape players, small dishes for receiving satellite TV, personal computers and modems, and videocassette players—information belongs to the people. The democratization of information is a force for freedom and growth, as the successes and failures of regimes become common knowledge throughout the world.

In helping to build, by its example, a consensus on the superiority of free markets, America is winning a global contest that is far more crucial than any military struggle. It would be a mistake for America to lose confidence in the soundness of its institutions just as the rest of the world is beginning to embrace them.

The U.S. in perspective

The American economy today is a grab bag of mixed results— things it is doing well, things that need substantial improvement. It's like a gigantic "good-news/bad-news" joke. Some of the signs of economic health are trending up, some down, and it's difficult to know which trends are short-lived, which are already reversing themselves without public notice and which will continue inexorably in the same direction. That's what makes forecasting so difficult.

Since your acceptance of our forecasts about America's future depends so much on assumptions about the present and recent past, it is worth taking some time to discuss where we are today . . . the strengths and weaknesses, the myths and realities, the false problems and genuine challenges.

One of the worst pitfalls in debates over economic performance is the failure to put big numbers into perspective. Nothing should be studied in a vacuum. The only way to get a fix on how well or badly the U.S. is doing today is by comparing its performance with some benchmarks, whether its own past performance or the current performance of other nations. If you think the budget deficit is "too big," we have to ask, "Compared with what—the deficit in 1979? 1983? Japan's today? The ideal of a surplus?" If you think American productivity growth isn't what it should be, we ask, "Compared with whose?"

The next two chapters will examine how America is doing today, as a domestic economy and as a participant in world markets. In these chapters and those that follow, you'll see a lot of comparisons with other nations. You'll see discussions of Europe's growing power, resulting from economic integration in 1992. You'll see comparisons with Japan in particular because it is the one nation that most people regard as America's most capable contender for world economic leadership in the 1990s. It certainly is that. But for many reasons we'll explain later, America is much better positioned to influence world growth and politics than Japan, whose contradictory stance toward the world is both international and insular.

2 Our Own Economy

Higher saving and investment ahead.

American standard of living will continue to rise.

U.S. productivity, highest in world, will grow faster.

Governments will curb spending and raise taxes.

The budget deficit will shrink, possibly disappear.

Inflation will average 4%, interest rates will decline.

GNP growth will average 3% a year in the '90s.

By most measures, this has been a decade of solid economic achievement for the U.S.—in total growth, industrial production, job creation, increase in personal income and the taming of runaway inflation. And the problems that have dogged the American economy in recent years—especially low growth in savings, investment and productivity, plus the budget and trade deficits—are on a path of gradual improvement. In light of this, we expect a continuation of strong growth in the coming decade, averaging about 3% a year. Annual growth will probably start a little lower than this early in the '90s, trending upward at mid decade.

Economic growth, past and present

The easiest way to measure how a nation is doing economically is to look at the trend in Gross National Product—the total value of the goods and services an economy produces in a year, adjusted for inflation. Changes in GNP don't tell you how the rewards of economic activity are distributed—how the pie is cut up—but they tell you whether the whole pie is growing or shrinking.

Let's put America's economic growth in perspective. Without knowing just how 1989 will turn out, it looks as if average annual growth in GNP for the decade of the '80s will finish out around 2.5%, with GNP closing in on $5 *trillion*—that is, 5,000 billion dollars. (The underground economy—barter, moonlighting for cash, dealing in drugs, illegal gambling and other transactions are not reported to the government and therefore are not taxed— might run another few hundred billion dollars, but no one knows for sure.)

In terms of America's recent past, average annual growth in the 1980s has been substantially lower than in the '60s and slightly less—and much less volatile—than in the inflation-wracked '70s. In the 1960s, the American economy grew at an average annual rate, adjusted for inflation, of nearly 4%. It was a decade of extraordinary prosperity, broadly shared, although the poverty rate averaged higher than today's. GNP grew steadily from 1961 through 1969, without a recession. It was the longest continuous economic expansion in American history, but it was pulled along by soaring military spending in Vietnam and social programs of the Great Society. By the end of the decade, an overheated economy sowed the seeds of inflation that would erupt in the '70s.

Economic growth slowed substantially in the America of the 1970s. Due to high inflation—caused by excessive monetary expansion and a tenfold hike in the world price of petroleum— nominal growth in GNP was robust, but after adjusting for inflation, real growth for the decade came in at an average annual rate of about 2.8%. There was a severe downturn in 1974-75. Productivity—the economy's output per hour of work—grew just 1% a year, less than half the rate of the '50s and '60s. Productivity growth was dragged down mainly by sagging capital spending and a wave of inexperienced workers—the Baby Boom generation, adult women seeking their first jobs and a high level of immigration. The two-income household became common, partly because of the rising aspirations of women and partly because of economic necessity in a time of skyrocketing living costs.

The 1980s got off to a shaky start, with a recession in 1980 characterized by "stagflation": the anomaly of negative growth at a time of 13% inflation and a prime interest rate that hit 21%. The Federal Reserve set out to wring inflation from the U.S. economy, and the result was the severe recession of 1981-82, when unemployment rose to nearly 11%, the first double-digit level since the Great Depresssion. American industry went on a drastic low-fat diet, cutting costs and restructuring to emerge leaner but stronger when the recession ended.

The Fed's bitter medicine worked, and inflation and interest rates began to wind down. Recovery from so severe a recession was bound to be vigorous, and this one was hyped by an extra stimulus, a sharp reduction of corporate and individual tax rates enacted in 1981. The economy began expanding in late '82, and the following years were marked by the longest continuous expansion of GNP since the 1960s. Productivity growth picked up a little from the 1970s but was still running less than 2% a year, with strong hikes in manufacturing productivity offset by very little growth in services.

Long, uneven GNP growth

One of the hallmarks of the long expansion of the 1980s—the longest peacetime expansion ever—has been the unevenness of the prosperity, by both region and sector. At no time in this decade has the immense engine of the American economy been firing smoothly on all cylinders. It has been a taking-turns, trading-places kind of national expansion, with a series of regional and business-sector recessions.

The petroleum industry and Oil Patch states boomed early in the decade, then took a dive when world oil prices collapsed. A rising stock market put the financial-service centers of New York, Boston and other major cities into clover. Office construction boomed, especially in Texas and along the east and west coasts, but was later cooled off by overbuilding and reduction of tax benefits. Agriculture suffered early on from sky-high debts and land prices, then gradually recovered. The trimming down of American industry, plus a falling dollar at mid decade, breathed new life into manufacturing for export. After the stock market crash in '87, it was time for financial services to take its turn at contracting, and retailing began to soften, too.

The unevenness of the expansion has probably been a key to its longevity—one sector's hardship balanced by a boom in another, keeping the national economy on a path of steady, low-inflation growth. Not once in the five years following the end of the '82 recession did *The Kiplinger Washington Letter* forecast a recession, even when growth slowed markedly in '85 and '86 and the stock market crashed in '87. Why? Because we saw room for continued growth—in availability of credit, employment, materials, factory capacity—and a trend toward progrowth government policies.

By the middle of '88, however, we began to alert our readers that the constraints on growth that you normally see after a very long expansion—rising interest rates, low unemployment, high plant utilization, shortages of raw materials, rising producer and consumer prices—were foreshadowing an end to this record-breaking expansion. Predictions of the expansion's demise have proved premature in the past, but we don't believe anyone has figured out a way to repeal the business cycle. Contractions of GNP will still occur from time to time. With smart management of monetary policy, they will be brief, mild interruptions of a long growth line.

Manufacturing: alive and well

One of the biggest misconceptions about the American economy is a widespread belief that America is "deindustrializing," that growth in service businesses has been accompanied by a shriveling of America's manufacturing. Related myths include the belief that manufacturing productivity is low in America and that service-sector employment means low-wage, dead-end jobs.

The deindustrialization myth is based on confusion between employment and output. Yes, the number of Americans working at manufacturing jobs did fall by about 1.9 million between 1979 and 1986, before turning up again during the export boom at the end of the decade. As a proportion of total American employment, manufacturing jobs fell from 27% in the mid '50s to about 16% in '86. (The drop has been even more pronounced in agriculture: In the 1920s more than 20% of the work force was in agriculture; today it's only 3%.)

But there has been an almost continuous annual rise in the value of American manufacturing. Its share of GNP has held fairly steady in the low 20% range since the '60s. The significant story is: A smaller and smaller number of manufacturing workers, armed with highly automated capital equipment, are producing more and more value. Between 1979 and 1986, for example, manufacturing employment *fell* 9% while output *rose* 13%. That's the definition of rising productivity, and it's good for America.

An underreported story of this decade has been the change in the composition of American manufactures—from low-tech to mid- and high-tech. It's true that the manufacturing of many kinds of simple products—clothing, tires, footwear, consumer electronics—has increasingly moved to other countries. But there are thousands of new kinds of American manufactures that have more than taken the place of the simpler goods we used to make in larger quantities. To get a handle on the broad definition of manufactures today, remember that computer software, an expensive mental process encoded on a cheap magnetic disc, is classified as a manufacture, and America is the unchallenged world leader in software.

The U.S. is the leader in worldwide sales of computers, research instruments, airplanes and aerospace equipment, pharmaceuticals, agricultural equipment and many other products. And there are even success stories emerging in the basic industries that some people have kissed off.

The American steel industry is coming back, closing down obsolete plants and modernizing with moves to continuous casting and other more efficient methods. Most of the minimills, which make specialized products such as rebar on a smaller scale, often from scrap, were profitable even during the severe slump in basic steel from '82 to '86. The American auto industry is regaining its health, thanks to better engineering, joint ventures with foreign makers and (early in the decade) strong government protection from Japanese imports. Another success story is the U.S. textile industry, where a high level of automation is producing fibers and cloth at very competitive prices. (It is already highly protected from imports, but its incessant plea for more barriers has been severely undermined by its soaring profits.)

Surging growth in services

No doubt about it, services ARE booming in America, and the lion's share of job growth has been in services. It's long been a law of economics that people spend proportionately less on goods and more on services as their incomes rise. America has been doing this for years, and now other countries are following its lead, as their standards of living rise. In Japan, between 1965 and 1980, employment in the service sector soared, at a rate three times FASTER than the percentage growth in service employment in America.

When you think "services," stop thinking first about low-value services like flipping hamburgers, washing cars and cutting lawns. Sure, they're services, but so are computer programming, law, financial planning, engineering, airline piloting, scientific research, health care, education, architecture and many other skilled occupations. Some service jobs ARE low paying, but some are very high paying, and the average is not much lower than for manufacturing jobs.

The myth about poor-paying service-sector jobs—the idea that the average manufacturing wage is some *multiple* of the average service wage—is based on faulty comparisons. Some people think that most manufacturing employment pays $20 or $25 per hour, like the dwindling union jobs in steel and autos that never were typical. And for service wages, they think of the minimum wage—a wage so low that even McDonald's often pays more to attract workers. Actually, the average hourly wage in manufacturing in America is about 20% more than the service-sector average—$10.00 per hour versus $8.00.

During the job-creation boom of the '80s, with services leading the way, the number of minimum-wage jobs in America has fallen by 25%, while jobs paying more than $10.00 an hour have grown by some 67%. Most of the new jobs are in the service sector, but over the last few years even manufacturing employment has risen, as capital spending and export sales have boomed.

Another rap on the service sector is that services aren't exportable, as manufactures are, so the U.S. isn't getting any benefit in the world economy from the strong growth in services. This just isn't true. Many kinds of services—education, entertainment, engineering and construction, data processing, financial and legal—are highly exportable, and America's international services earnings have been growing very well.

Productivity growth: mixed success

Productivity has something—but not much—to do with traditional concepts of industriousness in the labor force . . . punctuality, alertness, hard work. It has more to do with the work force's education and job experience. It has a LOT to do with the labor-saving equipment the workers are using. A high level of capital spending on automation, both in manufacturing and services, is the key to rising productivity. And rising productivity is the key to rising living standards, because an employer can afford to pay higher wages *and* maintain profits if output per hour is growing. On the other hand, if productivity is not rising, wage hikes will be inflationary, pushing up prices and wiping out real gains for workers.

Contrary to many people's impressions, American productivity—in all sectors combined, industrial, agricultural, services—is the highest in the world, and it's been growing, not declining. But growth in productivity has been uneven by sector. In the fast-growing service sector, where some businesses are difficult to automate, gains have been negligible. In manufacturing, gains have been very solid. U.S. productivity growth in manufacturing has averaged more than 4% a year since '84, ranking high among all industrial nations.

Obviously, American productivity *gains*—in a modern economy that is already very automated—haven't matched those in less-developed nations that have been moving rapidly from labor-intensive to automated manufacturing, but despite these gains, their level of productivity is still far below America's. For years, other large industrial countries were closing in on the world leader, America. By 1984, Japanese manufacturing productivity had risen to about 93% of ours, and Western European industrial productivity was about 85%. But the gap hasn't closed further since then, and the U.S. is still number one in manufacturing output per hour.

The slimming down of American industry in the '80s—closing of obsolete facilities, automation, trimming of labor forces, holding wage increases close to productivity gains—has done wonders for American competitiveness in unit labor costs. From 1981 through 1985, labor costs per unit produced in U.S. manufacturing rose a scant 1.7% per year, and since then they have actually declined. In a world context, with the low level of the dollar factored in, the decline in U.S. labor costs relative to Japan and West Germany has been dramatic. Today, in industry after industry, America is the world's lowest-cost place to produce goods—in some cases, lower than the Third World, due to higher automation. This has been a major reason for the enormous flow of foreign investment capital into America over the last few years.

In the 1990s it will be the service sector's turn to slim down and boost productivity. In recent years, even with the sluggish overall productivity growth rate in services, there have been a number of productivity success stories, in such services as communications, air transportation, data processing, petroleum pipelines, and even gasoline retailing (with automated gas-and-go stations). The big payoffs from computerization—in everything from insurance claims to design and engineering services—are still ahead.

The American standard of living

By most measures, the average prosperity of the American people has continued to rise—at an uneven rate, in fits and starts—throughout the last 30 years.

The personal-finance magazine we publish, *Changing Times*, makes an annual calculation of American prosperity using a new kind of index we created with the Washington economic-consulting firm of Joel Popkin & Associates. It is a composite index of household spending and net worth that cancels out the problems associated with relying just on income (cash versus noncash compensation, for example) or spending (which doesn't distinguish between paying cash or borrowing).

Since it tracks household net worth, it's a better gauge of living standards than an index based solely on spending without regard for saving. "Borrowing to spend for current consumption reduces your net worth by the amount that is borrowed," explains *Changing Times* Editor Theodore Miller. "So our Prosperity Index is a good measure of whether the average American household can afford the amount of spending it does without cutting into its net worth. If spending is occurring at the expense of wealth building, the index will decline, or at best, not change."

In fact, the *Changing Times* Prosperity Index—calculated back a few decades—has moved in an erratically upward line since World War II. It has tracked very closely with productivity growth. The sharpest temporary setbacks in the index occurred whenever inflation soared and productivity growth slowed— most noticeably in the mid-1970s. Even with growing consumer debt, the index has been steadily rising since 1983.

Statistics dealing with income, poverty and the distribution of wealth are full of traps, and if we've learned anything from our years of watching the economy, it is that you can find a set of government statistics to prove just about anything you want to say.

Many comparisons are the apples-and-oranges kind. For example, some Census Bureau figures on median family income in recent years have shown an inflation-adjusted decline between the early '70s and late '80s. But similar data from the Bureau of Economic Analysis—a sister agency of Census at the U.S. Commerce Department—showed family income at record high levels, because the BEA, unlike Census, included the value of noncash employer-paid fringe benefits, which have risen sharply in recent years.

How about the poverty rate? It declined for decades, bottoming out at about 11% in 1973. Then, with high inflation and slower economic growth in the '70s and early '80s, the poverty rate began climbing, hitting about 15% in 1983, after a severe recession. It's been declining since then, to about 13% today. But the official poverty rate doesn't take noncash income into account; if you add in benefits such as housing subsidies, food stamps, school lunches, medicare, and medicaid, the U.S. poverty rate is probably somewhere between 9% and 11%.

Sharing the wealth

Some portentous forecasts for America's future hinge on the spurious contention that income distribution in America has been skewing very sharply toward the wealthy in recent years. This impression was fueled by a statistically flawed report from the

Joint Economic Committee of Congress in 1986. The report was quickly retracted and revised. It turns out that the distribution of wealth and income in America has changed very little in the last 40 years. By income, the bottom fifth of households have typically received between 5% and 6% of total income, and the top fifth between 40% and 44%.

Wealth and income in America have ALWAYS been very unevenly distributed—it's a trait of a diverse, fluid, capitalistic society in which there is substantial economic mobility both up and down. More important, uneven income distribution in America has not been an impediment to a general rise in living standards for all Americans—rich, poor and in-between.

When author George Gilder discusses living standards in the U.S. and Japan, he doesn't focus on per-capita income, in which the rise of the yen gives the appearance that Japan is rapidly closing in on the United States. Instead, he looks at what income *buys* in each country, and he comes to the conclusion that average living standards in America are vastly higher than Japan's. Even more startling, "by most economic measures, the *bottom* fifth of U.S. families lives better than the *average* of Japanese families," he says. Compared with the typical Japanese family, the bottom fifth in America spend a lower proportion of their income on food (less than 20% versus more than 33%), have a higher percentage of homeownership (41% versus 33%), live in twice the square footage of housing and own more cars and TVs.

The middle class: alive and mobile

You've probably heard of the "shrinking middle class"—the supposed demotion of once middle-class families into the lower reaches of income. It's a myth. The "lower class"—defined in some studies as households earning less than $20,000 a year in 1986 dollars—stayed about the same in size between '73 and '86. The middle class—families making between $20,000 and the mid $50,000s—did in fact shrink, but because of UPWARD mobility into high-income classes. A Brookings Institution study showed strong 38% growth in the number of families earning an inflation-adjusted $50,000 or more between '73 and '86, due largely to the increase in working women.

Changes in the well-being of Americans have varied by age

group and sex. The elderly have fared very well in recent decades. Families headed by people over 65, historically concentrated in the lower-income classes, have been climbing into the middle class, thanks to inflation-indexed social security benefits, private pensions and rapid appreciation in home values.

As the elderly have moved up, their places in the lower-income groups have been taken over mostly by young mothers and their young children—typically, a woman who is unsupported by the children's father and is either unemployed or working at a low-wage job. It is a troubling fact that today a third of all children in our nation are living in households with annual incomes under $20,000, and one in five is living in a family below the poverty line of $12,100. Even more troubling is the likelihood that this problem is less susceptible to improvement by economic policies than by a change in social mores—especially a slowdown in the explosive rise in teenage pregnancy and non-support by young fathers.

The inflation-adjusted median earnings of full-time working women of all ages have risen steadily for 30 years. And the earnings of older male workers—say, ages 45 to 65—have risen, too. There is just one group that hasn't kept up with the general rise of earnings: men aged 25 to 44. Adjusted for inflation, their earnings today are LOWER than in the early 1970s, especially for young males who haven't gone beyond high school. The reason? The decline in the number of high-wage industrial jobs that young men of modest education used to find plentiful back in the '50s and '60s. "We're creating a lot of high-skill jobs for college grads and PhDs," says economist Joel Popkin (formerly of the U.S. Bureau of Labor Statistics), "but we aren't creating enough jobs for high-school grads to enable them to afford a middle-class life-style"—at least not on one family income. This isn't an indictment of American economic growth but a clear message to American families that education is essential to a better life.

The savings rate: how low?

The amount of income saved by individuals and businesses to invest for future needs is very important to economic growth, and the U.S. has clearly not been saving enough. A higher level of savings is needed to overhaul America's infrastructure of aging roads, utilities, schools and other public facilities. More savings are needed to continue modernizing American industry for world competition.

According to the Department of Commerce, American savings as a percentage of disposable personal income hit a modern peak at 9.4% in 1975. The savings rate has declined ever since and stood at 4.2% in 1988. When this figure appears on tables of international savings rates, it shows the U.S. savings rate to be the lowest among the major industrial nations. In '87, for example, Canada's rate was listed at 9.4%, Japan's 16.5%, West Germany's 12.2% and Italy's 23.5%. Closest to us at the back of the pack has been Great Britain, which had an official rate well above ours at about 5.6%.

But we're not at all sure that America's savings rate is really as low as it seems. For one thing, other countries' figures are based on a formula (devised by the United Nations) that produces a significantly higher U.S. figure than the Commerce Department's method—about 7% compared with 4%. And in all nations big-ticket spending—on cars and home renovations, for example—is counted as consumption, as if there is no residual value in used cars or lasting value from home improvements. In the affluent U.S., where these kinds of expenditures are unusually heavy, they depress the official savings rate more than in other nations.

In 1988, Kenichi Ohmae, managing director of McKinsey & Co. consulting firm's office in Japan, recalculated the U.S. and Japanese savings rates to reflect different cultural and financial-accounting practices in the two countries. His surprising conclusion was that there is very little difference in the savings rates between the two nations, and it's possible that the U.S. rate is higher than Japan's. The biggest reason: savings calculations are based solely on new money saved each year from discretionary income, without regard for appreciation in assets already owned. Americans have much greater assets per capita than Japanese—stocks, bonds, pension balances, insurance, and especially home equity—plus a higher average return on these assets, but official U.S. savings rates don't reflect this increase in value. After Ohmae's calculations appeared in the *Japan Economic Journal*, the Bank of Japan embraced his approach and put

Japan's and the U.S.'s annual savings rates at 16.7% and 14.7%, respectively.

Without getting into a statistical brawl, let's just assume that the U.S. savings rate *is* lower than in other countries, but probably not by a great margin, and that it ought to be higher. If it's any consolation, the U.S. has not been alone in experiencing a declining savings rate in recent years. It's been a broad world trend in this decade. Canada's rate has dropped more than four percentage points since 1980, France's five points and Great Britain's nine points. Only the Japanese and the West Germans have held their savings rates in roughly the same range during the '80s, reflecting the higher median ages of their populations. And there are signs that the Japanese are becoming more consumption-oriented, as urged by their government. As incomes rise, as their people demand a higher living standard, and as barriers to imports gradually decline, we expect their savings rate to drop some in the '90s.

Behind the savings rate

There are a lot of reasons for America's sluggish savings rate. The simplest explanation—that Americans like to live for the moment, borrow freely and indulge their tastes for consumer products and good times—has a small element of truth to it, but it's mostly a bum rap. There are much more valid reasons.

First of all, there's government policy, and you can start with the high federal budget deficit. Most of the loans made to Uncle Sam to fund the annual deficit come from American bond buyers, and to those buyers it's savings. But the government uses the borrowed money to meet its current expenses, so the money isn't savings to the economy, just more consumption.

Then there's the U.S. tax code, which doesn't encourage saving as much as it should, and actually rewards borrowing, by both individuals and businesses. In some countries with a high savings rate, such as Japan, a good share of an individual's interest income is not taxed. In the U.S., borrowing is subsidized by the tax deduction on interest. It's being phased out on consumer debt and reduced for mortgage debt, but it is still a disincentive to saving.

As for business borrowing, Congress encourages the use of

debt rather than equity capital by allowing the full deductibility of interest expenses but taxing profits twice, first as corporate earnings and then as dividends. The solution isn't to trim the deductibility of business interest (as some in Congress would like to do with debt used in corporate acquisitions), but to give shareholders a credit for corporate taxes already paid. And while they're at it, Congress could boost business investment by restoring the lower tax rate on capital gains, encouraging businesses to retain earnings for growth rather than pay them out as dividends and then borrow for expansion.

Another big factor in our declining savings rate is the demographic composition of America. Our biggest age segment is the Baby Boom group, ranging in age from early 40s to the middle 20s—the peak spending years. Families are forming, houses are being bought and furnished for the first time, children are being reared, with all the expenses of education, medical care, clothing, and so on. Traditionally, the savings rate of a family rises strongly when they're in their 40s and 50s, at first saving for college expenses and later for retirement.

Savings rates are related to the average age of a population. They are low in countries with a very young population, and America is on the youngish side. Rates are high in Western Europe, where an aging population is socking away money for their retirements—and, increasingly, stashing their savings in U.S. investments.

And savings rates are related to current economic conditions and what people see ahead. In most of the world, savings rates peaked in 1975, after two years of severe recession caused by the trauma of soaring oil prices. It was a time of pessimism—or at least of sobering uncertainty—about the future of the world economy. It's not a coincidence that savings rates have declined during the less-troubled years since, as people have become more confident of their future earnings and their ability to boost their savings later. For many Americans, homeownership *is* their savings plan. With home prices rising so strongly in most parts of America in recent years, they haven't felt a great need to set aside much additional cash for later use.

Higher savings ahead

Some forecasters doubt that the Baby Boom generation,

which as a group has not known severe economic hardship, will ever save at the same high rate as their parents, many of whom grew up in the Depression. They might be right, but we believe the U.S. savings rate WILL rise in the '90s, as the Baby Boomers put major purchases behind them and sock away money for their children's college education and their own retirement.

And we think Congress will help boost the low American savings rate with a few changes in the tax code. In a few years, there may be further cuts in mortgage interest deductions, especially for very large mortgages and for second homes. Congress may restore some of the old dividend-and-interest exclusion from taxation. There will be more experiments with tax-free or tax-deferred savings plans for college, like the new U.S. college savings bonds and a variety of state plans, and possibly an Individual College Account (ICA), similar to the tax-deferred IRA. As budget deficit pressures ease in a few years, Congress will lower the tax on capital gains, encouraging businesses to retain earnings for growth and stimulating investment in higher-risk new enterprises. There might even be some relief from the old problem of double taxation of corporate earnings.

In its quest for additional revenue to trim the deficit, Congress will do a few things that will indirectly encourage savings by taxing consumption, such as higher federal taxes on alcohol, tobacco and gasoline. It might bring back some long-gone excise taxes on luxuries such as jewelry, furs and entertainment tickets.

What about the quintessential tax on consumption—a broad, European-style VAT, or national sales tax on value added to goods at every stage of the production and distribution process? There will be plenty of discussion of a VAT in the years to come, but we think it *won't* be enacted. Liberals will say it falls too heavily on the poor, and everyone else will be terrified of a VAT's ability to raise mountains of revenue—too painlessly and automatically, without a vote of Congress—as GNP steadily grows.

Is debt too high?

Not only have Americans been saving at a less-than-satisfactory rate in recent years, but they've been borrowing very heavily, too. How heavily is open to debate. In absolute terms, individual, corporate and government debt are at all-time high levels. And this debt burden has grown dramatically in the decade in which the REAL cost of money—nominal interest rate minus the inflation rate—has been at record levels, and the tax deductibility of consumer interest and some mortgage interest has been trimmed by Congress.

Clearly, much of the strong economic growth of this decade—job creation, modernizing of business, a high level of consumption—has been supported by borrowing, mostly from American lenders but increasingly from abroad, where lenders are attracted by both high American interest rates and the stability and dynamism of our economic system.

We could debate endlessly whether today's American debt burden is (a) no problem at all, (b) imprudently but not dangerously high, or (c) a crisis that will bring hard times to America in the 1990s. We lean strongly toward the middle choice. The debt level is not a disaster in the making. None of the major categories of American debt—with the possible exception of corporate debt—is precariously high, compared with ability to carry and compared with underlying asset values.

But America will do better in the '90s if it can gradually reduce the level of debt, especially money owed overseas. This will help boost the national savings rate, free up interest expense for more productive uses and make all borrowers—individuals, businesses and government units—less vulnerable to the occasional shocks of economic downturns. Debt that feels easy to handle when incomes, corporate profits and tax revenues are rising can be a crushing burden when growth turns down.

Let's look at the differing pictures for individual, corporate and government debt.

Household debt

Individual debt is at record levels, but there is less cause for concern than meets the eye. The annual piling-on of new debt has been declining since a peak in '85, and there is no evidence that the debt load is unmanageable.

The rise in consumer debt in the '80s is largely the result of high consumption by the enormous Baby Boom generation in its household formation years—consumption that has been aided by energetic credit card distribution by financial institutions. (There are some minor statistical villains, too, such as defining all monthly credit card billings as new consumer debt, even though most users pay the balance each month with no interest charge.) How well is consumer debt being handled? Well, debt as a percentage of disposable income has risen in '80s, but the percentage of debt in default is close to the average for the last 15 years, so people seem to be doing about as well as they always have.

Another way to measure debt is as a percentage of assets, a net-worth calculation. This picture is very encouraging. The growth in family assets—home equity, financial holdings, pension balances—has been just as strong as the rise in debt. Taking out mortgage debt and home equity, consumer debt as a percentage of household assets peaked in '83-'84 and has declined since. Personal bankruptcies have soared since 1984, but this is due mostly to easier bankruptcy procedures, aggressive marketing by attorneys and hard times in a few energy-producing states. A final note on people's ability to handle their debts: The rise in two-earner families means that a temporary loss of one job, while obviously painful, doesn't totally cripple the family's ability to pay its bills.

Corporate borrowings

Businesses HAVE gone on a borrowing spree in the '80s, for lots of reasons. The strength of the business recovery since the last recession—higher profits from leaner operations, growing overseas markets, the desire to take advantage of new technologies—has made business owners and managers more bold about expansion. Most companies aren't borrowing to meet the payroll, but to grow, modernize or acquire an ongoing business.

Some of the expansion has been financed with retained earnings, but a lot has been with borrowed money, too, for several reasons. Nominal interest rates declined after the last recession, while corporate profits grew. And as we said, the tax code favors borrowing.

The corporate-debt level has been pushed up, too, by the merger-and-acquisition binge. The takeover wave resulted from the awareness of smart investors that the market value of many publicly traded companies was well below break-up value, or even below the value of the company intact, after a reasonable amount of cost cutting. With so much money to be made from restructurings, investors have been willing to pay lenders a sizable interest premium in the junk-bond market.

It's debatable whether the corporate debt load is excessive now, but there are plenty of signs it will be when the next recession comes. As David Hale, chief economist at Kemper Financial Services in Chicago, warned in late '88, the ratio of corporate interest payments to cash flow exceeded 20%, a level seen only twice since World War II, in 1974 and 1982, when interest rates were higher than today and the nation was in recession.

The default rate on the corporate debt—even junk bonds from takeovers—has been low in this decade, due to general prosperity. It will undoubtedly rise in the next economic downturn, and this shakeout will sober up bondholders and diminish the appeal of overleveraged takeovers. (Junk bonds—those rated less than investment grade—comprise more than 20% of all corporate bonds outstanding, compared with only 6% in 1980.)

Another restraint on the surge in takeover activity will be rising stock prices. As stocks sell for higher multiples of earnings, there will be fewer bargain candidates for acquisition. But mergers and leveraged-buyout activity will continue to be strong in the 1990s, with many more international deals made possible by currency fluctuations. Foreign takeover activity will move in waves from country to country, whenever a low currency (such as today's U.S. dollar) makes a given country's assets look tantalizingly cheap. The U.S. will continue to be a major player in corporate takeovers around the world, and Congress will reluctantly resist the urge to restrain foreign takeovers of American firms.

Federal antitrust policy will remain relaxed, in a realization that a company's world market-share is more important than U.S. market share. Our government will tolerate more and more combinations of American businesses that compete in the U.S. but need to forge alliances to do battle with even larger foreign corporations.

National debt and deficits

When people talk about debt, the debt they focus on most

often is the national debt (the federal government's) and the relentless annual additions to it—the federal budget deficit.

Let's put the budget deficit in perspective. We can't picture one billion dollars in our minds very well, let alone 100 billion. So we relate these enormous numbers to other even bigger numbers, by computing the budget deficit as a percentage of America's total economic activity, GNP.

Budget deficits have been a fact of life in Washington ever since the 1930s. In the 55 years since 1934, there have been only *eight* years in which the government did NOT run a budget deficit, and in the last 30 years, only two—in 1960 and 1969. There are plenty of excuses, including crises of depression, war and severe recession. But the fundamental explanation is simple: In a democracy, legislators find it a lot easier to promise government assistance than to raise taxes to pay for it. They get reelected by saying "yes" more than "no." And House incumbents of both parties, who have the worst deficit addiction, get themselves reelected at the rate of more than 95%.

Even Lord John Keynes, the much-misunderstood patron saint of flexible fiscal policy, wouldn't approve of continuous deficits. He urged budget surpluses in times of prosperity, with occasional deficits only when sagging private demand required a boost from higher government spending.

As with personal and corporate debt, it's all right for the government to borrow money—IF it's primarily for capital spending, rather than meeting current bills, and IF in good times the amount isn't growing much faster than other indices of health, such as GNP.

By that standard, however, government deficits have been excessive in recent years. In the years between 1947 and 1980, annual deficits averaged around 1.6% of GNP. Deficits rose steadily in the mid 70s, hitting 4.3% of GNP in 1976, after a severe recession had depressed tax revenues. By the last year of the Carter administration in 1980, the deficit ran 2.8%. The annual shortfall was pushed up in the early '80s by a combination of declining tax receipts (from the recession), the Reagan-backed tax cuts and rising federal expenses, especially for social benefits and defense. For the first five years of the Reagan administration, deficits averaged 4.7% of GNP, hitting a peak of 6.3% in 1983. But since 1983, federal spending hasn't grown as fast as tax revenues, so the deficit as a share of GNP has been cut in half, down to 3% or a little less—nearing where it was at the end of the Carter administration.

Is this a safe, acceptable level? That depends on the health of the economy. In a recession, with falling GNP, a higher level might be acceptable and even desirable, to pump up the economy. But in a strong, expanding economy such as America's today, the budget should be balanced—or in surplus. A number of other healthy industrial countries, such as Japan and West Germany, have been running budget deficits in recent years, but theirs are generally a lower percentage of GNP than ours, and their higher savings rates make the deficits more manageable. It's hard to feel a sense of urgency about the deficit when things are going reasonably well in the economy. But *continuous* deficits—as opposed to an occasional shortfall—are insidious, sapping savings and productivity growth. The long-term outlook will be brighter with a much lower annual deficit—or ideally, surpluses.

Federal spending growth

Of course, a deficit can be defined as either too little revenue or too much expense. There has been nothing feeble about the growth of federal tax revenues since 1983, but spending has risen even faster, and we think it's pretty clear where the problem lies.

In the short run, the American budget deficit could be erased very easily with an increase in taxes. But based on the past performance of Congress, higher taxes would not bring lasting relief from deficits. Why? Because government spending rises to meet—and usually exceed—the level of revenue that is available. As economist Milton Friedman points out, "Taxes have been going up for 50 years without any apparent success in eliminating deficits. That experience suggests that Congress will spend whatever the tax system yields plus the highest deficit the public will accept."

It would be better for the U.S. if the deficit were reduced with spending cuts—or at least serious restraints—rather than higher taxes. The supply-siders oversell their theory when they say that lower taxes bring *immediate* increases in total revenues, except in countries where tax evasion was rampant and rate cuts brought income into the open. There is usually a brief period of flat or falling tax receipts, such as the U.S. experienced in '82 and '83 (but it's debatable whether that was due to President Reagan's tax cuts or the recession he inherited). In the long run, however, supply-side theory is sound. As economist Alan Reynolds notes, the correlation between lower tax burdens, higher growth and ultimately more tax revenues is now being accepted and demonstrated throughout the world, in countries as different as Great Britain, Bolivia, Botswana, Israel, Mauritius and the Philippines.

One of the biggest problems with continuous budget deficits is the way they tie Washington's hands in dealing with recession. In the next recession, fiscal policy will be on the sidelines. Because of the deficit problem, one favorite method for fighting recession—raising federal spending to prop up sagging private demand—won't be feasible. Neither will the other traditional weapon—tax cuts to stimulate private spending. So it will fall almost entirely to the Federal Reserve to bring us out of a downturn with looser credit.

Lower deficits ahead

Somewhere between the two poles in the deficit debate—"the deficit crisis" and "deficits don't matter"—a consensus will emerge that the U.S. needs to work the budget deficit down, both in absolute dollars and as a percentage of rising GNP.

Congress will chip away at it with a combination of spending restraints *and* tax hikes. The President and Congress will be extremely reluctant to increase income tax *rates*, but the base of taxable income will be enlarged with trimmed deductions. And you can expect some higher and possibly additional excise taxes. President Bush is sincere about resisting higher new taxes, but he can't afford to look apathetic about the deficit. And the Democratic Congress won't risk ramming higher taxes down his throat and getting tagged by the voters as being protax. So they will all reach an accommodation on spending cuts and tax hikes that will make some progress in deficit reduction.

On the spending side, the rate of increase in defense spending will slow or cease for a few years because of the deficit, the

Pentagon's trouble in digesting the big increases of the '80s and better relations with the Soviet Union.

The best opportunities for budget savings, logically, would be small cuts in the biggest programs, which are entitlements—social benefits to which people are entitled by law, everything from social security and military and civil-service pensions to medicare, medicaid and welfare. (Of course, these are among the politically trickiest programs to cut.) The programs that involve direct payments to individuals consume about 43% of the federal budget, compared with 25% for national defense. All of these programs will be under pressure in the next few years, with a strong possibility of reductions in the social security cost-of-living adjustment (to less than annual inflation), more taxation of social security benefits and more capping of medicare and medicaid reimbursements to hospitals and doctors.

Do you know what the government's third biggest category of spending is, after social programs and defense? It's interest on the debt, a $171 billion cost that drains more than 14% out of the annual budget. And that figure rises when interest rates go up, as they did in '87 through early '89. Reducing the budget deficit will help reduce the interest share of annual government spending, but the actual amount of interest paid each year will continue to mount—along with the national debt—as long as there are budget deficits of any size.

So what are the prospects of serious deficit reductions over the next couple of years? Well, you can forget about a balanced budget; it's not going to happen any time soon. But the Gramm-Rudman-Hollings law, with targets to hit and automatic reduction mechanisms if Congress misses, *is* making a dent in the problem. We see the deficit declining to well under $100 billion over the next few years, occasionally rising when the economy softens and falling during recovery. Meanwhile, GNP will be growing in fits and starts, reducing the deficit as a proportion.

The social security trick

Some economists theorize that the American budget deficit will evaporate in the second half of the '90s, due to a tax increase that's already in place. They might be right, but this disappearing act will be a fake.

A few years ago Congress approved a plan of periodic hikes in the social security payroll tax and the amount of income to which it is applied. As these revenues mount faster than social security benefits, they are creating an ever-growing balance, which will total about $212 billion in 1990 and almost $12 *trillion* by 2030.

But the money isn't hoarded in a special fund; it's lent to the federal government, which spends it for current needs and gives IOUs—Treasury bonds—to social security. So the social security surplus will reduce the budget deficit each year—in '89 by about $56 billion. That's why the deficit will decline and might even disappear. But Congress shouldn't consider these excess revenues to be found money. Counting these surpluses twice— money to spend now, money still available later—could lull Congress into thinking it doesn't have to cut or restrain other parts of the budget.

Someday the government will have to pay off the Treasury bonds owned by social security, to provide the retirement program with enough money to support the enormous Baby Boom generation as it retires. The tax burden on workers early in the next century will be less painful if the *rest* of the federal budget— excluding Social Security—runs surpluses between now and then, gradually reducing the total national debt.

State and local budgets

We've talked a lot about the federal government's spending habits, but we shouldn't ignore the state and local systems. When you add all the debts and surpluses of all units of government in America, you find that America's total governmental debt is not out of line with that of other countries, where typically all the debt is concentrated in a single central government. Many states have been running operating surpluses in the '80s, mostly because capital spending (financed by debt) is put in separate budgets. But the operating surpluses are now waning, in part because the federal government is cutting back on programs and shifting responsibility down the line. So we foresee a trend toward higher taxes and employment growth at the state and local levels, which have been the star performers of government growth for years.

By the end of the 1990s, state personal income taxes will be virtually ubiquitous. Such holdouts as Texas and Florida, experiencing high population growth, will probably adopt income taxes to pay for infrastructure development, rather than continually jacking up sales taxes, which hit the poor harder than the well-off.

As for sales taxes, expect states to broaden the base without raising rates. The big target: services, with an end to exemptions for such services as cable TV, dry cleaners, car washes, beauty salons, advertising—and even the professions of law, medicine and accounting. Every proposed extension will bring howls and battles with the affected businesses, but governments will prevail in the end.

In recent years, differences among state tax burdens have had a lot to do with rates of business development, with the low-tax Sunbelt states having a big advantage over the North. In the 1990s, tax burdens will become more even around America, as the southern states scramble for money to handle high-growth problems of schools, roads and water systems, and as northern states get a grip on tax burdens that contributed to the original flight of jobs and population to the Sunbelt.

Inflation and interest rate outlook

In the '80s America has experienced inflation rates as high as 12.5% in 1980 and as low as 1% in 1986. In the 1990s we probably won't see such wide swings. The high inflation of the '70s and early '80s was mostly the result of soaring oil prices and overly expansive monetary policy. Conversely, tighter credit and the collapse of oil prices in the mid '80s were the dominant reasons for the sharp fall in inflation.

We expect inflation to average about 4% during the 1990s—a rate that is now termed "moderate," although in earlier decades it was regarded as runaway inflation. That was about the level at which President Nixon instituted wage and price controls in 1971.

There will be a lot of offsetting factors in the inflation picture for the '90s. On the one hand, energy prices aren't likely to decline from current levels, and will probably be rising gradually at mid decade. And tight labor markets later in the decade will put upward pressure on wages. On the other hand, there will be plenty of price-stabilizing forces at work, too, including productivity gains and tough worldwide competition in both manufactured goods and agriculture.

As for interest rates in the decade ahead, we believe they will average lower than today—both nominal and real rates. The biggest factors will be lower inflation (on average) and lower budget deficits, decreasing the government's demand for loans. Another factor will be abundant capital, from both retained U.S. earnings and overseas investors.

America at a crossroads

The 1970s and early '80s were a painful period of adjustment for America. But over the last few years American business has risen phoenixlike from the ashes of countless conflagrations: shut-downs, restructurings, modernizations, cost cutting. It is this self-renewing power of American capitalism—a kind of creative destruction—that, if allowed to operate with minimal governmental interference, enables the U.S. to adapt to new challenges.

A good deal of our economic growth in the mid '80s was the result of a level of consumption that was higher than national production, requiring an infusion of loans from abroad. It was a good thing for the world economy that the U.S. did this, as we'll explain in the next chapter. But this imbalance between consumption and production could not continue indefinitely, since it runs counter to the long-term interests of both the U.S. and its creditors. In fact there is already evidence of a tilt in the U.S. toward higher savings and slower growth in personal consumption. Over the past two years, America's growth in personal consumption has been the second-slowest among the world's large industrial nations.

Gloomy forecasters of America's future speak of curtailed consumption as if it will be a painful belt-tightening, a grim austerity imposed on the U.S. by foreign creditors. They foresee a long flattening in American living standards, or even a decline. We disagree. We envision a level of export-driven economic growth that will accommodate higher savings and investment with only modest restraint in consumption. For the American GNP to keep rising in the face of restrained domestic consumption, someone else will have to pick up the slack, and that someone will be the people of other countries, where savings rates will decline and consumption rise. (More on this in the next chapter.)

Make no mistake about it: A higher level of saving is essential to boost the U.S. investment rate, which in turn is essential to sustained growth in GNP, productivity and living standards. For the reasons we've discussed—some demographic, some economic and political—we believe higher savings and investment are on the horizon.

We don't think living standards are going to stagnate or decline in America in the 1990s, by any official measure of personal income, consumer spending or wealth. Having said that, we offer you a few thoughts on the whole concept of the standard of living.

Many Americans today define their spending choices—indeed, the actual amount of consumption—as essential to their idea of "the good life." This is especially common among affluent Baby Boomers who have never known difficult times. Many of them take for granted a degree of spending—on dining out, travel, entertainment, personal services, home electronics, private education, and many other things—that was available only to the very well-to-do a generation earlier.

As the financial realities of college expenses and retirement loom, many of these Americans will begin to question the necessity or desirability of their current spending levels. If their reordering of priorities results in less spending and more saving—as we believe it will—it may show up in official statistics as a reduction in their standard of living. But their wealth will be increasing, and this will be good for America's future.

Living-standard calculations based largely on consumption are too narrow. As we said in our discussion of the *Changing Times* Prosperity Index, most such measurements don't track the growth of household assets. And a spending-oriented index fails to take into account "quality of life" issues that are increasingly important to Americans—intangibles such as good health, leisure time, family closeness, environmental quality and the peace of mind (and financial security) that comes from investing.

In government statistics, the family that dines together at home is exhibiting a lower standard of living than the family that scatters its members among three restaurants each evening.

The family that forgoes an expensive new car in order to build its investment kitty is choosing a lower standard of living, too. Same for people who enjoy doing the maintenance and improving of their own homes; they are depressing their standards of living, as measured by spending forgone on lawn services, cleaning crews and remodeling contractors. The high-school youth who is home studying every night—investing in future earnings— manifests a lower current standard of living than the kid who's out cruising the mall, buying fancy clothes to impress school friends.

Obviously, in an economy in which two-thirds of the GNP is derived from consumer spending, robust consumption is crucial. What's more, we don't presume to pass judgment on anyone's spending priorities. The American consumer's range of choices is a keystone of personal economic freedom. (It's also the envy of the world.)

Nonetheless, there is a growing realization that an imbalance between consumption and saving has social and economic costs to America. Out of this realization will come a new equilibrium between current and future needs that will sustain the long, uneven trend line of rising American living standards.

3 America in the World Economy

Barriers to world trade and investment will decline.

U.S. will remain world's leading investor abroad.

Foreign investment in U.S. will continue strong.

America's exports will grow faster than its imports.

U.S. trade deficit will trend down, eventually disappear.

Value of U.S. dollar will rise by mid decade.

American share of total world GNP will remain stable.

When you think about America's role in the world economy, keep your eye on differences of scale—of sheer SIZE—between the U.S. and the rest of the world. By some measures, America is so dominant that one-to-one comparisons with individual nations are less meaningful than comparisons between America and the rest of the world *combined*.

The American economy is by far the largest in the world, a goods-and-services-producing (and consuming) machine of incredible size and variety, with annual GNP of nearly $5 trillion. It is bigger than the combined national economies of the European Economic Community. It is considerably bigger than Japan's economy, but by what degree depends on how you value currencies. Befitting its size, the U.S. economy owns virtually every superlative of international economic strength. For example, the U.S. imports more than any nation on earth—and also *exports* more. The U.S. is the world's leading investor in plants and equipment abroad—and also the country with the largest value of foreign-owned plants and equipment.

It is very difficult for the biggest entities—the biggest cities, companies and economies—to match the RATE of growth that small entities can achieve from their low starting points. Can IBM increase its revenues as fast as Compaq can? Can New York State grow as fast in population as Alaska or Utah? Rarely. But in absolute numbers—additional dollars of sales or numbers of new residents—the big guys may be growing more than the upstarts.

So it should not be surprising that the enormous American economy in recent decades has not always matched the percentages of economic growth logged by smaller, newly industrialized nations. But to log annual gains of 4%, 3% or even 2% on so enormous a base is pretty impressive. In fact, in this decade American growth has been exceeded only by Japan's among major industrial powers.

Take job growth in America during the 1980s. Since 1980, the American labor force grew from about 109 million people to more than 122 million in 1989—12% growth, compared with Japan's 8%. Since the end of the last recession in 1982, America has created more new jobs than all the nations of Europe combined *plus* Japan. The unemployment rate fell to about 5%, the lowest level in 15 years. An even more important figure—the employment rate, or percentage of all adult Americans in the labor force—rose to a record high of 65%.

Helping other nations grow

The U.S. emerged from World War II with the only major economy that had not been wracked by physical and financial ruin. Our dominance of the world economy was the result of the prostration of others. It was not a desirable situation for the world or for the United States, because the health of a prosperous nation depends to some degree on the ability of the rest of the world to buy its products. We deliberately helped the world rebuild itself, with the Marshall Plan in Europe, a benevolent occupation of defeated Japan and a massive program of assistance to the less-developed nations.

We succeeded beyond our wildest dreams, and rates of growth in many nations of the world began to eclipse our own—which wasn't anemic either. For example, during the 1960s and 1970s, when we were growing at about 4% and 2.8% a year, respectively, the less-developed nations, as a group, grew at rates in excess of 6% a year for 20 years, in large part due to American investment in their economies, by multinational corporations looking for less-expensive manufacturing sites. Third World growth fell behind the developed nations during the painful contractions of the early '80s but now, despite the burden of repaying foreign bank loans, growth rates are picking up again.

Meanwhile, Japan—the born-again miracle of postwar industrialization—was the fastest-growing major developed nation, albeit from a smaller base. But Japan's strongest growth rates were chalked up in the '60s and '70s, and in this decade its annual rates of growth have slowed considerably, to a level not much higher than America's.

Military spending and economic growth

One wild card affecting American growth in the 1990s will be national defense. In the decades since World War II, the U.S. has borne an overwhelming share of the Free World's military burden, giving other nations the freedom to devote more of their resources to consumer and industrial growth. This burden is likely to lighten in the 1990s, auguring well for higher U.S. growth.

By design, Japan has not been allowed to become a military power, and it spends only 1% of its GNP on defense. The U.S. is the dominant power in Europe's defense through NATO, allowing West Germany to spend about 3% of GNP on defense, with Great Britain and France running about 5% and 4%, respectively. Canada, our ally to the north, usually spends about 2% of its GNP on military needs.

Meanwhile, the United States has been spending about 6.6% of GNP for its defense and that of its allies. This is well above the 4.9% low in 1979, but below the 7.6% of the late 1960s and early '70s, when we were waging war in Southeast Asia. Look for our military spending to fall moderately from current levels, to about 5% of GNP.

The big military spenders of the world are the Soviet Union and the Warsaw Pact countries, which use vastly more of their national resources on the military than any other nations. The U.S.S.R. alone spends between 15% and 20% of GNP on defense. Soviet leader Mikhail Gorbachev clearly recognizes that the sick Soviet economy can't begin to make a serious recovery until the drag of military spending is sharply reduced, and this is the primary motive behind his arms-reduction initiatives and olive-branch overtures to Europe. If Gorbachev can survive the considerable internal challenges to his modernization program and really make significant reductions in Soviet defense spending, the United States will follow suit.

Regardless of the path of Soviet spending, the 1990s will see a broader sharing of the Western defense burden with European allies, because they can afford it. And you can expect to see some cautious steps toward a larger Japanese role, under close supervision by the U.S.—for example, in joint development of high-tech weaponry. But Japan's Asian neighbors—most of which were conquered by Japan during World War II—will be understandably suspicious of a rearmed Japan.

U.S. market share in the world

To assess how a company is doing, you not only compare its current sales and earnings to its own past performance, but you also compute its share of the market in which it operates. Market share gives you some sense of the company's importance in its field, but it's no sure indicator of financial health. For example, a company could increase its market share with a costly program of aggressive selling—and run itself into the ground. Or it could reduce capacity, increase its profit on each unit sold and boost earnings by willingly accepting a smaller share of the market. Other things being equal, we'd all like to have solid profitability *and* high market share.

At the end of World War II, the American share of aggregate world GNP was an incredible 40%—that is, the total production of goods and services in just one nation, the U.S., accounted for four out of every ten dollars of economic activity in the world.

It was inevitable that this figure should drop—after all, that was America's plan. By the early 1960s, after 15 years of postwar rebuilding, American GNP as a share of aggregate world GNP had fallen to a level in the mid- to low-20% range. Our share of market was picked up by other countries of the world, and the world economy was stronger for it.

If the American economy has been in a long decline for the past 20 or 25 years—as some observers say it has—there should be strong evidence that the American share of world GNP has declined steadily since the '60s. But—surprise of surprises— there seems to have been very little change in America's world market share in recent years. Our slice of total economic activity has kept pace with the growth of the entire pie, and that slice has run in the mid 20% range.

Changing currency values

But use caution with all such international comparisons; they aren't very reliable. It's difficult to compute GNP in countries where economic information gathering is rather primitive. And it's very tricky to convert the information to one relevant world standard. For example, one way to calculate the market share is to convert every country's GNP into a single country's currency, such as U.S. dollars. But with this method volatile currency swings can change the market-share result dramatically from year to year, even as volumes of total economic activity are fairly stable. For example, due to the sharp fall of the dollar in recent years, this method pushes down the U.S. share of world GNP, possibly to around 18%.

International currency values often fail to reflect the relative purchasing power of currencies in their home countries, so some economists prefer to calculate all the countries' GNPs on the basis of "purchasing-power equivalents." The PPE approach tends to increase the value of the dollar compared with, say, the yen—reflecting the very high cost of living in Japan. By this method, America's share of world GNP would have been 26% in 1987. So depending on which method you like, America's market share has gone up or down by a few percentage points since the 1960s. Either way, it's no cause for euphoria or alarm, but it undermines a central argument of the prophets of doom. We expect the U.S. market share of the world economy to remain fairly stable in the present range. Decline is highly unlikely, and there is a good chance it will rise a little through the decade ahead.

Unmistakably, the rising industrial powers of Asia—Japan, South Korea, Taiwan, Hong Kong, Singapore and others—have been growing at a much faster rate than most of the rest of the world, so their market shares have been increasing. South Korea saw its GNP grow almost *tenfold* from 1960 to 1987. Even using the purchasing-power-equivalent approach, which tends to understate Japan's GNP, Japan's share of total world economic activity soared from about 4.6% in 1960 to 9.4% in 1987, and it's probably over 10% today.

Where have their growing market shares come from, if not largely from the United States? Primarily from the Soviet Union, Great Britain and continental Europe (both the democracies and the communist states). In Europe and Britain, high tax burdens, soaring labor costs and social expenditures plus import barriers limited economic growth through much of the '70s and '80s. The countries of the European Community yielded about three points of world market share from 1960 to 1987, going from 25% to around 22% in 1987. But in the past year or so, growth-oriented policies have begun to boost the economic performance of Europe, and an integrated Europe will be a more formidable competitor in the Global '90s.

American competitiveness

Everyone knows that the U.S. buys more goods from the rest of the world than does any other nation, and we all know that we've been running a sizable trade deficit for several years.

So some Americans have extrapolated from that a mistaken notion that America just can't compete in international trade; that the rest of the world doesn't respect our manufactures; that we're not a capable exporter of much of anything, except maybe pop music, blue jeans and fast food.

The simple fact is, the United States is the world's leading exporter—the country that sells to the rest of the world the greatest value of goods and services in the widest range of categories. In terms of market share of total world exports, the U.S. holds about 18% compared with West Germany's 13% and Japan's 12%.

We lead the world in the overseas sale of airplanes, paper, chemicals, computers, scrap iron and steel, radar equipment and pharmaceuticals, to name just a few diverse products. The U.S. is the leading exporter of agricultural products because our shrinking farm population is so productive we can meet all our own needs and feed much of the world, too. We lead in exports of corn, soybeans, cotton and wheat, among other commodities. We are the world's low-cost agricultural producer, and our export lead would be much wider if our goods were not kept out of Europe, Japan and other nations by governments bent on protecting their overly large and inefficient agricultural labor forces.

World market share by industry

In some of the industries America dominates, U.S. market share is rising, and in others it is falling. The U.S. has clearly lost market share in many basic industries, such as clothing, footwear and basic carbon steel. The reason is usually the price advantage of overseas manufacturers, who are combining lower labor costs with increasing automation. The movement of basic manufacturing from high- to low-cost production centers has been a relentless worldwide trend since the dawn of the Industrial Revolution. It is folly to try to impede it. Since World War II, American businesses have been leaders in this ceaseless migration, even as they have continued to invest at home in high-tech manufacturing, in which the U.S. still has a comparative advantage. (It is estimated that American firms employ some 8.3 million people abroad in their foreign affiliates).

In some products—from cars to consumer electronics—the blame for declining market share falls squarely on American business. It was the result of slippage in engineering and quality control (as in cars), or failure to convert American technology into viable products (as in VCRs and compact discs, both pioneered in the U.S. but made almost exclusively overseas today.)

Because U.S. market shares in many industries—especially high-tech areas—have been so enormous, it's not surprising that they have been under considerable pressure in the '80s, as the ability to produce high-tech products has spread from nation to nation.

In 1981, for example, 41% of the world's total exports of computer parts and equipment were American; by 1985, this market share had fallen to 32%. Who picked up our decline? Japan doubled its share of computer exports from 6% to 13%, and the newly industrialized countries like South Korea, Hong Kong, Singapore and Taiwan doubled their share, too, from 5% to 11%. America has maintained market share in large, high-performance computers, but these nations have come on strong in the manufacture of personal computers, especially IBM clones, and commoditylike components such as semiconductors and circuit boards.

There have been similar stories in other high-tech fields. Between '81 and '85, the American share of total world exports in aerospace edged down from an amazing 49% to an almost-as-amazing 48%, in microelectronics from 26% to 23%, and in telecommunications from 12.4% to 11.8%.

But in some other high-tech fields, American market share is increasing. For example, a study by the British magazine *The Economist* estimated that U.S. share of world software markets rose from 67% to more than 75% between 1975 and 1985, and it is probably even higher today.

An export surge

The last several years have seen a great surge in American exports. The value of exports was up 12% in 1987 and another 27% in 1988. This performance would be even more impressive if there were not formidable barriers to all sorts of American goods in every country in the world.

The reasons for America's new export strength are many. The decline of the dollar gave America a strong price advantage over other countries' goods in all categories, but especially in commoditylike goods—chemicals and paper, for example—in which there is relatively little difference in design and quality.

But America's new strength in exports is due to more than the lower dollar. American product quality has been improving. Unit labor costs in U.S. manufacturing have risen only 7% in this decade, compared with increases of 18% in Germany and 50% in Japan (expressed in U.S. dollars; the contrast is even more dramatic with currency changes factored in). More small- and medium-sized American businesses, not just the giant companies, are awakening to the richness of export markets, and the U.S. is getting better at international marketing than it used to be. American firms are belatedly discovering that selling in other cultures is very hard work and that the world isn't going to beat a path to their door; they've got to learn the languages, customs and consumer needs of other peoples.

An appetite for imports

Of course, imports have been growing, too—at times much faster than exports, and that's what created the U.S. trade deficit. In 1988, however, a 9% growth in imports was swamped by the 27% rise in exports, trimming the deficit.

Yes, we Americans buy more goods from the rest of the world than any other country does, for three simple reasons: We can afford virtually anything we want, the goods are often priced at gift-horse prices and our government allows us to buy them. Before dismissing these factors as simplistic, consider how few other nations can match the U.S. on these grounds.

We've mentioned the scale of the American economy several times, and how its sheer size distorts comparisons. Take America's appetite for imports. Of course Americans spend more money on imports than any other people on earth; we spend *more money* on just about everything than anyone else does, because of our wealth. But it's a little-known fact that Americans spend a fairly low *percentage* of our incomes on imports, compared with what other people spend on imports in general, and especially imports from America.

There is no such thing as truly free trade anywhere in the world, and there is no country that doesn't practice any number of clever techniques—quotas, tariffs, government subsidies to hold down production costs—that work to restrict their citizen's access to low-cost (and sometimes higher-quality) products from abroad. We put high duties on certain kinds of foreign motor vehicles. We force American consumers to spend far more than necessary on sugar, to protect the American sugar industry from foreign competition. Same with certain kinds of steel, apparel, and many other products.

But compared with other countries, America is far and away the least protective, most open market in the world. Relative to other countries, our government is less inclined to coddle inefficient domestic businesses by keeping out the goods of other countries. And that's good for America, in the long run. At any moment, of course, it means that American business is under siege on countless fronts. When you combine the openness of our marketplace with its enormity and affluence, it's no wonder that the U.S. is the first export target of every country on earth.

The trade deficit

America has been running a merchandise trade deficit every year since 1976. Before that, trade deficits were rare and small. The deficit hit an all-time high of $170 billion in 1987, declining to $137 billion in 1988. We believe it's on a generally downward trend.

The popular explanation for our trade deficit is that we're bunglers at overseas marketing, our domestic manufactures aren't as good as imports and we're the Uncle Sucker of world trade, allowing other countries to dump their products here while they exclude our goods. It's also noted, with economic validity, that the trade deficit is a kind of mirror image of the federal budget deficit, with foreign countries lending us the earnings of their export surpluses to feed both higher federal government spending and the consumer's craving for imports.

There is often a kernel of truth in every myth, so there are plenty of examples to support this view of our trade deficit. But there are more contradictions. Take the arguments of low American product quality and inept marketing. The steady rise in American exports and America's high market share in numerous categories of goods, especially against import barriers, contradict these arguments.

How about the America-as-chump argument? Dumping—other countries' exporting goods at prices lower than the actual cost of production (subsidized by their governments) or just lower than the price in their domestic markets—is hard for American manufacturers to compete against, and that's why the government has methods for dealing with unfair-trade practices. But who's the sucker in this game, the country that dumps its goods on America at little or no profit, or the country that accepts these imports as a gift to its low cost of living? Maybe neither.

As long as the American economy and per-capita income are growing, we think the benefits of low-cost imports largely offset the damage done by dumping.

But a more important question is what American consumers do with the money saved by buying less-expensive imports. If they merely blow the savings on more and more consumption—whether imports OR domestic goods—then they won't be taking advantage of the gift from abroad. But if Americans invest the savings—channeling it into building America's comparative advantage in high-value exports—then the opportunity to buy low-cost consumer imports will be a boon to the U.S.

Overseas role in the trade deficit

We accept that federal deficits and overconsumption by Americans play a big role in the U.S. trade deficit, but another factor—much less appreciated by the American press and public—is the economic performance of our trading partners: oversaving and underconsumption. Their citizens have been relatively less able to buy imports than Americans have been.

Lower growth in the economies of some of our trading partners has simultaneously hampered demand for American goods and put pressure on foreign manufacturers to export to the U.S. In some cases—as in many less-developed countries—growth in domestic purchasing power has been sickly, and if their own citizens can't absorb the country's manufactures, exporting them is the way to make the economy grow. Exporting earns the country the hard currency it needs to buy capital goods for its manufacturing sector.

In other cases, mostly developed nations, governments have intentionally restrained domestic consumption to build export markets and accumulate foreign-trade credits. For example, standards of living in West Germany and Japan have not risen nearly as rapidly as their rates of growth and export success would suggest.

During the 1980s, America's appetite for imports has been a major force for growth in the world. In a blunt expression of this sentiment, *Wall Street Journal* Editor Robert L. Bartley says that in the 1980s, "the U.S. trade deficit was the only thing standing between us and a second world depression." American willingness to accept the excess production of manufacturers all over the world has given a lift to living standards everywhere, especially in the Third World. Don't think of this as American altruism. U.S. consumers are getting a good deal, and foreign-trade earnings enable other countries to increase their purchases of American-made goods, especially capital equipment.

Given the size of our market, and our enormous wealth as a nation, it would be damaging to the rest of the world—and ultimately to America—if the U.S. trade balance came rapidly into surplus. We don't want to oversell this point, however. The American trade deficit *was* too high a few years ago, and it needed to come down. Had the gap widened or even stayed at that level, the dollar would have continued to plunge, and this would have caused all sorts of problems, especially higher inflation and a slower flow of foreign capital to America.

The trade outlook

Trade imbalances have a way of correcting themselves through changes in currency values—assuming a country has products the rest of the world wants to buy, as the U.S. clearly does. The drop in the American trade deficit over the past few years is proceeding at a safely gradual pace. The lower value of the dollar is beginning to trim America's appetite for (or more precisely, its ability to buy) foreign products. And the lower dollar is enabling other countries to satisfy their desire for American goods. A rapid decline in the trade deficit would be a symptom of big trouble. The only way America could rapidly cut its consumption of imports would be through drastic protectionism or a sudden inability to buy imports because of a severe recession in the U.S. or the unwillingness of foreign lenders to lend us more money. Neither alternative is desirable—or likely.

The lower dollar has helped our foreign competitiveness, but there are dangers in a sharply falling dollar. It is both unnecessary and ill-advised for the U.S. government to drive the dollar down. At the level of early '89, it was already underpriced by purchasing-power comparisons. We believe the dollar will trade in the current range or a little lower in the early '90s, then trend upward by mid decade.

Looking further into the '90s, we see continued improvement

in America's products, export skills and production costs. The ability of its trading partners to afford U.S. goods is improving, and the basic trend in trade policy is toward more-open markets. All this foreshadows a long (albeit uneven) decline in the U.S. trade deficit, leading to a modest trade surplus by the end of the decade.

But it won't be easy. For one thing, there are a lot of goods Americans *have to* import, such as cameras, home entertainment systems and athletic shoes, because we simply don't make them in large quantities anymore. And another big factor is cars. We think U.S. automakers have arrested their slide in market share, but it's not going to rise dramatically. And finally, there's petroleum. Although America is still the world's second-largest producer of crude oil (after the Soviet Union), its energy demand is so great that the U.S. is also the world's biggest importer of oil (with energy-poor Japan number two). Energy conservation is so advanced in our economy today—with total use only a little higher than in 1980—that further cuts in oil consumption will be hard to achieve.

We foresee steady growth in exports, but in the short run American industry will have trouble matching the rate of growth achieved in the last years of the decade, due to tight capacity. Plants were running at 84% of capacity in early '89, unemployment was low and spot shortages were developing in a range of materials, from steel bearings and aluminum to resins for plastic.

As strongly as U.S. exports have been increasing recently, American manufacturers still have a long way to go to regain ground lost when the dollar was overvalued in the mid '80s. At 6.6% of GNP in 1988, merchandise exports accounted for a smaller share of U.S. output than in 1980, when they were 8% of GNP. By comparison, imported goods have tracked at a fairly even 9% of GNP throughout the decade. That's why economist Paul McCracken offers the dissenting view that the essence of the American trade problem "is not bloated imports but weak exports."

An overstated American trade deficit

A final word on trade data: It's pretty shaky, and most likely the American deficit of recent years has been substantially overstated, because U.S. exports are undercounted. Every country tracks imports very closely because of trade regulations—tariffs, quotas and such. And most countries except the U.S. have a good idea of their export volume because most foreign governments offer rebates of value-added taxes (VAT) to their exporters. But in America there is no such incentive for American firms to report their exports accurately—in fact, there is motivation to understate exports to cheat on corporate income taxes.

Due to errors in tracking exports, the U.S. trade deficit with Canada has been corrected downward several times in recent years. It's likely that similar problems exist in the computing of our deficits with other nations, too. Theoretically, the trade of the whole world should be in balance—one nation's exports being someone else's imports. But the whole world is paradoxically in deficit, and the reason is likely an undercounting of U.S. exports.

Does country of origin really matter?

In the tightly knit economy of the Global '90s, distinctions between exports and imports will become so blurred that the old definitions are becoming irrelevant. This is already a dilemma that fogs the whole debate over trade policy today.

At the turn of this century, everyone knew what an import was. It was a product made entirely in another country by a company that was based and owned there. When an American bought a product from England, it was understood that the earnings on that sale flowed there, for the benefit of English workers and English capitalists.

That all changed with the growth of multinational corporations after World War II. Multinationals based anywhere in the world do manufacturing at plants all over the world. Manufacturers buy components from many countries and assemble them into goods that can no longer be described as the product of a single country. And it's even difficult to describe a modern international business as being owned exclusively by investors in a single nation. It may be a joint venture, and its owners may include small stockholders all over the world. If you want, you can buy shares in Korean, Australian, Japanese and West German companies, through U.S.-based mutual funds that invest in businesses all over the world. Or you can buy individual shares in predominantly foreign-owned companies like Sony of Japan and Philips electronics of the Netherlands right on the New York Stock Exchange—the same way foreign investors buy shares in U.S.-based companies, adding buoyancy to our stock markets.

What does "country of origin" really mean anymore? Generally, a product is classified as an import if final assembly takes place outside the U.S. and it is sent into our country for sale. We call it an import even if the manufacturer is an American corporation and the profits flow back to the U.S., becoming a plus on our current-account balance. And we classify it as an import even if a substantial portion of the components inside were made in America by American labor. (The U.S.-made components inside count as American exports.) Conversely, a car made in America by Honda or Toyota is classified as a domestic product, not an import, even though the manufacturers are Japanese corporations, the parts are a mix of American and foreign components, and the earnings belong mostly to Japanese investors. And we consider an IBM personal computer to be an American product, because IBM is a U.S.-based corporation, even though three-quarters of the components inside are made in Asia. To get a handle on this crazy mix, consider that nearly 20% of all imports coming into the U.S. are made abroad by affiliates of American corporations.

Peter Drucker, of Claremont Graduate School in California, makes the point that American-brand products have a much higher share of the Japanese market than most people realize—as a matter of fact, he says, "about twice as much per capita than goods made by Japanese companies have of the American market." Japanese brands (regardless of where they're made) have large American market shares in several high-visibility categories—cars, consumer electronics and cameras. In Japan, American-brand goods enjoy market leadership in more categories, including large computers, software, candy and soft drinks, research instruments and pharmaceuticals. But these American-brand products are NOT American exports, so they don't improve our merchandise trade picture. Why? Because they're made in Japan by subsidiaries of American-owned corporations, which, Drucker points out, "tend to buy their machinery and tools from the U.S., creating high-value exports and well-paying American jobs." And the earnings of those U.S. multinationals in Japan improve the American balance of payments.

Trade flowing as freely as capital?

For a number of years investment capital has been moving around the world electronically with almost total disregard for national boundaries—and in enormous amounts. One *week's* value of international capital flow today exceeds the total *annual* value of world trade in merchandise.

In the Global '90s, we will begin to see much freer movement of goods, too, with less regard for national boundaries. When that day comes, traditional definitions of trade deficits and surpluses will become largely irrelevant, except as a way of informally keeping score. Editor Bartley of *The Wall Street Journal* believes that day has arrived. The American trade deficit is a "nonproblem," he says. "It is merely an artifact of history—a reflection of where politics has drawn lines on a map." That's true in economic terms, but politically the trade deficit will be a volatile issue in Washington until it shrinks to inconsequential size.

In the U.S. and other countries, a tentative transition to an eventual blurring of national boundaries can be seen in the boom in free-trade zones, any site—a city, industrial park or simply a single plant—where goods may arrive duty free from overseas, as long as they undergo some kind of value-added process and then leave the country as an export. The next step in free-trade policy would be loosening the requirement that the goods leave the country at all, but this is not likely to happen soon.

In Mexico along the U.S. border, especially in areas opposite Texas, there are more than a thousand *maquiladoras*, factories owned largely by American firms. The labor force is young Mexican men and women earning wages low by U.S. standards but attractive in Mexico. Using mostly American-made capital equipment, they assemble components from the U.S. and other countries into finished products—telephones, TVs, clothing, auto parts and the like—and then ship them back to the U.S. parent for sale in the U.S. and around the world. The U.S. components enter Mexico duty free, and the U.S. applies a low reentry duty only to the value added by the labor. Everyone benefits: Mexico, which gets jobs it desperately needs; American firms, which hold down production costs and improve their world competitiveness; and American labor, which gets the job boost from making components and, even more important, making the expensive machines the Mexican workers use. It is estimated that some 21,000 U.S. companies in 48 states supply components and machinery to the *maquilas*.

The *maquilas* of Mexico aren't taking many jobs away from American labor because those low-skill jobs already moved to Asia years ago. Instead, they are bringing low-cost assembly work back to North America from Taiwan, Singapore, Malaysia and other countries, while boosting high-skill employment in the United States, especially in design and engineering. This kind of joint manufacturing—with no or low trade barriers—could serve as a prototype for similar arrangements between the U.S. and other countries in Latin America. But we think it will be limited largely to Mexico because of proximity and the ease of transporting goods, not to mention the U.S. desire to help stem the flow of illegal immigrants by creating jobs in Mexico.

Lower trade barriers coming

America's greatest trade challenge over the next few years will be to open foreign markets to its goods, giving them a fair chance to compete in quality and price. Economists—and most government leaders, too—know that there is no contesting the merits of free trade versus closed markets, in terms of which system raises the living standards of ALL people in the world. Free trade wins hands down. But because of the electoral clout of threatened interests—whether they are farmers in Japan and Europe or steelmakers and automakers in America—protectionism often wins the political battles it cannot win on economic merit alone.

When you look at the headlines in the daily paper, it looks as if protectionism is on the upswing: a war with Europe over imports of American beef, conflicts with Brazil over U.S. computers and Brazilian orange juice, countless disputes over computer chips and cars and textiles. But a swelling total volume of world trade tells a different story. Barriers are falling and trade is booming.

The amorphous free-trade lobby—millions of people in America and the world whose livelihood depends on manufacturing for export and marketing imports and exports—is less organized than the protectionists, but its voice is beginning to be heard more clearly. All over the world, the message is sinking in: Free trade benefits everyone.

The U.S. pact with Canada, our largest trading partner, is a giant step forward for both countries. The Mexican government is beginning to loosen its restrictions on imported goods and foreign investment. European nations are in the process of eliminating trade barriers among themselves, and the next big step—still a way off—will be reducing barriers against non-European goods.

One of the biggest problem areas for the U.S. is protectionism in Asia, especially Japan, where there are still very formidable barriers to American-made goods and services of all sorts, from beef and lumber to cars and construction services. We're beginning to play hardball with our Asian trading partners, insisting on reciprocity, but so far our tougher stance hasn't made much change in Japan's resistance to imports. Forced reciprocity may occasionally require temporary trade barriers, but this tactic is risky.

More effective than all the negotiations will be the growing realization that trade restrictions take a toll on other peoples of the world. The Japanese, for example—especially their young, urban middle class—are waking up to the drastic costs that import barriers impose on their standard of living. Just as they have begun demanding a larger piece of the earnings pie—in higher wages—so are they beginning to seek wider access to inexpensive foreign goods. This trend, which is becoming visible throughout the world, will benefit the U.S. trade position in the Global '90s.

But don't expect miracles from reduced trade barriers alone. Some economists estimate that an absence of barriers to U.S. goods would reduce the current trade deficit only 15%, due to the most stubborn components of imports, especially oil and autos. Achieving a U.S. trade balance will require improvement on all fronts—quality and price of exports, marketing effort, lower trade barriers abroad and a reduced U.S. appetite for imports.

Is America a 'debtor nation'?

You've heard countless times that the U.S. is a "debtor nation" today, a dramatic reversal in 1985 of a solid creditor position maintained since World War I. The idea of our being deeply in hock to the rest of the world—coupled with anxiety over aggressive foreign investment in U.S. businesses and real estate in recent years—conjures up the specter of America's future as a giant "banana republic," a colony of Japan or Europe. We think this concern is unwarranted because the concept of a "debtor nation" is misunderstood, and—even more to the point—we might not even *be* a debtor nation in any sense of the term.

Here's what being a debtor nation means: The value of all foreign assets in the United States is said to exceed (in official tallies) the value of all American assets overseas. A big chunk of those foreign assets ARE conventional debts—money that the U.S. government and American businesses have borrowed from lenders abroad and must pay back from tax receipts and corporate revenues.

Another big piece of foreign assets in the U.S. are foreign deposits in American banks. Those deposits are defined as American debts, because they are liabilities on the banks' books and the money is immediately lent out to U.S. commercial and individual borrowers. (And sometimes it is lent out to foreign borrowers, as Middle Eastern oil earnings of the '70s were deposited in American banks and then recycled—in carelessly large loans—to Third World nations, which are still struggling to repay.)

Another big chunk of the foreign-owned assets in the U.S. are in no way debts that have to be paid back to anyone. They are equity investments in the American economy—controlling and minority interests in U.S. businesses, office buildings, farmland, etc. If they are profitable investments, the foreign owner gets dividends and rents, and some of that money does indeed flow out of the American economy.

Of course, American individuals and businesses also own enormous amounts of overseas assets, more than any other single nation's: manufacturing plants, real estate, stock in foreign companies, bank deposits and so on. These U.S. assets abroad are weighed against all other nations' assets in the U.S., and government figures say they fall short of the foreign-owned value. Hence America's official status as "debtor."

Undervalued American assets

But is the U.S. really a debtor by this standard? When you examine how the valuations are made, you find lots of softness. For example, many U.S. corporations value their overseas plants on the corporate books at acquisition cost rather than current value. Much of the American overseas investment occurred during the '50s, '60s and '70s at relatively low prices. And most of the heavy foreign investment in the U.S. has been in the '80s, at much higher prices. You can see how this would distort the comparison of current values.

Another reason to suspect that American plants and equipment overseas are undervalued is the disparity in earnings from those offshore businesses. Officially, the value of foreign plants and equipment in the U.S. was estimated to be $262 billion in 1987, and the value of American-owned businesses abroad stood at $309 billion, about 18% higher. But the $56 billion earnings on America's overseas businesses in '87 were *eight times* the scant $7 billion that foreign investors earned on their American plants. Many of the foreign-owned businesses in America are start-ups or recent acquisitions of low-profit American firms, and that explains some of the earnings gap. But it's hard to explain away so big a differential—unless American businesses overseas are highly undervalued.

Still more factors tend to undervalue American assets. For example, U.S. government gold reserves are valued on the books not at market rates (about $400 an ounce in early '89), but at $42.

Taking all this into account, it's likely America isn't a debtor nation at all, even by the official definition. That's a view that has been advanced very persuasively in a study by Charles Wolf Jr. of the RAND Corp. and Sarah Hooker of the University of Michigan.

Other economists attack not only the numbers but also the erroneous implication that being a debtor—as an individual or a nation—means that your wealth is decreasing. We know that's not true of ourselves when we use mortgage debt or a margin loan to buy real estate or stocks that appreciate faster than the carrying cost. And business managers know the value of leverage in increasing the worth of their firms.

"There is almost universal confusion between net debt and net worth, with the implication that the U.S. is 'poorer' if it has become a 'net debtor,' " says Herbert Stein, chairman of the Council of Economic Advisers under President Nixon. "If Americans build $100 billion worth of factories, financing half by their own savings and half by borrowing from abroad, Americans are richer by $50 billion, even though what has been conventionally measured as 'net debt' has increased by $50 billion."

So it all depends on why you borrow and how you use the money. A healthy debtor, whether an individual or a nation, is one who borrows mostly for long-term productive purposes (rather than just meeting current expenses), who can handle the repayment comfortably, and who keeps debts as a relatively low percentage of assets. While too much of Washington's borrowings have gone into consumption in recent years, America as a whole is still behaving like a smart borrower, using other peoples' money—foreign capital—to increase its total wealth.

Foreign loans to America

We're often asked about America's dependence on foreign loans, especially to cover the budget deficit in Washington. First off, some basic facts on the scale of the situation. The national debt is in the neighborhood of $2 trillion, compared with annual GNP of about $5 trillion. Big as it is, it's a smaller portion of our national income than the federal debt ran in the 1950s, when there was relatively little concern about it, and it's a percentage not out of line with other industrial countries today.

To an overwhelming degree, we owe this debt to ourselves—that is, about 84% of these bonds are owned by American individuals and institutions, not foreigners. Foreign lenders probably own something like 16%, or $325 billion. Some studies say foreign ownership of our national debt could be as little as 10% or as much as 20%, but in any case it's a small minority interest.

What are the odds that foreign investors would *stop* lending to Uncle Sam? Negligible, barring some worldwide economic collapse. There isn't another country on earth with a bond market big enough—and a need to borrow big enough—to absorb the excess capital (read "savings") of Western Europe and Asia, plus the wealth that continually (and regrettably) flees the developing countries of Latin America. And there isn't another market that gives lenders the U.S. combination of safety and high yield.

No, there's little risk that the money will dry up, but the volume of loans is another matter. Dependence on foreign lenders *does* make the U.S. vulnerable to the whims of world capital markets. If Japanese and German lenders decide to reduce their purchases of American bonds (for example, because of a concern that the dollar will drop more, devaluing their interest earnings), the U.S. Treasury would have to pay higher interest rates to keep the money coming. This would increase inflationary pressure in the U.S., slow growth and add billions to interest costs, not just for the U.S. government but throughout the economy. That's one of the best reasons for Washington to keep the budget deficit on a downward path.

Foreign assets in the U.S.

The value of foreign assets in the U.S. has grown dramatically in the 1980s, as our trading partners have plowed the earnings of their exports to America back into the U.S. economy.

It's hard to make an accurate tally of so many kinds of foreign assets spread around America, but the total probably comes to something like $1.5 trillion, more than seven times the approximately $200 billion in 1974. With international assets changing hands at quickening rates, the figures change constantly, but here's a stab at what the breakdown of that $1.5 trillion might have looked like in early '89:

Deposits in American banks	$450 billion
U.S. Treasury bonds	325 billion
Corporate stocks, bonds	300 billion
Whole firms, plants, equipment	300 billion
Real estate	125 billion
TOTAL foreign assets in U.S.:	$1.5 trillion

Some people seem to be worried about a pullout of foreign money—a quick sell-off that would depress the value of America's assets and plunge our economy into chaos. This worry focuses on the two-thirds of the $1.5 trillion in foreign assets that are highly liquid, easily sold in a matter of hours by telephone orders and electronic transfer—bank deposits, Treasury securities, corporate stocks and bonds. It's not a realistic worry. Sure, foreign investors *could* cash out quickly, but in the ensuing damage to the American economy their illiquid assets in America—$425 billion of real estate and entire companies owned—would plunge in value, too. And they're not so naive as to think their own economies could survive such a shock to the American system.

Investors—whether American or foreign—don't always act rationally. Sometimes they rush like lemmings to join a panicky sell-off. This can cause instability in international stock exchanges and bond markets, as evidenced by the role Japanese bond traders played in setting the stage for the stock market crash of October 19, 1987, by dumping U.S. bonds during the week preceding the crash.

But we believe that, on balance, the growing interdependence of national economies will cause more stability, not less. As the stake of foreign nations in our economy grows—especially through direct foreign investment in operating plants and equipment—their investors will grow more solicitous of America's financial health. And the U.S., as the world's largest overseas investor, has a similar stake in the prosperity of our trading partners.

America's investments abroad

The U.S.'s overseas assets are worth more than the overseas holdings of any other single nation on earth. For several decades—as a matter of fact, from World War I until 1985—the value of American assets scattered around the world exceeded the value of the ENTIRE world's assets in the U.S. We think that was a more troubling situation for world prosperity—and America's own—than the fact that this situation is now reversed.

In value of direct foreign investment, the U.S. is still the world's number-one overseas investor. As we mentioned earlier, the value of America's plants and equipment overseas was estimated at $309 billion at the end of 1987, compared with an estimated $262 billion of direct foreign investment in the U.S.

New American investment in operating plants and equipment overseas is still running very strong, growing at an average annual rate of more than 8% from 1982 through 1987. But foreign investment in the U.S. has been growing twice as fast—from a much lower base—increasing at an annual average rate of 16% in the same period.

Who are the biggest foreign owners of operating businesses in the U.S.? Contrary to popular impression, it's not the Japanese. Number one is Great Britain, followed by the Netherlands, with Japan a fast-charging number three. Japanese purchases and start-ups of businesses have tripled in value since 1982.

This surge has been greatest—and most visible—in such tangible assets as real estate and operating businesses. In real estate, purchases have been concentrated in a few American cities that are most familiar to foreign business people—New York, Chicago, Los Angeles, Washington, D.C., Boston, Minneapolis and others. Since American news media are concentrated in these same cities, Americans have gotten the impression that foreigners are becoming America's biggest landlords. In fact, foreign ownership of American real estate—millions of commercial, industrial, residential and agricultural parcels in 50 states—is still minuscule, possibly only 5% of the total.

There's a similar story in foreign purchases of well-known American businesses and in their start-ups of new plants. Foreign takeovers have focused largely on large, publicly traded firms, so the stories get a lot of attention in the press. In certain American industries, foreign firms *do* control a large and growing market share. According to many estimates, foreign-owned companies have about 50% of the U.S. cement industry, 33% of chemicals, 20% of metals, 10% of printing and publishing and 10% of electrical machinery, not to mention shares between 5% and 10% of many others.

But keep this in mind: In many countries without the size and diversity of the U.S., *big* business is synonymous with *all* business. Not so in America, where an increasing share of our economy—and especially our economic growth—is spread over thousands of small- to medium-sized firms, many of them in services and in emerging technologies. While there is beginning to be foreign interest in small U.S. firms—such as Japanese investment in struggling biotech companies—foreign investment has focused primarily on large industrial companies. The picture gets clearer when you look at the percentage of American workers who are employed by foreign-owned businesses. It's about 8% of manufacturing employment, but a scant 4% overall.

We all know that foreign-owned firms in the U.S. create jobs and pay wages just as American companies do, so why should anyone care about nationality of ownership? Well, there's the not-so-small matter of who gets the profits. Overseas earnings *can* be fully repatriated to the home country, but usually some portion is reinvested for further growth of the overseas firms.

American firms, which have been doing large-scale overseas manufacturing longer and more successfully than anyone else, tend to reinvest about 65% of their overseas profits in the divisions that generated them, bringing the other 35% back to the U.S. As for foreign owners of U.S. facilities, those percentages have been almost the reverse—63% sent back home, 37% left in America. But there are signs that with the growth of their U.S. operations and further reductions in production costs, a larger share of the profits generated in the U.S. will be reinvested here.

The benefits of foreign capital

The resentment of foreign investment in the U.S. reflects age-old feelings of xenophobia—a fear of things foreign, whether immigrants, imported goods or foreign ownership of American companies. Some people see all these forces as a threat to their control over their own destinies.

Back in the '50s and '60s, many Europeans felt threatened by the invasion of their continent by American multinational firms. In that era, America told other countries that our investment in their economies would be good for them. This wasn't a cynical rationalization. The argument was sound then and it's just as valid today: Inflows of capital are good for an economy, whatever their source.

On Capitol Hill these days, we hear a lot of loose talk about "economic nationalism," which encompasses both trade protectionism and vague proposals to somehow restrict foreign purchases of American assets, whether farmland, office buildings or entire companies. On the foreign investment issue, we can't envision any restrictions that wouldn't also curtail the freedom of Americans to sell their property to the highest bidder, so we don't think those proposals will go anywhere (except when there is a strong national-security angle, say, with a major defense supplier). The most the "nationalists" might get are tighter laws on disclosure of foreign ownership, to give America a better statistical picture of what's happening.

Just as Americans should use the money they save buying cheap imports to boost the U.S. investment rate, the same goes for the dazzling proceeds American stockholders get from selling their companies at high prices to foreign investors.

There's no problem with America selling a share of itself to investors around the world who can bring valuable resources to our table—money for growth, technology and expertise in international marketing, to name a few. But if the U.S. sellers squander the proceeds on current consumption, then America will miss an opportunity to build for the future and get further ahead of our competitors. If Americans invest the sale proceeds in starting or modernizing dynamic enterprises—both in the U.S. and abroad—then our nation will benefit enormously from overseas capital.

Foreign confidence in America

Before we leave this subject, another thought on what surging foreign investment in America really means. Each equity investment by foreign capitalists represents a careful judgment on where their money will earn the highest profit in the years ahead. Time and again, foreign investors all over the world survey the economic climate in their own countries—Germany, Argentina, France, Japan, Saudi Arabia, Canada, wherever—and decide NOT to invest at home.

Instead, they are deciding to put their money in America. There are many factors in the decision, including a desire to learn our rich markets up close, to benefit from our declining production costs and to hedge their bets on American protectionism by manufacturing in the U.S.

But the primary motivation is profit. They believe their money will earn a higher return in the United States, with safety unmatched anywhere else in the world. Their actions—a form of capital flight—pose problems of varying magnitude not for *our* nation, but for theirs. Each of these investment decisions is a vote of confidence in the future of the American economy.

4 The U.S.-Japan Technology Race

U.S. will keep its overall lead in science & technology.

Japanese aerospace will be up and running by '95.

U.S. and Japan will control 50% of all high-tech sales.

Superfast computers will give U.S. an edge.

A big battle shaping up in composite materials.

Japan and Europe will dominate high-definition TV.

U.S. will build on its lead in artificial intelligence.

If you think the '70s and '80s were packed with technological advances, wait until you see the next ten to 20 years. Bioengineering will improve health care, food production, and even plastics, glues and laundry detergents. Low-cost microprocessors—the guts of personal computers—will outperform and replace today's multimillion-dollar mainframes. There will be breakthroughs in superconductors that can transmit electricity with little or no resistance. And perhaps even energy supplies from nuclear fusion.

New technology will change the way you work. Voice-recognition computers will replace typists at many firms. Small, high-power computers will let you carry your office with you, perhaps in your pocket. At home, you'll be able to send and receive reports and pictures or look in on your grandchild's birthday party by pressing buttons on your superphone, the control center of the electronic home. (And you'll have more leisure time because of low-maintenance grass that will require mowing only three or four times a season.)

Major breakthroughs in technology used to come along about every decade. Now they seem to appear every month—not just in the U.S. but all over. Innovation no longer fits a neat progression from basic research to applied research to technological development to market. The steps are compressed and often nearly concurrent. The result is a fusion of technology and marketing.

U.S. versus Japan

The U.S. still holds an overall lead in science and technology, but the gap is closing, as other nations draw close and sometimes ahead in specific fields. An economically integrated Europe will be in better shape to compete in technology and will emerge as a high-tech power by the turn of the century. But by far our main challenger will still be Japan. Together, the U.S. and Japan will account for half of global high-tech sales, with the U.S. maintaining its lead.

How do the U.S. and Japan stack up in key technologies, considering both R&D and market positions? We talked this over with top scientists and engineers in industry, the universities and government. After picking their brains and listening to their reasons, here's how we size up the technology race.

U.S. Leads in These	Japan in These	Too Close To Call
Aerospace	Factory automation	Superconductivity
Supercomputers	Robotics	Fiber optics
Microprocessors	Ceramics	Composites
Computer software	Semiconductors	Telecommunications
Medical technology	High-definition TV	
Food technology	Other consumer	
Bioengineering	electronics	

As you can see from the table, the U.S. will enter the '90s with an advantage in breadth and depth of technology—everything from computers and aerospace to food and health, reflecting our long commitment to basic research. Japan's dominance in factory automation and consumer electronics reflects its ability to target and build on existing technologies, plus its willingness to plunge into research when it sniffs a big commercial payoff.

Maintaining America's lead

The scientists we interviewed think there's no reason to be gloomy about America's prospects in the Global '90s. The U.S. is the world leader in scientific innovation, marketing and distribution, and there are many reasons why this lead is likely to hold. As we discussed in earlier chapters, U.S. business investment will be on the upswing in the '90s. And there is a new focus on accelerating the transition from research to commercial uses and looking for long-term rather than short-term profits.

American universities continue to lead the world in basic research. Our top research universities, such as the Massachusetts Institute of Technology (MIT), Cornell, Carnegie Mellon, Cal Tech and Stanford, are the envy of the world. Scientists at these schools and many other top-flight American colleges enjoy an environment of financial support and research freedom that is unmatched overseas.

The 1987 Nobel Prize in medicine was awarded to Susumu Tonegawa, a molecular biologist who is a citizen of Japan. The Japanese greeted the announcement with a mixture of pride and embarrassed soul searching: pride that Tonegawa was the first Japanese citizen to win the medicine prize, but embarrassment that the research for which he won the prize was conducted not in his home country but at MIT and earlier in Switzerland. Tonegawa told us that he might not have been able to accomplish the same work in Japan, where consensus-based research tends to stifle innovation.

The U.S. has far more technical workers than any other country, and it replenishes its labor pool with a steady stream of skilled immigrants. The 3.6 million scientists and engineers employed by American business are more than twice the 1.5 million employed by Japanese corporations.

Another factor boosting our competitiveness in the '90s will be an easing of antitrust barriers and expansion of cooperative research, development and manufacturing facilities, according to Bruce Merrifield, assistant secretary of commerce for productivity, technology and innovation. There are now 125 industry consortiums involving 1,000 companies in the U.S. The biggest and best known is Sematech in Austin, Tex., which is developing equipment for making semiconductors, the directional chips in computers. There are similar centers for textiles, machine tools and most other major industries. Look for these to spread throughout the U.S. and overseas.

Also figure on closer ties between universities and corporations. Under a recent change in the law, U.S. firms get first crack at licensing university research developed with federal funding. This will end Japan's free lunch, Merrifield claims, and earn millions in royalties for the colleges. Within a few years, MIT will net an extra $50 million in such royalties.

Where we can do better

America still faces plenty of challenges in maintaining its technology lead in the '90s. The U.S. is beginning to upgrade science and math education in elementary and secondary schools, and this is coming none too soon, warns Erich Bloch, director of the National Science Foundation (NSF). "If we don't act, we'll be a second-rate power early in the next century," he warns. Research and education are closely linked: "If you cut one, you cut the other," he says.

The Council on Competitiveness, a private organization, points out that many nations, instead of trying to match America's scientific prowess, focus on acquiring new technology, rapidly translating it into commercial applications, then making improvements in response to market signals. The phenomenal success of that strategy, pioneered by Japan and followed by other countries, makes it clear that U.S. industry cannot expect to prosper by playing a designer role, inventing state-of-the-art products that can be duplicated elsewhere in a matter of months at lower cost.

U.S. companies must be hunters and gatherers of technology, not just generators, according to the Council. They must adjust to the fact that flows of technology and investment don't respect national borders. Japan has mastered technology transfer, paying three times as much for licenses, patents and royalties as it earns from selling its own ideas abroad.

In the '90s, the U.S. will take another look at how it allocates federal R&D spending. Bloch of the NSF believes we spend too much on defense-related R&D and not enough on technologies with no clear-cut military application. He says it's a myth that defense research is crucial to commercial technology—that the opposite is true. Civilian research is ahead of the Pentagon in computers and most other fields because it *has* to move faster.

In the final analysis, the U.S. will place its bets not on centralization of the technology commitment, but on the opposite: diversity. U.S. high-tech businesses will benefit from flexibility, openness and a traditionally American freewheeling style. As John Welch, chairman of General Electric, told *The Wall Street Journal*, "I can make a deal to put a plant in Spain without asking my government, my banker or even my shareholders. A Japanese company must consult its government. A German company consults its bank. I act."

The Japanese strategy

The U.S. invests three times as much in R&D as Japan, and Americans sometimes get the notion that Japan is a laggard in research, merely a clever copycat. But if you look closely, you'll see a different story. Less than 1% of Japan's R&D spending goes to defense, compared with 30% in the U.S. We take a broad-brush approach to research, while the Japanese are more selective, pinpointing specific fields for exploitation.

They have the advantage of total dedication and coordination among government, bankers and industrial conglomerates to capture and commercialize research. Time and again, they glom on to ideas developed in the U.S and beat us in the marketplace, as they did with color TV, VCRs and laser discs. *The Economist* describes the Japanese as "the magpies of the technological world."

They go at it systematically—shutting off imports and concentrating on the home market, then shifting to two-tier pricing, offering exports cheaper than the same stuff sells for in Japan. Semiconductors and advanced machine tools are examples.

In the '70s, Japan decided to go after semiconductors as part of its national industrial policy. At that time, eight of the top ten manufacturers in the world were American. By '89 eight of the top ten were Japanese, one was Korean and one American. The Japanese took control through predatory pricing. Hitachi sent a memo to its sales force, instructing it to sell chips 10% below Intel's price, no matter what Intel charged. As Intel whittled down its price, Hitachi would always go 10% lower. Intel filed for import relief, but by the time Washington acted, it was too little and too late. In '86 the Commerce Department worked out a microchip deal with Japan. It was a fiasco from the start, halting Japanese dumping in the U.S. but letting them grab markets worldwide and setting a floor under their prices, ensuring profits for their producers while we paid through the nose.

Japan pulled a similar stunt with advanced machine tools in the late '70s and early '80s, at a time when U.S. manufacturers had big backlogs of orders. The Japanese sent thousands of government-subsidized machine tools to the U.S., warehoused them, then approached U.S. customers, promising immediate delivery at bargain-basement prices. By the mid '80s the Reagan administration finally slapped quotas on some machine tools from Japan (and Taiwan). But the damage had been done; half the industry had gone out of business or been forced into joint ventures with the Japanese.

These are examples not of technological leadership by Japan, but of hardball international marketing. On the R&D side, the Japanese have used aggressive patenting to lock out competitors. While U.S. researchers have traditionally sought patents only for major innovations and product improvements, the Japanese flood the world with patent applications for even the most minor variations. Some are turned down, of course, but many more are granted, reducing the maneuvering room of Japan's technological rivals.

Now, for business and personal investing reasons, take a look at some key technologies and what's ahead in U.S.-Japanese competition.

No quick payoff in superconductors

In 1987, researchers at an IBM lab in Switzerland made a breakthrough in high-temperature superconductivity, the key to transmitting electricity without resistance, superfast computers, giant electric storage batteries and cheaper energy. Within weeks, Japan's Ministry of International Trade and Industry set up an R&D consortium on superconductors and followed with a flood of patent applications.

GE, Westinghouse, IBM, AT&T and others are making major commitments to superconductor R&D, and they plan to keep their research breakthroughs hush-hush—no more technology transfers to Japan.

Japan is now running neck and neck with the U.S. in this emerging technology, and trying to use the patent system to lock out U.S. competitors, a tactic it used with fiber optics and ultraviolet lamps. So far, the Japanese have filed more than 2,000 patent applications on the technology—a $40-million investment in filing fees, but chicken feed compared with the $25- to $30-BILLION market for superconductors by early in the next century. Japanese companies are working on market applications in tandem with their lab tests to beat U.S. manufacturers to market.

Major commercial applications of high-temperature superconductors are at least ten to 20 years off. Long dry spells in R&D seem sure. The danger is that the U.S. will lose interest when no quick payoff is in sight and that Japan will control one of the most important technologies of the future.

Factory automation

As in so many technologies, the U.S.-Japan race in factory automation is a mixed bag, with the Japanese ahead in some aspects and Americans in other areas. Japan has the jump on the U.S. in the breadth of its applications of plant automation—robots, flexible manufacturing and advanced machine tools. The U.S. has the edge in research and in computer-integrated ordering and manufacturing. Japan has more robots, but most run on U.S.-produced software. The most advanced plants in the world are in the U.S.—IBM in Austin, Tex., and Lexington, Ky.; LTV in Dallas; Allen-Bradley in Milwaukee—but Japan has more plants at a high level of automation.

Allen-Bradley's automated assembly lines for electrical relays and switches are state of the art—so flexible that the firm pays no penalty for making one of a kind rather than a large batch. Orders come in by computer and are relayed directly to the factory floor, where a bar code is imprinted on each unit as it starts down the assembly line. The code tells machinery along the way which parts should be added and where the screws go, allowing up to 700 variations in one product. A few hours after an order arrives, the goods are produced and shipped. Japan has nothing to compare with this, although it has more factories that are automated and its plants are set up for quicker turnaround from one batch to another.

U.S. companies will get a big payoff in the '90s from the record-high investments they've been making in cost-cutting and quality-enhancing equipment. In most industries, automation is a MUST for competitive reasons. And some items, such as integrated circuits, can't be made any other way.

The composites race

One of the major high-tech battles of the '90s will be fought over high-strength, lightweight composite materials, which combine two or more materials, such as carbon, glass, boron and Kevlar, to enhance the properties of each. Composites will be essential to the quality and performance of hundreds of products, ranging from planes to electronics.

The principal market for composites is now military and aerospace, in which the U.S. accounts for two-thirds of production and use. But Japan is a major player in high-strength carbon fibers and is further along than U.S. firms in adhesives for bonding composites in aerospace.

The main event will be fought over lower-performance, higher-volume composites that will go into thousands of products in the years ahead, including the walls of homes and auto and truck bodies. The trick will be to get costs down, through manufacturing processes, to the point where composites can replace aluminum, sheet steel and lumber for some uses.

The composite race is now a dead heat, with the U.S. having a slight advantage going into the home stretch because of its dominant role in aeronautics. Also, the Japanese don't seem to be targeting composites as they are ceramics.

Ceramics: U.S. leads in R&D, but that's it

In ceramics, the U.S. has the edge in research, but Japan is whipping us hands down in applying the research to marketable products. In fact, the U.S. is falling further and further behind.

As a result Japan will be selling high-performance ceramic auto engines in the '90s, at first heavy-duty diesel engines, then gasoline engines. Ceramic metal-cutting tools and drill bits will be big stuff by the mid '90s, with Japanese firms controlling the market. And in optics, Japan will lead in use of ceramics for TV, recordings, laser discs and other uses. Advanced ceramics will be the key to dealing with heat problems as integrated circuits keep getting smaller and smaller.

Can U.S. companies crack the market? Yes, but it will take a complete about-face. Most are downplaying ceramics while the Japanese are running flat out.

Next-generation TV

High-definition TV (HDTV), shown on a wide screen, will offer far more detail than ordinary TV, resulting in pictures as crisp as 35mm slides and sound as clear as compact discs. By the end of the '90s, you'll be able to watch HDTV in your living room. Japanese viewers, however, will be watching their baseball and movies on HDTV by '91. And shortly thereafter, Europeans will have their own system up and running.

While Congress, the Pentagon, the Federal Communications Commission (FCC) and the American Electronics Association were arguing over whether and how to develop HDTV in the U.S., Japanese electronics firms were beginning daily demonstration broadcasts. The Japanese have already spent $1 billion on HDTV and the Europeans about $100 million, while the U.S. is just dawdling along.

The FCC won't even settle on the U.S. transmission standard until '91 or '92. By that time, Japanese and European electronics firms will be working on the next generation of TV, perhaps holographic—three-dimensional pictures that will give you the sense of being on the football field or in the movie. So as we begin the decade, the U.S. is a distant third in the HDTV race but not quite out of it. Catching up is complicated by the fact that our home-electronics industry was decimated in the '70s. Manufacturing technology for TVs, VCRs and compact-disc players is almost nonexistent in North America.

HDTV is this country's last chance to get back into consumer electronics. And a lot more than home entertainment is at stake. HDTV requires development of high-capacity memory chips, advanced video tubes and other technology that will have a big impact in telecommunications, computers and military hardware. That's why it is essential for the U.S. to work on HDTV, even if we don't dominate sales of the sets. The Defense Department thinks HDTV is so critical for the long haul that it will bankroll a number of R&D projects. And our government will lend a hand in other ways, revising antitrust laws to let companies work together on developing, producing and marketing HDTV and setting up joint industry-government efforts to push the technology along.

The world may end up with at least three unique HDTV standards—Japanese, European and a U.S. system that will be purposely different to give Zenith and other U.S. electronics makers extra catch-up time. Present sets won't be made obsolete by HDTV; you'll be able to watch programs transmitted by the new technology but you won't get the superclear picture. It will be like the transition from black and white to color TV.

A different American standard won't provide an exclusive for a U.S. HDTV industry. Japan and Korea will simply set up separate assembly lines for making sets to receive HDTV in the U.S. or Europe. Will that leave U.S. electronics firms out in the cold? Probably not. AT&T-Bell Laboratories will make HDTV memory chips for Zenith in a joint venture that should capture a share of the market.

HDTV may be an opportunity to leapfrog Japanese technology, but it's a long shot. The Electronic Industries Association estimates that one-quarter of American homes will have HDTV by 2000, and 90% of the sets will be produced in the U.S. The catch is that most will be made in foreign-owned plants.

Information technology

The information revolution of the '90s will result from the melding of two powerful technologies: computers and telecommunications. Together, they will carry information in all forms over high-speed, high-capacity fiber-optic highways, making the world smaller and even more interdependent.

The U.S. is ahead of Japan in satellites and communications switching systems, but market access is a problem. Thus, we end up with a humongous trade deficit with Japan in telecommunications, even though our technology excels.

The driving force in communications in the next decade will be fiber optics—flashes of laser light sending information along networks of hair-thin glass fiber, handling vastly more data than traditional copper wires. For example, a single optical fiber can carry 12,000 phone conversations, compared with 48 for regular wire. In another five or six years, fiber-optic cables will run under all the oceans and throughout the Caribbean, having a multiplier effect on the amount of information that flows worldwide.

New-style computers

Computers of the '90s will be smaller, faster, more powerful and probably cheaper. And the U.S. will retain its lead in overall computer technology.

Today's most advanced computers will be obsolete by the mid '90s. Changes will keep coming at whirlwind speed. A new generation of inexpensive microprocessors—the operating core of computers—will make dinosaurs of million-dollar mainframe computers. A number of companies are already replacing their mainframes with microprocessor-based systems. By the early '90s, you'll be able to buy desktop computers that handle 50 million instructions per second, twice as many as current mainframes.

There will be tens of millions of transistors on each computer chip. New materials such as gallium arsenide will help make computers faster. And later on, superconductivity will enhance their speed.

Japanese semiconductors

Although the U.S. pioneered transistors and integrated circuits and is still on the leading edge of research, Japan dominates commercial production and exports of semiconductors, the chips that are the workhorses of computers. It controls 85% to 90% of the world market for one-megabit dynamic random access memory (D-RAM) chips, the most advanced products now available. The U.S. share of the pie is less than 10%. Gordon Moore, chairman of Intel, told us that Japanese dumping pressured American firms out of the D-RAM business in 1984-85. Now Intel, Motorola, Texas Instruments and Micron Technology are reentering competition and pushing for a joint production arrangement, which Congress may approve within the next year or two.

Through cooperative industry-government efforts such as Sematech, a strong R&D push in individual companies and changes in antitrust laws to permit joint production, U.S. firms stand a chance of closing the semiconductor gap with Japan by the mid to late '90s. By then, worldwide sales will run around $200 billion a year, which is five times as high as the current market. Semiconductor competition will soon advance to a new level: the four-megabit chip. Development is already well along in the U.S. and Japan.

U.S. supercomputers and software

American firms such as Cray and IBM will face stiffer challenges from Japan in supercomputers. A Japanese company, NEC, recently announced a machine that does 20 BILLION calculations per second, but a unit even more advanced is being developed in this country. Leadership in supercomputers is crucial to our economic fortunes in the '90s because high-performance computing will be used for everything from designing cars and planes to formulating pharmaceuticals, dyes and fibers.

America is the undisputed world leader in software, for everything from personal computers to supercomputers, in countless applications ranging from telecommunications to computer-assisted design and manufacturing. But the Japanese are working around the clock to catch up. One of their "solutions" is to promote joint ventures with U.S. software producers. Howard Yudkin, who heads the Software Productivity Consortium, thinks U.S. managers ought to get away from the "not-invented-here syndrome" on technology transfer and be less concerned about risk avoidance. "We're often dealing with a short-term mentality," he explains. "The payoff will be longer term."

Look for major advances in so-called expert systems and artificial intelligence (AI)—complex computer software that can sift through information and simulate rational thinking, giving computers a depth of information and analytical skill approaching that of an experienced professional in a given field of knowledge.

AI will provide the smarts for advanced manufacturing, ordering parts and directing assembly. It will assist air-traffic control, select military targets, assign credit ratings and help diagnose illnesses. Other expert-system software will teach children in class, coach attorneys on legal strategies and devise investment plans. The possibilities are endless.

Despite challenges from Japan and others, the U.S. has a solid lead in artificial-intelligence technology and should be able to build on it between now and the new century.

Aviation and aerospace

For years there has been talk of a hypersonic "Orient Express" that would zoom from Los Angeles to Tokyo in two or three hours, making several round-trips each day. That may come in the early 2000s but not in the '90s.

The major changes in the decade ahead will be in technologies such as composite skins to make planes lighter and more fuel efficient, optical processing and artificial intelligence to improve safety and new engines for better performance with lower fuel consumption (including some with propellers). One of the innovative new entries will be tilt-rotor, vertical-takeoff-and-landing planes now being built for the military. They'll eventually be used commercially for short-hop travel between nearby cities.

The U.S. will need technological breakthroughs to stay ahead of competition from the Airbus Industries consortium in Europe and Japan's targeting of aircraft development and production. Japan will emerge as a major competitor for Boeing, Lockheed and McDonnell Douglas by the mid '90s. Also, many foreign airlines that buy from Boeing and other U.S. producers want at least part of the work done in their countries.

For America's future competitiveness and trade balance, it is essential that the industry build on its global lead. Our aerospace industry contributes a sizable trade surplus year after year, $18 billion in '88 and probably about the same in '89. U.S. aircraft manufacturers have traditionally exported a good share of their production, both military and civilian craft.

Commercial space launches

The '90s will see intense competition among private firms in the growing field of commercial rocket launching to carry communication satellites and research experiments into space.

Communication and tracking satellites will remain the dominant interest of business in space during the '90s. Data transmission will expand worldwide. Satellites will keep watch over ships, trains and trucks, and portable phone connections will be possible from almost anywhere by '00.

U.S. aerospace firms will rent facilities at Cape Canaveral, Vandenberg Air Force Base and elsewhere for commercial launches. They will have to compete with Europe's Ariane space-launch project, The Soviet Union and emerging industries in Japan, China and even India. Japan has licensed technology from the U.S.-made Delta rocket and is modifying it for launches. And the Chinese are already quoting launch prices at 50% less than their U.S. competitors. (Discount space shots. What's next?)

Cooperation in space

Look for more cooperative space exploration—a dozen or more countries getting together to share know-how and costs and to build better relations. For example, space agencies from 22 nations will observe the 500th anniversary of Columbus' discovery of the New World with an International Space Year in '92, concentrating on the greenhouse effect, ozone depletion and other ecological threats.

And work will begin in the '90s on a manned space station for earth observation, telecommunications, satellite control, processing of materials and other uses. The U.S. will deal with Canada, Japan and nine European countries as part of a 30-year agreement.

U.S. and European space scientists are planning an umanned probe to the rings of Saturn and an instrument landing on Titan, one of Saturn's moons. Also during the '90s the U.S. will get started on a new generation of unmanned space explorers. The Magellan launch in early '89 was the first U.S. interplanetary probe since 1978. It will arrive at Venus in 1990.

Recent failures won't sidetrack Russia's space effort. Military and scientific uses of space are very important to the Soviets. Expect joint U.S.-Soviet space planetary probes and scientific projects, but that doesn't mean space competition will disappear. Both nations will expand their space programs for intelligence gathering, ballistic missile defenses, offensive arms, communications and antisatellite lasers.

By early '90, the Hubble Space Telescope will be put in orbit, extending the observation powers of astronomers to seven times present levels. And a gamma-ray observatory is scheduled to be scanning the universe within a year or so.

Work will get under way in the '90s to return astronauts to the moon early in the next century. The next generation of manned missions to the moon will be used to exploit its resources and establish a permanent research station there for trips to Mars and beyond by 2050.

5 Shifting Global Markets

U.S. and Japan will start thousands of joint ventures.

Europe '92 will be the toughest trade challenge to U.S.

U.S. trade with Canada and Mexico will nearly triple.

A U.S.-Pacific Rim trade deal will be worked out in '90s.

Third World debt will be stretched out and written down.

The Soviet economy won't get on its feet by 2000.

China will emerge as the new manufacturing hub of Asia.

Small Asian nations will grow the fastest in next decade.

While the U.S. has been getting its act together in the '80s, so have many other nations. With trade and international investment accelerating, no one wants to be left in the dust. Throughout the world, governments are getting ready to participate in the trade boom of the Global '90s.

Success will require more speed, agility and aggressiveness than ever before. Sleepy domestic industries will be less protected by benevolent governments. And governments will be held more accountable for the performance of their nations' economies, both domestically and in world trade.

More than ever before, economic power in the '90s will count for more than military might. That's why the Pacific Rim nations will be on the ascent as powers and the Soviet Union will be on the decline. Indeed, global economic power will be the foundation upon which world influence rests, in both diplomacy and military affairs.

This realization has led to a worldwide surge in economic experimentation, focusing on free-market mechanisms. It is also leading to new alignments of nations, within regions and among regions—new trade pacts among allies, opening of trade between former antagonists, sharing of security burdens. Every new trade agreement will be designed to give its members competitive advantage and, in the process, will put nonmembers at a disadvantage.

With growing world integration will necessarily come a loss of national autonomy—not just for the U.S. but for every nation. "The U.S. economy (like most other economies) has become far more subject to international forces that are beyond the pale of political control," says Richard McKenzie, of the Center for the Study of American Business at Washington University in St. Louis. "Integration means that domestic fiscal, monetary and regulatory policies are now being guided more by international economic forces and less by domestic political constraints. Politics is having to yield to economics."

To do business in the '90s, you'll have to adjust your thinking. The old ways of doing business will be out. There will be whole new ways of dealing with customers and suppliers. This will entail more than learning foreign markets. Americans will have to make the effort to learn the languages of their customers around the world, just as Japanese businessmen have learned ours. They'll have to switch to metric measurement, if they haven't already, and make other adjustments to world markets. This chapter will give you an overview of significant economic and trade developments, showing you how the U.S. and your industry may fit into these shifting patterns.

The broad trends

Economic growth rates will improve throughout the world, but wide variations will persist. The fastest-growing economies will be Asia's rapidly industrializing nations, such as South Korea, China, India, Singapore, Taiwan, Malaysia, Thailand and Indonesia. Latin America and Africa will lag behind, but there will be a few bright spots on each continent.

In the U.S., world trade will account for an increasing share of the economy, rising from 16% to at least one-fifth of American

GNP by 2000. Exports will grow faster than imports, so the trade deficit will narrow and probably disappear by the late '90s.

Count on more regional trading blocs, similar to Europe '92 and the new U.S.-Canada trade pact. A U.S.-Pacific Rim arrangement is a good bet in the next ten to 15 years—a treaty that might include Japan, Taiwan, Korea, Singapore, Indonesia, Malaysia and Thailand. The U.S. will strengthen its ties to Mexico and the rest of Latin America, but we don't foresee free-trade arrangements similar to those that exist with Israel and Canada.

Economic unification of Europe in '92 will be the toughest nut that U.S. traders will have to crack in the '90s. Once you strip away the rhetoric, Europe '92 is designed to benefit European companies and restrain competition from the U.S. and Japan. Look for a unified Western Europe to expand its trade with the Eastern Bloc. Europe will use economic chips in dealing with the Eastern Bloc on political matters, as in relations between West Germany and East Germany.

The Third World "debt crisis" will be gradually alleviated by rolling over current debts into new loans with longer terms and lower interest rates—essentially a planned write-down (and occasionally, a total write-off). Most big banks have already heavily discounted these "assets." The U.S. government will encourage banks to make new loans to developing countries by offering some kind of repayment guarantee, probably through the World Bank or International Monetary Fund. All of this will improve the liquidity of the Third World—and the capacity of those countries to buy from the U.S.—but it will take years.

Japan, the world's second-largest economy and the largest lender, will pose an increasingly serious challenge to the U.S. in a number of key industries. It will continue to achieve strong economic growth, but at a lower rate than in the past few decades, reflecting the maturing of its economy. It will have to contend with rising production costs; the limits on growth imposed by its geographic smallness, aging population and modest natural resources; and the demands of its citizens for a higher standard of living. It will move more and more of its production to lower-cost overseas sites (including the U.S.), just as American firms began doing in the '60s and '70s and continue to do.

The Soviet Union and Eastern Europe will improve their economic performance, but not as much as their leaders hope.

They will also increase their dealings with the West. Mikhail Gorbachev's policies of *perestroika* and *glasnost* have raised economic and social aspirations in both Russia and Eastern Europe, but this will go only so far; the satellites won't be allowed to shift out of the Soviet orbit.

The U.S. will be the only truly global power, involved in all regions of the world with a combination of economic, military and political leadership. The Soviets will be a superpower in terms of military strength, but they will lack the economic and technological vitality for global leadership. Japan has the economic power, but it will not be trusted with a major role in regional security. While many nations will try to copy its export-driven growth, Japanese society is not a compelling model for world emulation, comparable to America's message of economic openness, creativity and personal liberty.

Trade versus security

In the Global '90s our relations with the rest of the world will hinge more on trade and economics, less on military and political considerations. For years, trade played second fiddle to security and foreign policy. So what if we lost a billion dollars in sales here and there because of a ban on grain sales to the Soviet Union, trade embargos on South Africa and Rhodesia, limits on high-tech exports to communist countries? We were so dominant in world trade we could easily shrug off a few lost export opportunities to make an international statement. Today U.S. trade is in deficit, and America has learned there are many other nations waiting in the wings to make the sales we decline to make for reasons of national security or morality.

Count on a growing conflict between U.S. commercial and military interests. Some of the conflict will arise in Europe, because of better relations with the Soviets and the fact that Western Europe and Japan are keen on trade with the Eastern Bloc. Other tensions will arise in our dealings with the Japanese. For example, we want Japan to help us with the economic burden of world security and development assistance. But should we develop weaponry with the Japanese if that gives them access to American technology, making them a tougher competitor in commercial aircraft and computers?

Washington has had trouble balancing economic and military concerns. By contrast, the Japanese define national security mainly in terms of economics and trade, and they take advantage of the differences that exist between U.S. government agencies. The Japanese are assisted by thousands of American lobbyists, lawyers and public relations advisers, including former White House aides, members of Congress and U.S. trade negotiators. They spend more to lobby Washington than the U.S. Chamber of Commerce, National Association of Manufacturers and other major business groups *combined*, according to Pat Choate, vice president for policy analysis at TRW Corp.

Now take a look at what's happening in other regions of the world, and the implications for American trade.

CANADA

U.S.-Canada trade amounts to some $160 billion a year—the most between any two nations—and will probably *triple* by the turn of the century, mainly because of the 1988 trade agreement. We already do more business with the province of Ontario than we do with ALL of Japan.

The new trade deal will create jobs and business on both sides of the border and make North America more competitive in world markets. It will get rid of practically all tariffs by 1999. Canada's are twice as high as ours, so we get a big break on that score. In the short term, at least during the '90s, Canadians have more to gain than the U.S. because they'll get freer access to the world's richest market, a country with 250 million people, compared with Canada's 26 million. Long term, the U.S. stands to benefit through access to Canadian resources—natural gas, oil, lumber and uranium.

Within each country the impact of free trade will fall differently on various industries. For example, Canadian manufacturers of steel, newsprint and aluminum are among the most efficient and competitive in world markets and stand to benefit from the agreement. On the other hand, Canadian food processing, brewing, textile, furniture, computer and electronics firms will run into stiffer competition from U.S. companies. The pact will lead to mergers, especially in Canada—companies getting together to tackle the much-expanded consumer market.

The first stage, January 1, 1989, ended levies on computers, motorcycles, phones, aircraft, stereos, ski equipment and skates. The next stage will be a five-year phaseout of duties on furniture, paper and paperboard, chemicals, radio and TV sets and telecommunications gear. There will be a speed-up of this schedule for some items, eliminating tariffs within the next few years. Finally, a ten-year phaseout is scheduled for some of the more sensitive lines, such as steel, copper, zinc, textiles, clothing, shoes, drugs and cosmetics. In addition to ending tariffs the agreement will reduce nontariff barriers and establish a U.S.-Canadian arbitration board for settling disputes, such as differences over plywood and farm goods.

MEXICO

Mexico will continue to be our third-largest trading partner, behind Canada and Japan. Total U.S.-Mexican trade is now $45 billion a year. Expect it to top $130 billion by the end of the '90s because the Mexican government will open up to more foreign investment, production sharing and two-way trade, and it will loosen its grip on key industries. The U.S. will try hard to prop up the Mexican economy, recognizing that tough times there could trigger deep political and social unrest that could eventually strike against our country.

Mexico will aggressively pursue American investment to bolster its wobbly economy, whittle down debt and create jobs. With a very young population, it needs investment today to make jobs for tomorrow. To attract investment, President Carlos Salinas de Gortari is shedding red tape and restrictions on foreign ownership and will expand protection of intellectual property, such as computer software and manufacturing processes. And more state-owned industries will be privatized.

Mexico's population will zoom from about 90 million in 1990 to 110 million by 2000, adding as many people as the U.S. during the same period, even though Mexico is a much smaller country. Of the 110 million, 60 million will be age 24 or younger—meaning greater pressure for emigration to the U.S. in the early years of the next century.

Production sharing by U.S. and Mexican firms already runs

close to $10 billion a year, counting the 1,400 *maquiladoras* and other joint-assembly arrangements. Launched in 1965, the *maquiladora* program lets foreign businesses set up factories in Mexico free of the general prohibitions on such enterprises, as long as the products are exported. U.S. companies can send machinery, raw materials and semifinished parts into Mexico duty free and later import the assembled products, paying re-entry duties only on the value that's added at the plants. Most of the *maquilas* are U.S.-owned, but an increasing number of foreign firms, especially Japanese, are opening manufacturing facilities in northern Mexico.

American electronics, auto, clothing and consumer-appliance firms were the first to arrive in the Rio Grande Valley of Mexico. Now agricultural and food-processing *maquilas* are sprouting, too. Cheap labor is the one thing these plants have in common. All told, *maquiladoras* employ 350,000 Mexicans, accounting for 15% of all manufacturing jobs in that country. And another 100,000 Americans work in supplying the plants. Those figures may triple during the '90s.

Will the U.S. hammer out a trade agreement with Mexico, similar to the U.S.-Canadian free-trade pact? No, certainly nothing as comprehensive. The economies of the two countries—especially labor costs—are vastly different. Mexico is traditionally paternalistic; its industries are hooked on government subsidies, and Salinas can't reverse this in the near future. The U.S. can't simply open its borders to EVERYTHING Mexico wants to sell, at any price. But there will be more industry-by-industry trade deals on steel, textiles, electronics, auto parts, food, chemicals and pharmaceuticals.

SOUTH AND CENTRAL AMERICA

Long term, South America carries great potential for U.S. business. But short term, most of the countries will be severely limited in what they can buy from us because of heavy debts, economic stagnation and political instability. Even assuming that the debts will eventually be written down or written off by U.S. banks, Latin America will continue to run huge trade surpluses with the U.S. throughout the '90s.

Take Brazil, for example, the eighth-largest market in the free world. Its two-way trade with the U.S. hit an all-time high last year, $14 billion. The catch is that $10 billion of it was products it sent here—shoes, Volkswagens, auto parts, orange juice, radios, iron and steel, coffee, and other goods. Saddled with debt and lacking sufficient investment to develop its extraordinary potential, Brazil will sell more than it will buy from us for many years to come.

Argentina is in the same boat. Debt relief will help but won't work any miracles, so its economy will have to be export driven. Venezuela, the third-largest market for U.S. goods in the Western Hemisphere, will retrench in the next three to five years to get its budget in shape and attract foreign investment. But it is beginning to privatize petrochemicals and other industries and will probably get its house in order by the late '90s.

Of the major South American countries, Colombia and Chile are in the best shape economically. Colombia has grown every year in the '80s, has a trade surplus of $10 billion and no serious debt problems, but it is overly dependent on drug trafficking. The drug trade and roaming guerrilla gangs have soiled the country's reputation in recent years and scared off foreign investors. If its government gets a grip on these problems, Colombia will emerge as the crown jewel of South America by the late '90s—and as a good customer for U.S. business.

Chile likewise enjoys strong economic growth with budget and trade surpluses. Its big challenge will come after current president, General Augusto Pinochet, steps down, when it will attempt to increase democracy and political freedom without turning away from the free-market programs that have been the key to its economic success.

More help for Central America

Though U.S. foreign-assistance programs won't be stepped up greatly during the '90s (due to the U.S. budget deficit), Central America will get a bigger piece of the pie. Many of the ideas of the 1984 Kissinger Commission report will be put in place, leading to greater economic engagement and targeted aid in the Central American democracies as a way of heading off communist overtures and lifting living standards.

The U.S. will work with Japan, Taiwan and other industrialized countries to bolster market-oriented economies in Honduras, El Salvador, Guatemala and Costa Rica, thus creating examples that Nicaragua may aspire to. The economic turmoil in Cuba, Russia's key client state in the Western Hemisphere, together with some improvement of Central American living standards, will keep other countries from falling for totalitarian regimes.

It's a good bet that Panama will recover after military strongman Manuel Noriega gives up control and private investment returns. The U.S. will hand over control of the Panama Canal at the end of the '90s, as agreed. Still, as the Noriega episode shows, the U.S. will have to get more involved and be less reactive when advancing its interests in Latin America.

THE EUROPEAN COMMUNITY

Taken together, the 12 nations of the European Community and the U.S. produce two-thirds of the noncommunist world's GNP. Viewed as a single multination market, Western Europe is both America's largest customer and largest competitor. U.S. trade with Europe (especially exports) has been booming recently and will probably double by '95. Thus, major economic changes there are bound to affect trade and investment prospects for thousands of U.S. businesses.

Before looking at the implications for the U.S., keep in mind that Europe '92 is still controversial within Europe; there is no unanimity that it will be good for most European businesses. It will take a while for things to fall in place, and there will still be wide cost disparities, jealousies and charges of unfairness. For example, Spain and Portugal will have labor-cost advantages over the others. And companies that have enjoyed protection and even subsidies within their own country will suddenly face stiff competition from firms based in other European nations.

What's at stake for the U.S.

The coming integration of Europe is the single most important challenge to U.S. trading interests as we enter the '90s. "No other issue places a greater demand for cooperation between the U.S. government and the private sector—not market access to Japan, nor controls on exports to the U.S.S.R., nor the rise of

Asia's newly industrializing nations to trading prominence, not even what to do about Latin American debt," says Lionel H. Olmer, a former under secretary of commerce for international trade.

Europe '92 will create the largest trading block in the industrialized world, an internal market of 320 million people without barriers, dwarfing Russia's market of 285 million, our 250 million and Japan's 122 million.

To give you an idea of what's at stake, business between the European Economic Community (EC) and the United States— combining annual flows and current values of fixed assets— already amounts to over $1 *trillion*, broken down like this:

Annual U.S. exports to the EC	$ 76 billion
EC exports to the U.S.	$ 89 billion
Value of U.S. plants and equipment in the EC	$122 billion
Value of the EC's direct investment in the U.S.	$158 billion
Annual sales by European divisions of U.S. firms	$450 billion
Sales by U.S. affiliates of European companies	$340 billion

Our two-way trade with the European Community comes to $165 billion a year. That's $5 billion more than our trade with Canada. What's more, the U.S. has become a magnet for European investors. Well over 300 U.S. firms were bought by British investors alone in a six-month period in 1988, at a value greater than $20 billion.

American response to Europe '92

Officially, the U.S. government supports Europe '92. "An economically stronger, more competitive and technologically innovative Europe is in our strategic and economic interest," says Commerce Secretary Robert Mosbacher. "A single European market open to the world provides the best basis for growth in global business and multilateral trade cooperation." But the unanswered question is, will Europe *be* "open to the world?"

Many U.S. managers who know the ropes there think that the

new single market will enhance trade opportunities and eliminate nuisances such as bewildering licensing requirements and differing technical standards from one country to the next. They see it as improving economic growth within Europe and as a plus for U.S. firms that do business there.

In fact, major U.S. corporations that already operate all over Europe, such as IBM, Ford and Honeywell, may be better off in the new pan-European economy than European firms that are accustomed to doing business in only one country.

But there's no doubt that Europe '92 is driven largely by fear and insecurity among the 12 member countries that they won't be competitive with the U.S. and Japan in industries such as telecommunications, computers and semiconductors unless they unite. Europe '92 is NOT driven by a sudden conversion to Adam Smith and wide-open markets.

Protectionism in Europe

Europe's only previous effort at creating a single market—the Common Agricultural Policy—resulted in a massive loss of markets by U.S. farmers and agribusiness, former Under Secretary Olmer points out. "Thus, if we were to draw a lesson from the agricultural unification of Europe, we should indeed be wary of concluding too quickly that EC 1992 will benefit the U.S. business community," he notes. Europe's current agricultural policy may be the single largest trade barrier in the world, costing U.S. farmers billions of dollars each year.

Judging by recent EC policies, Europeans think they need government intervention or they will fall further behind in technology, innovation and profits. Without such protection Europeans figure that they will be second-class citizens in the world economy of the 21st century. The big threat to U.S. business is that Europe will bargain away the legitimate interests of outsiders as it tries to balance the political interests of the EC's 12 member countries (plus probably two more after '92—Austria and Norway).

"Fortress Europe may not be a realistic outcome, but selected protectionism—defended as temporary measures for import-sensitive sectors (automobiles, computers, semiconductors, telecommunications, textiles and agriculture, to name only the obvious)—will be defended as necessary," Olmer states. Japanese companies may be even more of a target of selected protectionism than U.S. firms, with the EC restricting imports from Japanese subsidiaries in the U.S.—cars, photocopiers, integrated circuits, VCRs and other goods.

Among U.S. industries that will face big hurdles because of European unification are telecommunications, apparel, financial services and electronics. Europe will use standard-setting government procurement and "reciprocity" to head off outside competitors. In setting a common policy in TV programming, for example, Europe has agreed to limit the proportion of the programming day devoted to shows from the U.S. And it has been proposed that non-EC banks desiring an EC-wide banking license must pass a "reciprocity review." If the EC follows through on this, there will be new barriers to entry of all non-EC banks, financial-service firms and insurance companies.

Because of such problems, U.S. business will have to work closely with government trade representatives and Congress to get a fair shake in European markets. They will be stressing that today's global interdependence results from market forces, not government intervention, and that the best bet for Europe is free world commerce, not inward-looking protectionism. If Europe agrees—and that's a big IF—the coming changes would benefit both the U.S. and Europe.

THE SOVIET SPHERE

The Soviet Union is a first-class military power with a third-class economy. To maintain its military prowess, it has always been willing to sacrifice its people's living standards. Now it's trying to build up its economy without losing military superiority. That will be a tough trick for a country that has trouble keeping meat on the table.

The results of Gorbachev's economic reforms will be slow and uneven in developing. And many proposals will never see the light of day. Consumer goods in Russia will remain scarce and shoddy well into the 21st century. Meanwhile, Gorbachev will angle for more help from the West—credit, products and especially, know-how. Soviet debts to the West increased $17 billion during Gorbachev's first four years in office, and they'll increase a lot more. His main objective in the '90s will be to give his economy a badly needed jump start.

Gorbachev is already finding out that a little freedom can be a dangerous thing—dangerous to the stability of a repressive regime. He has led the Soviet people to expect a pace of improvement in living standards that will be impossible to achieve in the short run. His reforms have angered and threatened government bureaucrats who owe their comfortable existence to the status quo. If unfulfilled public expectations lead to social unrest and open challenges to the regime—as in Poland—Gorbachev's rivals will blame him and maneuver to oust him. It's not a foregone conclusion that he and his reforms will survive.

The Eastern Bloc

As the Soviet Union scrambles for trade and economic assistance from the West, its satellites in Eastern Europe will do the same, like railroad cars following the engine. The trouble is, Hungary, Poland, Czechoslovakia, Yugoslavia, Bulgaria and Romania don't have the resources to export and earn the hard currencies they need. They will try for autonomy on trade but will be thrown back to relying on Russia for many basics, especially energy. With the exception of East Germany, the East Bloc satellites will remain in an economic twilight zone.

East Germany can make it on its own and will strengthen its ties with Western Europe. Unlike other Eastern Bloc satellites, it isn't overloaded with debt and has succeeded in developing healthy export markets for precision instruments, sophisticated machine tools and other goods. And East Germany has backdoor access to the European Economic Community, due to its special relationship with Bonn. There's tremendous trade between the two Germanies, with an understanding that Germany is united for trade purposes, at least. Economic ties may eventually lead to some form of political confederation of East and West Germany, but that's a long shot for the '90s.

Trade with the West

U.S. trade with Russia gets a lot of attention in the papers and on TV, but it's small potatoes compared with the business that we do with most other countries. Total two-way trade with the U.S.S.R. is only $3.5 billion. We sell the Soviets $2.8 billion in agricultural products and equipment and buy $580 million in petroleum products, chrome, magnesium, vodka and furs.

Look for growth in both exports and imports in the '90s, but the U.S. will still sell more than it buys. There will be strong growth in joint ventures—food, Fords, floppy disks and other items—now that ways have been found for U.S. firms to repatriate their profits in dollars. But total business with Russia will still be small compared with China, Korea or Western Europe.

Gorbachev will buy turnkey plants and glom on to Western technology by hook or by crook. To improve the lot of Soviet consumers, he'll set up assembly-line poultry factories, welcome Ford Motor Company to Russia and let the Japanese make TVs and VCRs there. Companies considering deals with the Soviets should remember that the Russians want control, 51% or more in partnerships. And cash earnings are often hard to come by. They'll try to pay off in products and keep the dollars at home.

To earn hard currency for improvements at home, the U.S.S.R. will peddle more oil and gas, gold and other resources. But that won't be enough. Moscow will need billions in Western loans, credits and guarantees, and it will no doubt get them. Russia hasn't welshed on its debts since it repudiated the pre-Revolution Czarist loans years ago. After it makes good on Czarist bonds that are held by the West, the Soviets will seek credits and "most favored nation" status from the U.S., and probably get them, at least on a trial basis. U.S. and European bankers, who have run out their string in Latin America, consider the U.S.S.R. quite creditworthy, and will trip all over themselves to provide the money Gorbachev wants.

There's no guarantee that Western credits will turn the Soviet economy around. Loans certainly didn't do the job for Poland, Yugoslavia or Romania. The system itself—the lack of incentives—is the problem. That's why it's unlikely the Soviet economy will get on its feet in the next ten to 15 years.

Soviet agriculture

Gorbachev's move to dismantle his agricultural bureaucracy—by gradually shifting toward some semblance of "free market" farming and allowing farmers to lease state land for life and pass it on to their children—shows how frustrated he has become with his own rickety economy.

After a transition period, he believes Russian farmers should have "complete freedom" in marketing their crops and livestock, including the right to sell directly to processors, farm markets and restaurants. (Farmers have been promised this right in the past but in practice, Moscow takes most of their crops.) They now deliver their goods to the government at fixed prices to fulfill quotas set in Moscow.

Why did Gorbachev pick food for his grand experiment with market orientation? Because he knows it best, having served as the party's agricultural secretary through the crop failures of the '70s, massive grain purchases from the West and bungled distribution schemes.

And Gorbachev knows that more and better food is essential to improving living standards. He told a party meeting that, "the essence of economic change in the countryside should be in granting farmers broad opportunities for displaying independence, enterprise and initiative." That's an admission by the General Secretary of the Communist Party that the 1929-33 collectivization of Soviet peasantry was a blunder and that communism isn't working.

Gorbachev learned his market lessons during the rough and tumble U.S.-Russian grain deals of the early '70s. In the first round of purchases, buyers from Moscow hoodwinked U.S. sellers by keeping the extent of their massive orders secret to avoid running up prices. For several weeks, they cleverly played off one U.S. company against another, using the advantages of a centrally run system against the vulnerabilities of a free market.

But that trick never worked again. Using space satellites and other means, U.S. grain merchants kept close tabs on Soviet crop conditions, and an elaborate sales reporting system was set up through the Department of Agriculture. Soon, Gorbachev was admiring not only the productive might of the U.S. but also the advantages of a private system and the financial acumen and marketing skills of U.S. agribusiness executives, some of whom he still consults on a regular basis. The flaws and contradictions of his own economic system were driven home in a powerful way, an experience that's now leading to the biggest changes ever in the Soviet system, extending far beyond agriculture.

U.S.-Soviet military tensions

Forecasts for the coming decade must include some assumptions about matters other than trade and economics. One assumption we're making is that regional fighting and wars will be part of the '90s just as they've been part of every other decade in this century, but that there will NOT be a global or nuclear war.

No doubt the Soviets are tempted from time to time to use their raw military power as a way out of their economic and political mess; after all, they've sacrificed so much to build their arsenal. If they decided to, they could clobber the West, because we have no nuclear shield and won't have one in the '90s. The Strategic Defense Initiative will remain largely a research project. But the Soviets know that the West would smack them right back with missiles aimed at their cities, factories and military installations—leaving the "victor" with nothing but ruins.

Does that mean nuclear war can be ruled out? No. Even though we believe it's very unlikely, a hard-line Soviet regime, frustrated by economic failures and perhaps threatened politically, might unleash its ultimate weapon. And about 15 more countries, including some in the Third World, will develop ballistic missiles capable of carrying chemical or nuclear warheads. Given a certain predictability in the U.S.-Soviet rivalry, the greater threat to world security may come from the spread of nuclear weapons among smaller nations and the incessant threat of terrorism, which gets more sophisticated every year.

That's why we'll spend 5% of our GNP for defense in the '90s. For the U.S., the challenge of the '90s will be to achieve more security from fewer resources (partly through our lead in technology) and to get Japan and our NATO allies to pick up a bigger share of defense costs.

Defense sharing will move forward, but very slowly, and the U.S. will still have to bear the lion's share of the burden. The Japanese are more inclined to push commercial interests than chip in for defense. And Western Europe has been taken in by the charm of Gorbachev; it seems inclined to look upon the Soviet Union as benign and nonthreatening, no worse than the U.S.

Gorbachev's reforms depend on substantial trade and economic relations with the noncommunist world. For the Soviets, that world is mainly Western Europe.

Peace through deterrence

At the heart of U.S. national security interests is one constant: Only Russia has the military might—nuclear and conventional capabilities—to inflict devastating damage on the U.S. and its allies. This will be a fact of life well into the 21st century, even though nuclear-arms reduction agreements of the past few years have been a giant step in the right direction. For the U.S., this fact means the same measured efforts that have maintained peace through deterrence will have to continue. It does not mean everything in our national security interest hinges on U.S.-Soviet relations. Our strategic defense concerns are wider and more complex than simple competition between the U.S. and the U.S.S.R.

The world of the 21st century will be multipolar and diverse. Other power centers will emerge as more important players— the unified Europeans, Japan, China, India, Israel, certain Arab states, and the Asian "tigers" such as Korea, Taiwan, Singapore and Thailand. Our strength and resources, geopolitical position and strategic interests mean that we'll be involved globally in many spheres at all times. This is the framework for America's responsibilities and challenges in the years ahead.

The good news in U.S. security for the '90s is that we and other democracies *have won* the Cold War with our common efforts and values. It's not overstating things to say that democratic institutions have shown they work better for the common good than totalitarian systems. If the U.S.S.R. stays on the course of Gorbachev's liberalizing reforms, imitation will truly prove to be the highest form of international flattery. The main task will be to maintain the consensus on strength and deterrence, which has preserved peace for some 45 years.

JAPAN

As living standards continue to improve in Japan and consumer spending grows (encouraged by the government), a more-balanced Japanese economy will emerge—a little less export-driven and more oriented to domestic spending. The need for better housing, roads, trains and telecommunications to link Tokyo with the rest of the country will increase. The Japanese will gradually consume more and save less. And many of the barriers to imports of American food, electronics and equipment will be broken down—but not without a struggle over every small gain.

Currency swings and production costs

Japanese businesses will keep the competitive heat on the U.S., regardless of the exchange rate between the dollar and yen. The decline in the dollar against the yen has made a terrific difference in relative production costs between the U.S. and Japan. In February 1985, one dollar bought 260 yen; four years later, it bought only 130. As a result, U.S. unit labor costs in manufacturing sank 28% below Japan's, making the U.S. the low-cost producer among the industrialized nations and egging on the Japanese to build more plants in the U.S. and purchase American companies with their strengthened yen.

Many problems that infected U.S. industry in the '70s—runaway labor costs, militant unions and aggressive foreign competition—are now confronting Japan. While Japan's business groups are targeting inflation threats as "public enemy number one," the Japanese Private Sector Trade Union Confederation lists higher wages and benefits as its top objective, making that country's exports less competitive. Already, appreciation of the yen and huge trade surpluses are pricing Japan out of the labor market in Asia, giving an edge to Taiwan and Korea and forcing Japan to move production abroad, to less-expensive Asian and Latin American countries (and to the U.S. too).

But Japanese firms have so far shown an amazing ability to hold market share in the face of rising prices and currency. Many of them are planning on the yen going as high as 100 to the dollar (some even say 80), and they think that they can sell goods in the U.S. at that level, either by shaving their profit margins or maintaining them through productivity gains.

The U.S.-Japan trade deficit

The U.S. trade deficit with Japan—now more than $55 billion,

40% of our worldwide trade deficit—will narrow significantly but won't disappear. It took a long time to build up, and it will take just as long to chisel away. The last time we ran a trade surplus with Japan was in 1964.

It may surprise you that we're already selling a lot to the Japanese: $38 billion worth of airplanes and parts, chemicals, computers and office machinery, logs and lumber, corn, soybeans and other products in '88. Trouble is, we're importing so much more: $93 billion in cars, TVs, VCRs, compact disc players, computers, fax machines, copiers, cameras—you name it.

In the years ahead, the Japanese will import more from the U.S. and the rest of the world, but it's debatable whether the U.S. will consume less Japanese-brand merchandise. Americans might end up buying fewer Japanese imports—but more goods made by U.S. subsidiaries of Japanese firms.

The fuss over a joint U.S.-Japanese effort to build 130 FSX advanced fighter planes may prove to be a watershed in U.S.-Japan relations. The U.S. military wanted the deal as a major step in military burden sharing. The Commerce Department opposed it, on the grounds that it would give away too much U.S. technology that could be used by the Japanese to develop their own commercial aviation industry. But the differences were eventually accommodated.

After many years of foregoing such deals, the U.S. will enter hundreds of joint high-tech manufacturing ventures with the Japanese where mutual commercial benefits are at stake. These will cover everything from high-definition TV to biotech and superconductivity. Both sides will have more to gain than to lose.

Japan as lender, investor, donor

For years Japan's strong exports and high savings rate have been generating more capital than it can invest at home. So its businesses scour the world for investment opportunities as lenders and equity investors in operating businesses.

Japan is playing a big role in financing the U.S. budget deficits by purchasing billions in U.S. government securities—20% to 40% of the successful bids at recent Treasury note auctions. (That's one reason the White House and Treasury handle Japan with kid gloves.) Japan's investment in U.S. businesses and real estate totaled $33.4 billion in 1987. Meanwhile, U.S. companies were investing $14.3 billion on such facilities in Japan. That amount would be even higher if it weren't for barriers to U.S. investment there.

Japan is now the leading contributor of nonmilitary foreign aid in the world, surpassing the U.S., even though our economy is twice as large. That's one reason Japan will demand more say-so in running the global economy, throwing its weight around at the World Bank and International Monetary Fund and in economic matters throughout Latin America and Africa. The Japanese will push their ideas on Third World debt and other matters, whether we like them or not.

But Japan won't get a free ride. Americans will insist that the Japanese pick up a bigger share of the defense burden—bigger than the $2.5 billion that they're now paying to support American forces there, roughly $45,000 for each U.S. serviceman in Japan. "Are we really going to keep 25,000 troops in South Korea and 50,000 in Japan when we owe them a trillion dollars?" asks Clyde Prestowitz, a former top Commerce Department official. The answer may be a resounding no.

In the '90s, Japan's immense economic influence will give it more political power in the Pacific, and its military role will increase gradually, especially in northern Asia, a fact that won't set well with Korea, China and others. Japan will be acquiring more sophisticated and mission-capable aircraft, naval vessels and high-tech weapons, largely from the U.S. This will help our trade balance with Japan and ease our military costs in the Pacific, although not as much as we'd like.

ASIA'S NEW INDUSTRIAL STARS

The smaller economies of Asia will experience the world's highest growth rates in the Global '90s, taking advantage of the combination of low-cost labor and high investment in automation by multinational companies from the U.S., Japan and Europe.

Given the rising importance of the Pacific nations to America's economic well-being and the proliferation of joint ventures and other arrangements expected between now and 1995, a U.S.-Pacific Rim free-trade agreement is already being chewed over by our government and is a good possibility by 2000.

Labor costs in Korea, China and Singapore are less than a third of the $12-an-hour average in Japan, so a lot of the manufacturing is shifting to those countries. Korea will continue to beat Japan on prices if not on quality. The Koreans are just plain out-hustling the competition, with employees working an average 2,800 hours per year compared with 2,200 in Japan, 1,880 in the U.S. and 1,700 in Europe. A six-day, 72-hour workweek is not unusual in Korea. But the unions are taking a more strident, hard-boiled approach on political and economic matters and threaten to slow that country's huge productivity gains.

Taiwan won't be left in the dust by Korea, China or anyone else. Its huge capital resources and free-market system ensure it will be one of the principal trade centers of the Pacific well into the next century. Look for closer trade ties between Taiwan and China before Hong Kong reverts to Chinese sovereignty in '97.

Indonesia is a sleeping giant with a large, highly skilled labor force, plus oil, rubber, mining and other industries. Malaysia, following the Korean model, is developing an auto industry, has plenty of tin and rubber, and is aggressively seeking foreign joint ventures for manufacturing. The Philippines hope to get things off dead center with economic assistance from Japan and the U.S. and more political stability. Thailand is one of the brightest spots in Asia—a boomy economy, flourishing agricultural exports and plans for new manufacturing facilities to serve Japanese auto-makers and others. Long before the end of the '90s, U.S. relations with Vietnam and Laos will be "normalized"—diplomatic and trade ties renewed.

India, the world's largest democracy, is a land of opportunity for American business. But it's also a tough place to do business because of protectionism, red tape and corruption. The best bet is to work with a reliable Indian partner. Two-way trade with India is close to $5.7 billion. We buy $3.2 billion in cut diamonds, apparel and textiles and sell $2.5 billion in equipment, farm products and fertilizer. India's close ties with the Soviet Union limit our sales of sensitive electronic gear there.

CHINA

If it remains on course—after catching its breath from recent overstimulation—China will emerge as the new manufacturing hub of the Far East in the '90s, using Hong Kong as its financial center after the takeover in '97. You'll see more and more manufacturing shifting there from higher-cost countries such as Japan, Korea and Taiwan.

Despite all the hoopla over doing business with Russia, the fact is that China is a much better bet for U.S. exporters and investors. If you want to see economic change, look to China, not the Soviet Union. The Chinese are trying to develop an export-driven economy, using Hong Kong, Korea and Taiwan as models. Manufacturing centers are popping up all along China's coasts. The Chinese have a tradition of trade and entrepreneurism going back centuries and they're willing to take risks to reap profits. They're miles ahead of the Soviets in understanding how markets work and in making deals.

But China's is still a centrally controlled socialist economy, so changes must suit government planners. The bureaucrats think things got out of hand in 1988, that the economy grew TOO fast, firing up inflation, causing bottlenecks and shortages, encouraging corruption—and diminishing their control over Chinese society. So they cooled things off a while, postponing construction and other projects. Once inflation is tamed and other pressures subside, the forward push will continue.

Soaring trade and investment

America's trade with China is four times as large as trade with Russia and will keep growing faster. Look for annual increases of 15% to 20% through the '90s. (The 1988 increase was 40%.) America's two-way trade with China is now over $14 billion—$5 billion in U.S. exports to China, $9 billion in imports. They buy computers, industrial equipment, planes and other transportation equipment from us. We buy clothing, textiles, petroleum products, footwear, fish and other products from them. In the decade ahead, China's manufactured exports, plus sales of its oil, titanium and other minerals, will earn it the trade income it needs to become a customer for U.S. financial services, transportation firms, medical care, equipment makers, agribusiness, hotel chains, ad agencies and others.

China will open up to more Western high-tech investment, anxious to create jobs and higher living standards for its 1.1

billion people (who continue to reproduce at rates far above what the government wants). China has already attracted U.S. firms in energy exploration, electronics, textiles and pharmaceuticals. IBM and Hewlett-Packard are getting set to make components in China and will work with private firms there in cracking other Asian markets. There's a potential gold mine of talent in programmers and data processors.

All told, several hundred U.S. firms have invested over $3 billion in China. Many have set up offices in Beijing to untangle the many restrictions that are imposed on outsiders. To clarify the rights of foreigners in China and improve the business and investment climate there, the U.S. and China have worked out a series of bilateral agreements on trade, taxes, financial and transportation matters and liberalized controls on our exports of high-technology items to China. The dollar value of approved licenses for U.S. technology exports to China, including computers, analytical instruments and telecommunications equipment, jumped from $400 million in '82 to $3.5 billion in '86 and will probably top $20 billion by 2000. The way has been cleared for vastly expanded U.S.-China trade in the coming decade.

AUSTRALIA AND NEW ZEALAND

Australia and New Zealand have been shedding protectionism and cutting tariffs, positioning themselves to be increasingly important players in Pacific-Rim trade throughout the '90s. As modern, English-speaking societies, they will be convenient regional hubs for U.S. and European bankers, insurance, telecommunications and other service firms doing business in the Pacific. Both countries will also build up tourism and their manufacturing industries, especially apparel and food processing, while trying to lessen their dependence on raw commodities. Because they don't have big domestic markets, their manufacturing will focus on exports. Australia's headstrong unions may hamper its efforts at industrial development.

The U.S. now enjoys a $3-billion trade surplus with Australia, selling $7 billion in planes, computers, chemicals, machinery and high-tech products, and buying $4 billion in wool, lamb, beef, aluminum and petroleum goods. Australians like American products, preferring them to Japanese items. The U.S. will continue to run at least a small trade surplus with Australia. Foreign investment in that country has been booming—$25 billion in 1988, a 25% increase from the year before, with much of it by Japan. The Japanese are snapping up land, office buildings, resorts and hotels, similar to their shopping sprees in Hawaii and California.

New Zealand is a small country—3.3 million people and 80 million sheep—that will run a small trade surplus with the U.S., selling us beef, lamb, mutton and wool and buying planes and computers.

THE MIDDLE EAST

Because of its strategic location next to the Soviet Union and its role as the world's largest exporter of oil, the Mideast will continue to occupy the attention of the U.S. and the rest of the world throughout the '90s. Politically, the Mideast and Persian Gulf will remain a powder keg.

The U.S. will be the only outside power that can play a brokering and mediating role in disputes between Israel and the Palestinians and the Arab nations, although the Soviet Union will try to get its foot in the door. The U.S. will continue to rely on Israeli strength as its security proxy in the region, but we will also attempt to deal fairly enough with Israel's Arab neighbors to maintain influence with them.

Strife-torn Lebanon will not regain its prominence as a banking and investment center. Its political and territorial existence will be determined largely by the outcome of the Palestinian problem, the future of Islamic fundamentalist fervor and the policies of Israel, Syria and Jordan.

Although Islamic extremism will outlive Khomeini, it's likely that U.S.-Iranian relations will improve in the '90s. For Iran, rebuilding trade and financial ties with the U.S. and other Western countries is essential for stabilizing its economy. For the U.S., better relations with Iran will help offset Soviet influence in the region and make it easier to deal with Islamic forces elsewhere in the Middle East. This will be part of our government's effort to avoid a repeat of 1970s-type oil crises. A more serious threat is the spread throughout the region of nuclear and chemical weapons—and the missiles for delivering them.

The mid '80s plunge in oil prices made a dramatic overnight change in the global power of the Arab world. A decade ago many Americans were concerned that Mideast investors would buy up the world. Today the Arab nations face budgetary problems similar to those of governments elsewhere.

In the '70s and early '80s, the oil-producing nations were generating more income than they could possibly spend on building their own societies, even considering the lavish rate of spending that prevailed. They poured billions into construction projects—roads, bridges, government buildings, housing, colleges and power plants, keeping Bechtel and other U.S. contractors busy. They still had billions left over, which they used to buy into petrochemical processing and real estate around the world. Many of the petrodollars deposited in American banks were lent to Third World nations. Repayments are now overdue—a problem for American banks, not the Mideast.

Today, OPEC nations are struggling to maintain an orderly world market in petroleum, trying to regain their grip on prices and supplies. It's not working very well, but the Middle East remains the world's dominant exporter of petroleum, and gradually rising world demand will firm up prices in the '90s.

Saudi Arabia will still be our number-one trading partner in the Middle East. U.S.-Saudi two-way trade is $10 billion a year, of which we import $6.2 billion in oil and petroleum products. In turn, they buy $3.8 billion in cars and trucks, aircraft parts, cigarettes and appliances. The U.S. trade deficit with the Saudis will probably rise in the '90s, due to our increasing dependence on imported oil.

Two-way trade with Israel will keep growing at a good clip, spurred along by the free-trade agreement. The U.S. now exports $3.2 billion in military equipment, radio navigation aids, machinery, electronics, grain and soybeans. From Israel, we buy $3.1 billion in cut diamonds, jewelry, aircraft parts, electrical equipment and chemicals.

AFRICA

You have to look hard to find bright spots in Africa, a vast region of 52 countries and 650 million people that's still emerging from colonialism as we approach the '90s.

But the future looks better than the present, partly because a growing number of African nations have seen the failure of state-run economies and are moving toward free markets and private initiatives while seeking foreign investment. It will be a slow process—beset by heavy debts, racial and political unrest and other problems—but there is a rising level of appreciation for democratic principles and private initiative.

As other parts of the world have developed and built higher living standards, the poorest continent on earth has endured a slump in per-capita food production, declining commodity prices, mounting debt burdens, disease, wars and natural disasters.

American industry depends on imports of chromium, platinum, manganese, cobalt, palladium and other metals from Africa. But our overall trade with Africa is a drop in the bucket compared with the business we do elsewhere. During the '90s, Africa will account for less than 5% of our total imports and exports.

North Africa

In North Africa—culturally and economically more a part of the Mideast and Europe than Africa—Egypt is weighed down by debts and buffeted by political turmoil. It ranks second only to Israel in total aid received from the U.S. It will be angling for foreign investment and agricultural assistance as a way out of its current jam. Algeria and Tunisia have substantial trade with the U.S., centered on petroleum. The U.S. accounts for half of Algeria's crude-oil exports. Morocco is the world's leading exporter of phosphates and is expanding its chemicals, cement and machinery industries.

Trade with the sub-Sahara

U.S. exports to sub-Saharan Africa are slightly less than $4 billion. Our imports total $9.3 billion. U.S. economic and food aid is around $1 billion a year, not counting the costs of refugee programs that we support under United Nations assistance.

South Africa, the richest and most industrially advanced nation on the continent, has been ostracized by much of the world because of apartheid. No one knows for sure what will happen in the next few years, let alone over the coming decade, but apartheid probably won't survive to the turn of the century. Responsible black and white leaders in South Africa stand a good chance of working out a peaceful settlement and making constitutional changes that will end the political stalemate and preserve the economic viability of the country, which is rich in gold, diamonds, chrome, platinum, copper and other goods. Business people and investors who are on the scene are betting on such a solution, by buying up companies as fast as they're put on the market by foreigners.

Nigeria is another country with great potential and plenty of oil and natural gas. But it's staggered by debt problems, corruption and mismanagement. With fresh leaders, it could do a turnaround in the '90s.

Other African nations—including Zambia and Zaire—have minerals but need technicians and capital to make things go. Their mines are crippled and will remain so until their governments take steps to guarantee that investors can operate them without interference and with some prospect of profits.

That's typical of the whole continent. There are problems galore, but there is also great untapped potential: hundreds of millions of people who, given education and incentives to earn, could be vastly productive; millions of acres of land rich in minerals and forest products; prime agricultural areas that are ready for development at a bargain price. If this is the American century, and the next the Asian century, then the following one might well be the African century.

6 The Changing Population Mix

<u>U.S. population will grow about 8% in the '90s.</u>

<u>And it will **NOT** decline in the next century.</u>

<u>Immigration will give the U.S. a competitive edge.</u>

<u>Population will drop in Europe and Japan after 2000.</u>

<u>U.S. Hispanic population will be world's fifth largest.</u>

<u>Normal retirement age will move toward 70.</u>

<u>Fewer marriages, divorces and births in the '90s.</u>

<u>But 12 million more households by the year 2000.</u>

You can project population changes into the next century and count on them because the trends are already well established. The vast majority of people who will make up our country in the early 2000s are already here. You can tell *now* how many teenagers there will be, how many people in their twenties, how many in the middle-age groups and how many retired and older people. For all these groups, there are certain special needs and special markets.

U.S. population will grow more slowly in the '90s than in the '80s, and after 1995 it will grow even more slowly than during the Great Depression of the '30s. But we WILL grow, and our population growth rate will exceed that of the other major industrialized democracies. In fact, some industrial powers, such as West Germany, are already declining in population while others, including Japan, will start losing population in the early 2000s.

As a nation, we'll begin the '90s with 250 million people. By '95, U.S. population will be about 260 million. By 2000, probably 270 million. Our population will grow 8% in the next decade, compared with 10% in the '80s.

A U.S. population decline?

U.S. adults are reproducing at less than replacement level. That is, today's American woman will have, on average, about 1.8 children in her lifetime. This low fertility rate has prevailed since 1973. The odds are good that access to legal abortion will be somewhat curtailed in the next few years, on a state-by-state basis, but that won't change the fertility rate much. (Today, there are about 1.6 million abortions each year, four for every ten live births.)

Even though the fertility rate is less than the 2.1 considered to be replacement level, the enormous size of the Baby Boom generation has kept births well ahead of deaths, and this "natural increase" in population should continue into the first quarter of the 2000s—even without high levels of immigration.

The fertility rate has never been this low before. It dipped during the Great Depression but was still above the replacement level. Even so, there were dire warnings then of a shrinking population later in the century. But a decade later, the postwar baby boom got under way, keeping American population growing robustly.

The Census Bureau is projecting a decline in U.S. population beginning 50 years from now, based on slightly lower fertility rates and on lower immigration than there is today. Given those assumptions, this projection is certainly sound, but the assumptions don't make sense to us. The Census Bureau is underestimating the surge of immigration that America will experience to alleviate labor shortages, and the likelihood that fertility will tick up a little (partly because of immigrants).

The odds are that during the '90s there will be a tremendous amount of publicity on the aging of Europe and Japan and the harmful effects this will have on economic growth. This, in turn, will START a trend toward more immigration and higher birthrates in the U.S., beginning in the late '90s and extending into the next century.

We're not saying that people will decide to have babies to make the demographic charts more reassuring or to do their bit for economic growth. An uptick in fertility is more likely to come from people emigrating from Mexico and other places with higher fertility rates; an improving economy; more flexibility in the workplace for employees with children; and better tax incentives for having kids—all of which are likely in the years ahead.

In the meantime, births will drop from 3.9 million at the end of the '80s (the highest in 25 years) to around 3.4 million by 2000, mainly because there will be fewer women in prime childbearing ages, the early twenties to early thirties.

Help wanted: immigrants

Our ace in the hole early in the next century will be immigration, which will account for over a third of our population growth in the '90s, and even more as we move into the 21st Century.

Although immigration is often considered a time bomb that will go off in the '90s, the truth is that it will be a positive force in American society, not to mention an absolute necessity for economic growth. We'll NEED immigrants as much as they will need jobs. They'll help us counter the effects of an aging population, fewer births and fewer workers to support each retiree.

Bear in mind that the U.S. will age quite slowly over the next ten to 20 years. The share of the elderly population will remain virtually unchanged until 2011, when the first wave of Baby Boomers hits 65. That's when we'll need a fresh infusion of people for the work force.

By contrast, Japan and Europe are already aging at a fast clip because their births dipped after World War II while ours were increasing explosively, and when their baby booms did come, they didn't amount to much. By 2020, the median age in West Germany will be 47. In Great Britain it will be 43, in France 42, and in Switzerland 46. In Japan, it will be about 44 and in the U.S., around 40 (compared with 33 now). The U.S. will have three workers for each retiree, down from five now. Japan and West Germany will each have two workers per retiree.

The simple fact is this: The U.S. is the only nation that welcomes hundreds of thousands of immigrants each year and offers them the promise of citizenship. In the past five years we've absorbed more immigrants than ALL other industrialized nations combined. In the rest of the world, aliens are merely guest workers—needed but not welcome.

Our long history of accepting and assimilating new Americans will make us a stronger nation, with a work force that includes the full range of skills and wage levels. There will be problems galore, especially educational needs and finding the right level of welfare support that provides a safety net without undermining the immigrant's incentive to succeed. Gradually, the new Americans will be woven into the national fabric, just as the waves of Irish, Germans, Chinese, Italians, Poles, Greeks, Cubans and other nationalities were earlier.

The world perspective

Racially homogeneous Japan, on the other hand, has a bad case of xenophobia and a clear set of policies against foreigners. Very few foreigners are accepted permanently, unless they're married to Japanese or have worked for a company there for many years. There are many Filipinos, Taiwanese, Pakistanis, Thais and others working as housekeepers and laborers in Japan, but they get the heave-ho after a few years. A nation that distrusts and fears foreigners isn't about to roll out the red carpet for immigrants.

Western Europe is in a similar position, turning a cold shoulder to Turks, Greeks, Algerians and others who take menial jobs and then show signs of sticking around. Even with a creaky-old population, Western Europe won't open its doors to immigrants or do much to encourage bigger families.

West Germany is already losing population and will continue to do so well into the next century. It has the lowest fertility rate in the industrial world, 1.3 children per woman. With fewer people coming along, Germany won't need more houses or schools. Its farmers won't have to produce as much food. Its stores won't have as many customers. Its economy will become more and more dependent on exports. Fertility is nearly as low in Denmark, the Netherlands, Italy and France.

On the other hand, the fertility rates of the Soviet Union and most Eastern European countries are well above the replacement level. So sometime in the next century the West will be losing population while the Soviet Bloc will be gaining.

Then there is the Third World of less-developed nations. A quick glance at the table below tells a story of rapid population growth in the countries that should be getting a grip on their population explosions—China, India, Mexico, Iran, plus other nations of Asia, Africa and Latin America. Thanks to better medical care, public health and agricultural productivity, mortality rates will continue to plummet. But government birth-control programs meet with only modest success in countries where a large family, especially of sons, is still considered a parent's old-age security program.

Population Forecasts by Country (in millions)			
	1985	**2000**	**2025**	**2050**
No growth				
West Germany	61	59	53	46
East Germany	17	17	16	16
U.K.	57	57	57	55
Italy	57	58	56	52
Low to moderate growth				
France	55	59	62	61
Canada	25	28	31	30
Japan	121	129	130	126
U.S.	239	270	305	310
Soviet Union	277	308	344	363
High growth				
China	1,040	1,274	1,537	1,637
India	765	996	1,312	1,525
Mexico	79	110	154	182

In the last 20 years, the focus of concern has shifted from preventing famine toward job creation and economic growth.

Prophecies of widespread starvation, which some expected to be caused by soaring population and stagnant agricultural production, turned out to be baseless. World agricultural production has more than kept pace with population, due to continuing strides in food technology. Most famines in the world today are due to varying combinations of cyclical droughts, war and governmental corruption and incompetence. Arguably, tomorrow's agricultural crisis may be overproduction and fierce export competition, driving down commodity prices.

It is jobs the Third World is starving for today—decent living for its young populations. The illegal-alien pressure on the U.S. border with Mexico is primarily caused by the shortage of good jobs in Mexico; promoting economic growth on our southern border would be the single best immigration-control policy we could develop. The Salinas government agrees, and that's why it's embarking on a gradual opening of that highly controlled economy to foreign investment, imports and a new spirit of free enterprise.

In the table on the opposite page, notice the shortening time interval between each additional one billion of world population. It took 48 years to double from two billion in 1926 to four billion in 1974. The doubling interval from three billion in 1960 to six billion in 1998 will be only about 38 years. But in the late '90s world population growth will begin to slow, and the plus-one-billion intervals will begin to lengthen again. Why? It's partly because of the pressures of overcrowding, but more the result of the reduced fertility rate that usually accompanies rising education and living standards.

Immigrants keep coming

Even with stronger job creation and rising living standards in the Third World during the 1990s, the United States will still be a magnet for ambitious people from all over the world.

We believe that immigration in the '90s will run about 820,000 a year, divided between 620,000 legals and 200,000 illegals. (We're assuming that the new immigration regulations won't substantially slow the flow of illegals.) Emigration by U.S. citizens will continue to run about 200,000 a year, mostly older former immigrants who will return to their homelands for re-

How World Population Will Grow

Population	Year	Elapsed Years
1 billion	1805	Indefinite
2 billion	1926	121
3 billion	1960	34
4 billion	1974	14
5 billion	1987	13
6 billion	1998	11
7 billion	2010	12
8 billion	2023	13
9 billion	2040	17
10 billion	2070	30

tirement, armed with social security and pension income, which goes a lot further in most other countries.

So net inflow—immigration minus emigration—will run about 620,000 a year in the '90s, a little higher than at the end of the 80's, and then move much higher after 2000. That's our own judgment, based on the fact that there will be a need for more immigrants and plenty of younger foreigners willing to take jobs here. On the other hand, the Census Bureau projects that immigration will decline from now on.

Nearly half of legal immigration each year will be people let in under one or another section of the "preference system"— children, spouses and parents of earlier immigrants. There will also be a steady stream of political refugees, mostly from Southeast Asia. And we'll be partial to skilled immigrants who can help fill labor shortages in our economy, such as nurses, engineers, scientists and teachers. India, the Philippines and other countries have plenty of scientists who want to come to the U.S, but many of their governments will accuse us of fostering a brain drain.

There's a good chance immigration policy will be changed in the '90s to allow more Europeans to enter the U.S. Because European immigration was so low in the '60s and '70s, "family reunification" preferences have skewed immigration volume toward Asia and Latin America and blocked Europeans from entering.

Learning from immigrants

For some two centuries the best and brightest from all over the world have made America their preferred destination for a new life, and this will continue in the Global '90s. The new immigrants will provide fresh vigor and enthusiasm and an appreciation of our freedoms. They will be young, forward-looking, optimistic, full of entrepreneurial spirit.

Next time you go to a high school or college graduation, look at the top students. In most places you'll find first- and second-generation Americans, especially Asian-Americans, represented FAR out of proportion to their numbers in the class. More than half of the students in science and engineering graduate-degree programs at American colleges are from overseas. Many of these bright young people choose to remain in the U.S. to work.

There is a message here for native-born Americans: It's past time to get *our* act together and rekindle the spirit of self-reliance, commitment to family, hard work and high educational standards for our children. These are the values that immigrants expect to find in America—and often do, especially compared with the societies they left behind. But too often immigrants are surprised by the degree to which Americans take those values for granted and end up teaching them to us by their example.

Why do Asian-Americans attain higher levels of education and income than other Americans? It probably has something to do with the close family ties among Asian-Americans and the emphasis put on schooling and entrepreneurial achievement in their families, the same as was true of earlier generations of immigrants and their offspring. It's not because Asians or any other group are inherently superior in intelligence or gumption.

High levels of immigration have always shaken up native-born Americans, especially those on the lower end of the economic ladder. It is they who feel most pressured by job competition from waves of immigrants who are anxious to find work and get off to a fresh start.

The effect on black Americans

In America today and throughout the '90s the most pressured of native-born Americans will be low-income blacks. The economic advancement of black Americans has been dramatic in the last several decades, but it has not been as fast as it might have been or can be in the '90s.

Although racial prejudice has declined since the '60s, it has by no means disappeared, despite this country's best efforts to create a fair and compassionate society. Through the '90s it will still be an impediment to the economic progress of blacks.

But it won't be the main one. The outlook for generations of black children will remain bleak until the cycle of single-parent households, poverty and welfare is broken. Over 60% percent of black children are born to unwed mothers, compared with 16% for whites. Teenage pregnancies are twice as common among blacks as whites—23% of black births compared with 11% of white births. And 51% of black kids live in households without a father. All too often the same youngsters follow the familiar pattern of dropping out of school and into a life with little hope of getting ahead.

Looking to the '90s, there will be a reexamination of the federal role in assuring equal opportunity for all. There'll be more focus on education as the way for youngsters to escape the poverty rut. Where there is a clear showing of intentional discrimination against specific groups of workers, the courts will still require remedies, perhaps even quotas. But expect fewer general affirmative-action programs, because we don't think there will be as much blatant discrimination as in the past.

Generally speaking, there'll probably be fewer minority preferences in hiring, government contracting, college admissions and so on. And some minority-group leaders think that may not be so bad. Robert Woodson, who is chairman of the Council for a Black Economic Agenda, puts it like this: "If black America is to achieve its rightful place in American society, it will not be by virtue of what white America grants to black Americans but because of what black Americans do for themselves. We must end our preoccupation with what white America feels about or does to us."

The melting pot bubbles on

Even more than now, in the Global '90s America will be an ethnic and racial melting pot, a nation of nations. In 1989, minorities totaled about 24% of our population. By 2000, that percentage will rise to about 29%, divided about like this: blacks, 13%, Hispanics, 11%, all others (mostly Asians), 5%. The percentage of Asians could reach 7% by 2020, mostly through high levels of immigration. California will eventually have a majority of minorities.

By the end of the '90s, the number of Hispanics in the U.S. will increase about 50% to 30 million people. They will account for 16% of the school kids and 18- to 24-year-olds entering the labor force, military service and colleges. The relatively young Hispanic population will make up 20% of growth in the labor force by the beginning of the next century. Your own company may have to offer English courses for its recently arrived Latin employees.

We already have the sixth-largest Hispanic population in the world, surpassed only by Mexico, Spain, Argentina, Colombia and Peru, and we'll probably pass Peru by the end of the '90s.

There will be a more Latin flavor to the foods we eat, the clothes we wear, our schools, the workplace, sports and music. And our politics will be more attuned to the needs of the new immigrant population, the new voters. The seven states with the largest Hispanic populations—Texas, California, Florida, New York, Illinois, Arizona and New Jersey—accounted for 180 of the 270 electoral votes needed to win the 1988 election. With the population shifting to the South and West, Hispanics will have more electoral votes in '92.

In Congress, there will be more surnames like Garcia and Martinez, Matsunaga and Saiki. There may even be a minority member on a presidential ticket in '92, '96 or '00.

More social stability

Traditional American values and mores have been thrown for a loop in the past 25 years, a time of unprecedented change and turbulence. We've been through the "counterculture" and drug explosion, the divisiveness of Vietnam and Watergate, strides in civil rights, the sexual revolution, the hardest economic times since the '30s. We've absorbed the surge of women into the workplace and adjusted to a high level of immigration. This turmoil has been accompanied by explosive increases in teenage pregnancies, broken marriages, single-parent households and latchkey children.

The '90s will mark a period of more stability, more maturity, more pulling together as a people than we've seen in the past two decades. Even young people seem to be returning to more-traditional values.

Take a close look at the table below. The figures hold a lot of significance for people engaged in every line of work. The table tells at a glance which age groups will increase or decrease in actual numbers and percent of population.

Population Breakdown by Age, 1990 to 2000

(in millions)

Age	1990	1995	2000	Share of Total 1990	2000
Under 5	18.4	17.8	16.9	7.4%	6.3%
5-13	32.4	33.9	33.5	12.9	12.5
14-17	13.2	14.5	15.3	5.3	5.7
18-24	26.1	24.3	25.2	10.4	9.4
25-34	43.9	41.0	37.1	17.5	13.8
35-44	37.9	42.3	44.0	15.1	16.4
45-54	25.5	31.3	37.2	10.2	13.9
55-64	21.4	21.3	24.2	8.5	9.0
65-74	18.4	18.9	18.2	7.3	6.8
75 and older	13.2	14.8	16.6	5.3	6.2

The low birthrate of the 1970s means a smaller proportion of young adults in the '90s, and that should translate into more stability in the workplace and the home. Even street crime, mainly caused by young adult males, should decline, assuming progress against drug use.

There will be fewer young people trying to land their first jobs, a more-experienced and productive work force, fewer people in the prime marrying and divorcing ages. The Baby Boomers, now 25 to 43 years old, will be at the peak of their family responsibilities. Their spending power will be great, but they will also pick up the sagging American savings rate as they put money aside to prepare for their children's college education and their own retirements.

In recent years we've been consuming more than we've produced, spending more than we saved. Much of that was caused by absorbing the youth bulge in the population, with high spending on schools, cars, clothes and then housing. Under such circumstances it was natural for consumption to rise and savings to fall, even if we overdid the spending side. We're at the turning point now, a time when the Baby Boomers will contribute to better productivity, a stronger economy and higher savings.

There will be fewer toddlers and young adults, more teen-agers and middle-age career couples. And there will be more blended families—stepchildren, half-siblings and multiple sets of grandparents.

Try to apply these facts to your business or profession. They give you some idea of the potential demand from different age groups for any line at any time: baby food and diapers; school supplies; clothes for children or teens; sporting goods for the young; colleges; homes for new families; furniture and appliances; cars and vacations for the middle-aged; and housing, recreation and other services for millions of new retirees.

For example, consider the birth wave of 1954-64, the only stretch when births ran over four million a year; people born then are now 25 to 35 years old. Carry that wave forward through the years for a glimpse of future demand. People in that age bracket are now early in their careers, marrying, raising families, buying their first homes. They are conservative in their political and economic views, liberal in their social views.

In ten years, they will be 35 to 45 years old, established in their jobs and entering their most productive years. Twenty years from now, in 2009, they will be middle aged, nearing their peak earning power, buying upscale homes and all the fixings. And in another ten years, in 2019, they will be going to retirement parties and drawing down the social security trust fund.

Well-heeled older Americans

In your sales and marketing strategies, don't overlook people 50 and over. That age group is often brushed off by Madison Avenue as too dowdy, tight with a dollar, set in its patterns of product preference. Instead ad agencies and marketing executives go chasing after Baby Boomers, who have less buying power and lower net worth.

Look at the table below, put together by the Conference Board's consumer research center. It shows that older people have financial assets and net worth far out of proportion to their share of population.

Age	Share of Households	Financial Assets	Net Worth
Under 35	29.6%	6.9%	7.3%
35-49	26.4	16.1	23.2
50-64	22.9	37.2	37.0
65-74	12.6	29.1	23.4
75 and older	7.3	10.1	9.1

As you can see, people age 50 through 75 are substantially better off in net worth than younger households. Because there are fewer two-income households in this age group, their total income is often lower than that of Baby Boom households, but their major expenditures are behind them and their discretionary income is higher. Their kids have been raised, 70% own their homes, and they have plenty of time. Marketing research shows they are just as receptive to new products and brands as young people are. They are good prospects for investments, time-saving services, quality merchandise, fancy homes and cars. The 50-and-up crowd dominates the travel and tourism market.

There will be 3.5 million more people 75 and older by 2000. Better health care is adding years to life, and it also adds life to the years. The 75-year-old of 2040 will be as fit as the 60-year-old today. Older people will be healthier, able to work longer and able to live more fully. Families extending four or five generations won't be unusual. More than ever before, grandparents and GREAT-grandparents will be a big part of a child's life. Think of your own grandparents. If they lived well into their sixties or seventies, they probably looked and acted like old codgers. Thanks to better health care and diets and less backbreaking work, most grandparents and great-grandparents will lead active and enjoyable lives and be prime prospects for travel, low-maintenance one-story houses and labor-saving products. Businesses that ignore these customers will be missing the boat.

Since 1950, the number of people 65 and over has more than doubled. The 85-and-over crowd has increased almost five times, and the number of centenarians has grown more than ten times. There are now more than one million Americans 90 and older. By 2000, there will be almost two million. And there will be more than 100,000 centenarians. The Census Bureau figures that by 2080 the U.S. will have almost a million and a half people age 100 and older. The vast majority will be women.

With people living and staying well longer, and with growing concern about the social security system's ability to meet the surge in obligations after the Baby Boomers retire, there's a good chance that normal retirement age will be phased upward to 70. The rising affluence of older Americans will make retirement at 65 or earlier very appealing, even with actuarial reductions in their benefits. But the plain fact is that many older people will be needed in the work force, and employers will encourage them to stay on past 65.

Fewer and later marriages ahead

Wedding bells won't ring as often in the '90s because there will be fewer young eligibles. In fact, remarriages will account for a third of all weddings, even though remarriage after divorce will be less frequent.

Young couples will continue to postpone marriage but probably not much beyond the present ages, 24 for women and 26 for men the first time around. (For comparison's sake, in 1959, women were marrying at 20 years of age and men at 22½.) This trend to delayed marriage has implications for business and family life in the '90s.

Later marriage means young folks have more time to pursue education and careers, size up their earning potential (and that of their future spouses), and learn what the world is all about. There's an inverse relationship between marrying age and the risk of divorce. Women who marry in their teens and men who marry at 20 to 24 have the highest divorce rates.

There are more eligible men than women in the marryingest ages, 20 to 35 years old: 118 unmarried men for every 100 women. Best places to look for a husband will be Alaska, Nevada, Wyoming, Washington and North Dakota. They will have the highest ratio of men to women. And for a wife, consider New York, Florida or Pennsylvania. (Statistically, that is.)

About 90% of today's young people will eventually marry, down from the traditional 95%. That doesn't seem like a big difference, but it means a DOUBLING of never-marrieds in the population in the years ahead.

That's one reason why the number of households will increase substantially, while average size will remain small, although it probably won't shrink much from the present 2.6 persons. We'll have about 12 million more households by the end of the '90s, about 106 million in all. That compares with 14 million more during the '80s and 17 million more during the '70s.

Singles, "mingles" (people living together, romantically attached or otherwise), childless couples, divorced men and women, empty nesters and widows and widowers account for most of the trend to smaller households. Small households will mean good demand for condos, apartments, townhouses, furniture, small appliances, no-fuss meals in small portions and convenience services of all types.

The number of divorces has peaked and will decline in the '90s because of the drop in marriages, the trend to older brides and grooms, more recognition of the heavy emotional and economic costs of divorce and better working conditions for mothers. We'll still have one of the highest divorce rates in the world. Nearly HALF of this year's marriages will end in divorce. About 60% of married women 36 to 43 years old—the vanguard of the female employment surge of the '70s—will get divorced.

Births are topping out

If you sell products or services for babies and preschoolers, you had better be making hay now, because your market will be much smaller in the '90s. On the brighter side, the trend to more dual-income parents and small families means more spending per child, on clothes and toys, schooling, tutoring, day care, summer camps, everything.

More than half the women who have had babies in the past year and nearly 60% of the mothers of preschool kids are in the labor force, up from 12% in 1950. That's why the politicians see child care as a sure vote-getter. Young mothers have less time for running households but contribute mightily to household incomes and to the demand for housecleaning services, catalog sales, easy-to-fix meals and similar conveniences. Average income if both husband and wife work full-time is around $49,000; if only the husband works it's $37,500. Wives earn more than their husbands in 20% of the families where both work.

Help wanted: elementary teachers

Now apply the birth trends to school enrollments to see what happens:

Grade-school enrollment (5- to 13-year-olds) will increase. It's now around 32 million and will build to almost 34 million in the mid '90s, staying near that level until 2000. By 2010, the elementary-school population will ease to 31 million. The early '90s will be a good time for new teaching grads to hit the job market.

High-school enrollment, about 13.5 million, will drop to 13.2 million in 1990, then start upward, reaching 14.5 million in '95 and 15.3 million by 2000. By 2010, it will be back to 14.7 million.

Colleges have done a good job of keeping their enrollments up, considering that fewer young people are coming through the pipeline. They've stepped up recruitment efforts and attracted many more graduate students, silver-haired scholars, homemakers and others who are coming back to finish up degree work or seek retraining for a second or third career. But their enrollments will suffer in the early '90s when there will be even fewer high school grads and the limits are reached on attracting older students back to campus.

Where the growth will be

Perhaps you're wondering whether job opportunities would be greater if you moved to some far-off place. So you may want to know something about areas that will grow fastest and what special opportunities they offer for jobs and business. You may also want to know something about places that will shrink or lag behind in rate of growth because declining or lagging areas will offer fewer opportunities.

You should understand that pulling up stakes and heading for the growingest areas is not a surefire formula for success. A place that looks attractive to you no doubt looks the same to thousands of others. You will have to do your homework and check the local demand for the particular skills you offer and the kind of work you're in. Everyone knows that Southern California will keep growing at a good clip, but that doesn't mean that EVERY business that opens up there will make a go of it. You might be better off staying put, especially if you're well rooted.

Don't use sheer population growth as your main guide to relocating yourself or your business, or opening branch facilities. It is the KINDS of people—both workers and customers—and KINDS of opportunities—the local demand and competition from similar businesses—that will be the most important factors in your success.

The Sunbelt will continue to lead the nation in rate of growth in the '90s, as it has for several decades. Of the northern states, only Alaska, New Hampshire, Delaware and Maryland will top the national average of 8%.

But the Sunbelt's growth advantage over the rest of America will diminish a bit in the coming decade. The cost of doing business in the Sunbelt is rising steadily: Land, labor, taxes and energy are all increasing and the competition for scarce water in the Southwest is becoming more intense. The business-development climate of the southern states, in general, is still superior to the North, but the degree of advantage is shrinking, especially as land and labor costs in the North come back into line, competitively.

The manufacturing and export boom at the end of the '80s has brought new life to many Frostbelt cities. Keep in mind that some slow-growth big northern states will add more new residents in the '90s than most of the small Sunbelt states whose rates of growth will be much higher.

State-by-state growth

Look at the table of state population change on the following page. See how your state, or some other where you're thinking of moving, will fare—not only in percent of growth but in actual numbers of new people as well.

State Population Change, 1990 to 2000
(U.S. Average, 8%)

	Numbers	%		Numbers	%
Arizona	866,000	23%	Massachusetts	207,000	4%
New Mexico	336,000	21	Missouri	191,000	4
Nevada	227,000	21	Minnesota	166,000	4
Florida	2,597,000	20	Oregon	111,000	4
Georgia	1,294,000	19	Arkansas	102,000	4
Alaska	111,000	19	Idaho	30,000	3
Hawaii	204,000	18	Washington, D.C.	30,000	3
New Hampshire	191,000	17	Oklahoma	91,000	3
California	4,374,000	15	Kansas	37,000	2
Texas	2,499,000	14	New York	213,000	1
North Carolina	793,000	12	South Dakota	6,000	1
Virginia	720,000	12	Louisiana	3,000	.1
Maryland	545,000	12	Illinois	− 32,000	− .3
Utah	215,000	12	Kentucky	− 12,000	− .3
Colorado	379,000	11	Michigan	− 43,000	− .5
South Carolina	357,000	10	Wisconsin	− 24,000	− .5
Delaware	68,000	10	Indiana	− 48,000	− 1
New Jersey	647,000	8	Montana	− 11,000	− 1
Washington	334,000	7	Ohio	− 162,000	− 2
Mississippi	178,000	7	Nebraska	− 32,000	− 2
Tennessee	294,000	6	Pennsylvania	− 324,000	− 3
Alabama	229,000	6	Wyoming	− 13,000	− 3
Connecticut	166,000	5	North Dakota	− 31,000	− 5
Maine	59,000	5	West Virginia	− 134,000	− 7
Rhode Island	47,000	5	Iowa	− 209,000	− 8
Vermont	29,000	5			

The fastest-growing in percentages are often states that don't have many people now. For example, Alaska will grow 19%, but by only 111,000 people, not enough to make up a medium-size city. By contrast, New York's mere 1% growth will mean 213,000 more people, roughly the same gain as that of higher-growth states such as Nevada, Hawaii, Utah and Mississippi.

These states will add the most people: California, Florida, Texas, Georgia, Arizona, North Carolina, Virginia and New Jersey. One of every four Americans will live in California, Texas or Florida. And these states will lose the most people: Pennsylvania, Iowa, Ohio, West Virginia, Michigan and Indiana. (By the way, Utah has the highest fertility rate. Lowest fertility rates are in West Virginia, Kentucky, Tennessee, North Carolina, Missouri, Massachusetts, Rhode Island and Connecticut.)

These will be among the fastest-growing metropolitan areas, with population increases of at least 15% to 20% in the '90s— twice as fast as the national rate: San Diego, Los Angeles, Riverside/San Bernardino, Oxnard/Ventura, Fresno, Bakersfield, Sacramento, Las Vegas, Phoenix, Colorado Springs, San Antonio, Austin, Dallas, El Paso, Orlando, Naples, Tampa, Fort Myers/Cape Coral, West Palm Beach/Boca Raton, Atlanta, Charleston (S.C.), Charlotte, Raleigh/Durham, Norfolk/Virginia Beach and Washington, D.C.

As with states, the high-growth-rate cities will be dominated by the Sunbelt, but a number of northern metropolitan areas will also gain people. These will include Boston, Hartford, Rochester, Philadelphia, Columbus, Chicago, Indianapolis, Minneapolis/ St. Paul, Kansas City, Seattle, Tacoma and Portland, Oreg.

Politics of population

Sunbelt states will benefit from reapportionment after the censuses of 1990 and 2000. In '92, as many as 18 House seats and electoral votes will shift from the Northeast and Midwest to California (5 more seats), Texas (3 or 4), Florida (3), Arizona and Georgia (1 or 2 each), Virginia and North Carolina (1 each). These additions will come at the expense of New York (loss of 3 seats), Pennsylvania (2 or 3), Ohio, Michigan and Illinois (2 each), Iowa, Kansas, Massachusetts and West Virginia (1 each) and possible losses in Montana, Kentucky and Wisconsin.

On the surface, that should favor Republicans—Democratic centers in the North surrendering seats to more-conservative areas. The actual impact, however, depends largely on who draws the lines for redistricting. Democrats will have the advantage on that score because they'll control more state legislatures and governorships.

Probably another dozen congressional seats and electoral votes will be switched after the census in 2000. Once again, the big winners will be California, Texas, Florida, Arizona and Georgia, plus Virginia, Maryland and North Carolina. Their gains will come at the expense of New York, Pennsylvania, Ohio, Michigan, Illinois, Iowa, Minnesota, Kansas, Montana, Kentucky, Massachusetts, West Virginia and Louisiana.

One wild card in upcoming reapportionment will be the use of microcomputers to size up population shifts and composition and to challenge proposed redistricting. By redrawing districts in different shapes, political and special interest groups will be able to use computer graphics to get instant readouts of voting patterns, ages, incomes and racial mix. By bending district boundaries into the right configuration of geography and demographics, politicians will be able to make their opponents disappear. As a result of such gerrymandering, dozens of reapportionment plans will end up in the courtroom after the '90 census.

7 The Health Revolution

<u>Biotech will conquer many diseases, including AIDS.</u>

<u>U.S. leadership in health care will boost exports.</u>

<u>Health care costs won't rise as rapidly as in '80s.</u>

<u>Employers will shift more medical costs to employees.</u>

<u>Federal health insurance for all won't be enacted.</u>

<u>Retiree health benefits will be cut back.</u>

<u>More physicians will be on salary, not self-employed.</u>

<u>Clot-dissolving drugs will replace coronary bypasses.</u>

Health care is in for drastic changes in the next ten years, in terms of how the industry will operate and the use of technology already in the pipeline. Here's the big picture:

The aging of America will put special strains on the medical system because the elderly are the biggest users of health care. The demand for nursing homes and hospices will soar; so will the need for day-care centers for senior citizens in good health. Many diseases now largely untreatable, including AIDS, will be brought under control through new medicines, especially those developed through biotechnology.

The rise in medical costs will continue to surpass the general rate of inflation in the '90s, but will slow a bit from the skyrocketing pace of the '80s. The biggest factor in moderating health care inflation will be a greater emphasis on cost containment. Federal health insurance for the elderly and low-income Americans will not be extended to all citizens. Employers will shift more of the cost of medical care to their employees through higher deductibles. Big insurers and the federal government increasingly will cap reimbursements to both hospitals and physicians, forcing them to lower their fees, limit unnecessary tests and services or collect more from the patient, or—probably—some of each.

Hospitals, facing enormous cost pressures from government and competition, will consolidate, close or specialize in certain kinds of care, so that not every expensive machine and procedure will be available at each hospital. There will be a rising percentage of doctors and other health care personnel in the population, and more and more physicians will be salaried employees, rather than self-employed.

While these transformations are taking place, increases in life expectancy and reduction of death rates for most major diseases will continue at an accelerated pace. The reasons for this faster rate of improvement are many—some technological, some relating to increased awareness of the causes of diseases, some resulting from improved access to health care, especially for low-income people.

The U.S. will maintain its lead in medical research and technology. And our exports of health equipment and drugs will grow in the '90s. Computer technology that makes it possible to send information on a patient across town for expert consultation also makes it possible to send data across a continent or around the world. International consultations will be quite common, and medical centers in the U.S. will be the hubs for such activity. However, the Japanese will challenge us in selected areas. For example, they're well along in use of lasers for heart surgery and computers for monitoring patients, and they could move ahead of us in the most important area, genetic engineering. The Japanese government has targeted biotech for all-out development in the '90s.

The next frontier for medicine will be understanding how life and disease function in the cells. This will allow doctors to attack disease at its roots rather than just dealing with its symptoms.

By 2000, products derived from biotechnology will account for 15% to 25% of all drug sales. But before you rush to invest in start-up genetic-engineering companies or specialty firms with just one or a few patented products, keep in mind that old-line drugmakers such as Merck, American Cyanamid and SmithKline will also be into biotech in a big way. Biotech accounts for a small part of their annual revenues, but they have the financial staying power that small firms don't. Investing in genetic engineering will be a high-risk proposition throughout the next decade, with some firms hitting it big and more being absorbed into larger companies.

Disease prevention

Over the past nine decades, life expectancy has increased by more than 60%. Babies born in 1900 had a life expectancy of only 47 years. Today, due to the conquering of infectious diseases and strides in public health and nutrition, life expectancy at birth is 72 years for men and 79 for women. Baby boys born in 2000 will have a life expectancy of 74 years, baby girls 80 years. By 2070, life expectancy for men will be 77, for women 84.

The greatest improvements in American health in the next decade will come not from treatment of disease but from the prevention of it, through sensible eating and drinking habits, a lower incidence of smoking, regular exercise, life-styles that minimize mental and physical stress, and earlier diagnosis and treatment of problems. The American Medical Association estimates that 55% of all disease, disability and death is attributable to life-style. In short, more life-enhancing steps are available to the individual, through his own free will, than any medical center can offer at any cost.

For example, a much lower incidence of smoking (already in decline) will sharply reduce the incidence of cancer, heart disease, high blood pressure and stroke. Excessive exposure to the sun accounts for most of the half-million cases of skin cancer each year; more public awareness of the dangers of sunbathing, plus the wider use of sun-blocking lotions, will reduce this problem. The incidence of hypertension will decline as the connection to overweight, high salt intake and smoking becomes better known. Earlier testing for high cholesterol, coupled with dietary changes, will lower the risk of heart disease.

In nutrition, the trend will continue to foods lower in calories, fat (especially saturated fat), cholesterol, salt and sugar, and higher in fiber and complex carbohydrates. That's good news for sellers of whole-grain foods, dried beans, cereal and low-fat dairy items, fish, poultry, lean meat, fruits and vegetables. Food manufacturers will start using synthetic fat substitutes in ice cream, potato chips, french fries, bakery goods and other items as soon as these substances get approval from the Food and Drug Administration (FDA). And more attention will be given to obesity as a factor in diabetes, high blood pressure and stroke, heart disease, cancer and gallbladder disease.

More employers will offer fitness and "wellness" programs, including company-paid or subsidized annual physical exams, prenatal courses, and aerobics, antismoking, weight-loss, drug and alcohol-abuse programs. They will be viewed as part of company strategy to hold down medical costs. At some firms, cash bonuses will be paid to employees who stay healthy.

Note in the table below that eight of the ten leading causes of death in our country have some link to smoking, the foods we eat, or excessive consumption of alcohol. The eight causes account for 75% of all deaths.

Major Causes of Death in the U.S. in 1987

	Number	% of Total
Heart disease*	759,400	35.7%
Cancers*	476,700	22.4
Strokes*	148,700	7.0
Accidents**	92,500	4.4
Chronic obstructive lung disease	78,000	3.7
Pneumonia and influenza	68,600	3.2
Diabetes mellitus*	37,800	1.8
Suicide**	29,600	1.4
Chronic liver disease and cirrhosis**	26,000	1.2
Atherosclerosis**	23,100	1.1

  *Related to smoking and diet
**Related to alcohol abuse

Infant mortality

One of America's most tragic health problems is an infant mortality rate that is one of the highest among industrial countries. Infant mortality in the U.S. has declined sharply in this century, with the rate per 1000 births cut in half between 1970 and 1987. It will probably continue to decline in the decade ahead, but it's unclear how much more improvement is possible until America gets a grip on the underlying causes, which are related more to social forces than medical policy.

Most of the doomed babies are born premature and underweight to teenage and low-income women who neglect their health during pregnancy. Better programs of prenatal education and care will help reduce infant mortality some, but not as effectively as a pendulum swing away from early sexual activity and peer-group acceptance of teenage pregnancy.

New kinds of drugs

New drug therapy will minimize or even eliminate illnesses that have afflicted us for hundreds of years. For example, researchers have developed a treatment that halts the spread of spinal osteoporosis and reverses bone loss. It involves use of sodium fluoride in delayed-release form, plus a calcium supplement. The breakthrough promises relief for the five million Americans, mostly elderly women, who suffer from the disease.

New medicines will also be coming along for lowering cholesterol and blood pressure, for regulating heart rhythm, and for treating cancer, diabetes, Parkinson's disease, arthritis, ulcers and other problems. Mental-health specialists expect further progress in psychoactive medications and faster-acting antidepressant products.

Generic drugs will account for a bigger share of pharmaceutical sales in the next ten years, perhaps as much as 50%, mainly because of cost-containment pressures from insurers and the government. The larger proprietary-drug companies will become more involved in generics, and, in turn, the generic houses will become more like the rest of the industry, with a heavier commitment to research. To encourage more drug research, the government will agree to lengthen the period of patent protection for new products if drugmakers agree to hold their prices down.

Manipulating genes

Biotechnology, the key to controlling the behavior of individual cells, offers the most promise for advances in treating disease. It will help combat leukemia, for example, by regulating white blood cells, and it may have a role in treating AIDS by destroying the virus and then regrowing the immune cells. Within the next 20 years, it's a good bet that an AIDS vaccine and a cure for AIDS will be available. There'll be a huge market, since the disease has spread to more than 100 countries, straining medical facilities and budgets.

Diabetes is a biochemical disturbance, and researchers think that more-effective pancreas transplants will be feasible in the '90s to help overcome the illness. At a minimum, there will be simpler ways to take insulin: nasal sprays, capsules and eye-drops, or cell implants that will produce insulin. There's also hope for the 100,000 kidney-dialysis patients through more successful transplants. And biotech may help regenerate the spine and other parts of the central nervous system. New technology may allow repair or replacement of disease-causing genes before problems arise. And within a couple of years, the FDA will approve a clotting protein for hemophiliacs. Biological products will also be developed for healing wounds, burns and ulcers.

Advances in vaccines depend largely on progress in biotechnology. There may even be a vaccine for Alzheimer's disease, if researchers can find a clear link to a virus. There's talk of nerve transplants and other approaches, but at this point not enough is known about the disease. Unless a cure is found, the number of Alzheimer's patients will increase as the population ages.

Expect breakthroughs in nerve regeneration as scientists make further advances in understanding the nervous system and brain. As a result, fewer accident victims will become invalids.

Coronary bypass operations will be replaced by clot-dissolving drugs and less-invasive catheter-based procedures. Enzyme treatment was a factor in the speedy recovery of Chicago Bears' coach Mike Ditka after a mild heart attack midway through the 1988 football season. Less than two weeks after his attack, Ditka was back running the team. That made believers out of many doubters. Progress in predicting heart attacks and strokes will save many lives.

Look for biotech to contribute better drugs to control harmful cholesterol, perhaps aimed at receptors that make it easy for the liver to break down and eliminate fatty deposits in the arteries.

Throughout the '90s, genetic engineering will fuel political and ethical controversies over use of fetal tissue in transplants, in-vitro fertilization, in-utero surgery, preselection of the sex of a child, freezing of germ cells and embryos, and embryo-transfer banks. How far and how fast these developments go will depend largely on government policymakers. So far, government officials have taken a hands-off approach because they don't want foreign companies to get a jump on U.S. biotech firms.

Mechanical devices for health

The use of artificial hearts—a very expensive and iffy treatment—has dropped off in the last few years, but it will pick up in the '90s, as many of the technical problems are worked out and the shortage of healthy hearts for transplants worsens, due to the aging of the population. But it may be well into the next century before totally implantable artificial hearts that won't require any connection to tubes and machines outside the body become a reality.

Demand will also be strong for mechanical devices such as booster pumps and pacemakers for patients who aren't to the point of needing an artificial heart. Artificial limbs and other sophisticated prostheses will look and perform nearly as well as the real McCoy. Implantable drug-infusion systems and hearing aids, artificial blood and bones from bone banks will be commonplace.

New laser techniques

Lasers will be used more widely as a tool in general medicine for such jobs as stopping bleeding ulcers, opening blocked windpipes, reconnecting nerves and getting rid of birthmarks, polyps and warts. New laser techniques for correcting intrauterine problems will reduce the number of hysterectomies and relieve menstrual pain. Along with fiber optics, lasers will be used to analyze and separate individual cells and measure blood flow. They will also aid delicate surgery on cancerous tumors, the knees, spinal discs and eventually the heart. And they'll be used to stimulate inert drugs in the body. Further ahead, lasers will be an essential tool of genetic engineers.

Strides in imaging

In 20 years, we've moved from x-rays to computerized tomography (CT) to magnetic-resonance imaging (MRI), which produces extraordinary pictures of the internal body without the risk of x-rays. The next step up the imaging ladder is positron emission tomography (PET), which shows the brain, heart and other organs in action.

With PET, doctors will be able to pinpoint a certain area of the brain as responsible for specific problems and then develop remedies. They'll track how your brain metabolizes sugar, drugs and other chemicals, looking for very subtle changes, including early clues to brain tumors, schizophrenia, epilepsy, alcoholism or Alzheimer's. Computers will note any changes from previous examinations, just in case the doctor misses them.

MRI will be refined to track phosphorus and dozens of other chemicals in the body, making it easier to detect specific problems. There will also be cheaper diagnostic tests for identifying individuals who have a predisposition toward cancer or heart disease. They will be watched closely and treated as needed.

Improvements in imaging and the reading of these pictures may offer new insights into predispositions to mental illnesses and drug and alcohol abuse.

Computers all over

Computers will play a big role in medicine. They'll even be used in hospital rooms to monitor patients continually. Nurses won't have to wake you up to take your blood pressure, pulse or temperature; instead, they will have constant readings right at their work stations.

Computers will also regulate dosages and watch for incompatible drug combinations. Those wrist bands that hospital patients wear will carry a bar code. When doctors drop by, they will run a scanner over the bar code and then look at the patient's chart on a computer screen. These automated information systems will be more accurate, legible and consistent than current systems and should improve productivity and care while reducing costs.

As the shortage of nurses worsens and their pay increases, hospitals will invest in more and more automation of this sort. Hospital registered nurses now spend about 30% of their time on paperwork. Computers will free up more of their time for working with patients and for other duties.

Heart patients are already being monitored by phone, radio and such devices as CardioBeepers, used in conjunction with cardiac drugs.

Computerized cataloging of imaging, both MRI and PET, will eliminate the need for filing x-rays, which are often lost or destroyed after several years. Doctors will be able to watch how your heart pumps, compared with a year or so earlier, and will be able to send such imaging almost instantly from one hospital to another or to another doctor's office.

Understanding cancer

For years, researchers have taken a shotgun approach to cancer, trying everything, probing everywhere to understand the disease. Out of this has come the variety of chemical, radiation and surgical therapies that—coupled with strides in early detection—have extended the lives of cancer victims substantially. Today, nearly 55% of all cancer patients live five or more years after detection. That will improve to 70% by the turn of the century because of better cancer prevention and breakthroughs in vaccines and drugs.

The overall death rate from cancer has risen about 9% since 1955, but the cancer death rate for people under age 55 has fallen in the same period. When you remove smoking-related lung cancer from the equation, the U.S. cancer death rate declined 13% between 1950 and 1985.

Years ago, youngsters with leukemia were considered hopeless cases because there was no cure in sight. Now the vast majority of children suffering from leukemia can be saved. There has also been major progress against lymphomas such as

Hodgkin's disease, and cancer of the ovaries, stomach and cervix, along with marginal success in dealing with breast, colon and lung cancers.

Researchers believe their storehouse of information will pay off in promising new cancer treatments, medicines and vaccines. Biotechnology and use of the body's own immune system offer the best possibilities. And early detection techniques will improve, saving thousands of lives each year.

Net: It will be a decade of progress against killer diseases such as cancer, AIDS and hypertension.

High-tech dentistry

Fluoridation, better dental hygiene, and lower birth rates means fewer children's cavities for dentists to fill and more people going through life with their own teeth. So dentists will pay more attention to the needs of young adults and the elderly—gum diseases, adult orthodontics, crowns, oral surgery and aesthetics, even to the point of engineering better smiles for their patients.

Computers will become as common as drills at the dentist's office. In making ceramic crowns, for example, dentists will prepare the tooth the same as usual, but instead of making a mold, they will use a laser or other light beam to tell the computer the exact shape and size needed. The computer will do the designing, then signal another machine to start carving the crown. The whole job will be finished in less than an hour and there will be no need to mold and cast metals and porcelain at a dental lab or make repeat trips to the dentist.

In cosmetic dentistry, patients will be able to see on a computer screen how they'd look if their teeth were reshaped or recolored. And the results of surgery will be simulated by computer. Patients with extreme buck teeth will be able to see how their looks would change if they elected to have oral surgery.

Electronic anesthesia will come into its own in the '90s, replacing the dreaded needle. The new technique will overload the nerves with electronic impulses, thus deadening pain. Patients will regulate the painkiller themselves with a handheld device. And electronic braces, powered by a tiny battery, will straighten teeth twice as fast as those used today.

Lasers will be used for sealing root canals and for hardening tooth enamel. And they may eventually replace the drill for smoothing out crevices and vaporizing tooth decay in cavities. With lasers, there's no noisy whine, no vibration and no pain. There will also be expanded use of dental implants, in which teeth are anchored into the bone with titanium screws or glued to the remaining stubs.

Even with fewer cavities, there will still be plenty of market potential for the profession: About half the people in the country have NEVER been to a dentist. And with more adults keeping their teeth for a lifetime, those teeth and gums will need lots of maintenance.

Who will pay the bill

Advances in health technology won't come cheaply. Spending on medical care already claims 11% of our Gross National Product. That's more than $2,000 per person. By the turn of the century, health care will be a $1.3-trillion-a-year business.

As the table below illustrates, health costs have been climbing faster than the general inflation rate throughout the '80s. As a result, the government and insurance companies will focus even more on what hospitals, doctors and laboratories charge. Also under scrutiny will be costs at outpatient clinics and shopping-mall medical centers, which are expanding rapidly and aren't subject to federal-fee controls.

Year	Overall Inflation	Medical Costs
1981	8.9%	12.5%
1982	3.8	11.0
1983	3.8	6.4
1984	3.9	6.1
1985	3.8	6.8
1986	1.1	7.7
1987	4.4	5.8
1988	4.4	6.9

The big increases are in hospital bills (up 10.4% in 1988 alone), physician fees (a 7.5% increase) and prescription drugs (7.8%). It's true, of course, that care is improving, new equipment and other technology are VERY costly, doctors must pay huge liability insurance bills, and new drugs take years to develop, test and market.

The aging of America compounds the problem of holding medical costs in line. Older people are the heaviest users of health services. Although they make up only 12% of the population, they account for 30% of all hospital admissions, 20% of doctor visits and a third of total medical expenses. Health care use and costs are highest among the very old and in the last year of life.

For those reasons, health costs will keep running ahead of overall inflation in the '90s. But we believe that the rate of increase will moderate a little in the next decade, as preventive medicine takes hold, health continues to improve, and—most importantly—insurers and the government clamp down on medical charges through "managed care" and other approaches.

Employers, socked by annual double-digit increases in their insurance costs, will shift more of the health burden to employees via higher deductibles (including hospital and surgical expenses), cost sharing and other measures. Employees will be forced to make more trade-offs between medical and other benefits. Some firms are adding $2,000 or so to workers' pay and telling them to shop for their own insurance. That gets the monkey off the company's back, but employees don't make out as well, and in today's tight labor market, most workers expect (and 75% receive) at least some company-paid insurance.

In the next ten years, employees will pay a bigger share of health insurance premiums and hospitalization and surgical costs, perhaps with a cap on annual out-of-pocket expenses of $2,000 to $3,000. Unions will seize on such developments in their organizing efforts, especially in attempts to sign up white-collar workers. Health care is sure to emerge as a more critical issue in labor negotiations.

The trend will be to a managed fee-for-services approach and away from anything-goes, seat-of-the-pants health care systems. Employers will turn to specific-service contracts or to preferred-provider organizations (PPOs)—a fancy term for a simple concept. It means a company, often through an insurance firm, cuts its own deal with local hospitals and doctors to care for employees and their families at a set fee. Big companies are doing this now. In a few years, midsize and even smaller outfits will be seeking bids for their health contracts. If you're an employer, check this out and perhaps get into a PPO pool.

Insurers will do more second-guessing of tests and other services at hospitals, outpatient clinics and doctors' offices, often through the use of a computerized data base loaded with detailed information on medical procedures. Insurers will require pre-certification before a doctor can send a patient to the hospital. There will be closer scrutiny of the need for disk and lens-extraction surgery, prostatectomies, angiography and heart by-passes. Insurers will also question cesarean births, which cost $3,000 to $3,500 more than normal deliveries and are often prescribed for scheduling convenience or because the doctor believes they are less prone to complications than is vaginal delivery.

Insurers and employers will use a "gatekeeper" physician to control costs—a doctor who will monitor the medical history and care of each worker's family. The gatekeeper will order testing, make referrals to specialists, and recommend hospitalization, surgery or outpatient care. This and similar approaches to managed care will muzzle some of the run-up in insurance and medical costs.

One possibility in ten to 15 years is a computer network that would include virtually all doctors. They would feed in details on each of their patients and the treatments. The system would chew over data, looking for patterns of success or failure, then make suggestions. Doctors don't like people looking over their shoulders, but they'll have to get used to it.

The federal role

Government intrusion is likely to increase, for the simple reason that Uncle Sam—through medicare for the elderly and medicaid for the poor—is picking up more of America's health care tab than any other insurer.

While some in Congress and the administration struggle with ways to better manage what Washington does already, others are seeking to expand coverage with long-term health care and nursing home care, expansion of medicare and medicaid, and either mandatory employer-paid health coverage or some sort of national health insurance. Administrative costs for health care are already $25 billion. They would shoot higher under national health insurance.

In a few years, physician fees for medicare will be limited by new federal schedules, similar to those that apply to hospital charges now. They work much like the book rates that insurers use in dealing with auto-repair shops. The government will set the level of reimbursement for a particular service, a take-it-or-leave-it proposition. Most doctors will take it because medicare will account for 30% to 40% of their incomes. Of course, they can try to charge more, but that will have to come from the patient.

Long-term nursing home care has Congress stumped. A lot of members would like to crank up a federal program, but they don't know how to pay the annual bill of $40 billion to $50 billion when everyone's worrying about budget deficits. So in the short term Congress will simply encourage insurance companies to set up more-affordable plans for nursing home services and home care. Later in the '90s, it may approve medical IRAs or other tax incentives for long-term care.

Physicians, hospital administrators and other health professionals will be watching Massachusetts' new mandatory health-insurance plan carefully, as a possible model for a federal law. Employers in that state must either provide health insurance for their workers or kick in to a state-run risk pool for individuals who aren't covered. The state government is liable for any shortfall. Congress and the President are much more likely to go for this type of approach, even though business strongly opposes it, than they are for straight-out national health insurance or socialized medicine, with health care professionals working for the government, as in Britain. Within a few years, it's likely that all companies will have to pay for at least some of their employees' health coverage.

Employers face another gigantic problem in the '90s: unfunded medical benefits that have been promised to their current and future retirees—obligations that have already forced some companies into bankruptcy. Thus, the trend will be to defined-contribution care for retirees rather than defined benefits. Companies will specify in dollars how much they'll chip in for health care.

That means retirees will have to assume the inflation risk. Employers will also raise co-payments that retirees must make on hospital services and will link company contributions to length of service.

To minimize the impact on retirees, Congress will probably approve pension-type tax incentives for funding of retiree health benefits by employers, and possibly a tax-deferred medical IRA. But don't hold your breath. It will be well into the '90s before Congress gets anything worked out.

More doctors per patient

The number of physicians and the physician-to-patient ratio will continue to increase over the next 20 years. The American Medical Association estimates that there will be 653,000 doctors in 2000, one for every 413 persons in the U.S., up from 563,700 doctors, or one per 443 in 1990. By 2010, there will be 715,200 doctors, or one for every 397 people. Over the next 20 years, the number of foreign-born physicians with U.S. citizenship will more than double. Distribution of health professionals will continue to be a problem; most new doctors head for the cities and suburbs, and not enough set up shop in small towns and depressed rural areas.

There will be across-the-board increases by specialty, but the sharpest percentage gains will be in doctors who practice emergency medicine, pediatrics, anesthesiology, general internal medicine, radiology and the new interdisciplinary field of geriatric medicine.

Due to a strong supply of physicians, increasing restraint of doctors' fees and exploding malpractice premiums, it is likely that the average inflation-adjusted income of physicians will rise very slowly during the '90s. Early in the next century, there's a strong possibility that a majority of American doctors—although still the best paid in the world—will be salaried employees of hospitals and prepaid health plans, rather than self-employed practitioners.

The role of nonphysician health professionals, especially registered nurses, will be expanded in the years ahead. The recent shortage of nurses, which is still predominantly a female profession, is caused by a combination of factors, including expanding career choices for smart young women in other fields and the low pay that nurses have traditionally received relative to the amount of education their job requires. As with all other labor shortages, it will be gradually reversed by steady increases in nursing pay in the '90s. Meanwhile, hospitals will hire more nurses from the Philippines, Ireland, Latin America and elsewhere.

Defensive medicine

It's no news that premiums for malpractice insurance have headed skyward in recent years, and there's no relief in sight, as long as America remains the most litigious society on earth. Undoubtedly more genuine malpractice is being punished today than in decades past, but it's equally true that competent doctors (and their insurers) are often penalized by patients (and juries) who refuse to accept that life is full of unseen risks, insisting that someone is to blame for everything.

As a result, doctors are practicing more defensive medicine, scheduling redundant tests and taking every precaution imaginable. (Some estimates indicate that tests account for half of all health care costs.) The liability crisis is one reason why more physicians will crawl under the protective umbrella of institutional practices, clinics, Health Maintenance Organizations (HMOs) and the like, rather than start their own practices.

The proliferation of new technology probably has something to do with the surge in malpractice suits. Heart bypasses and use of MRI scans, for example, have spread far beyond the role that researchers originally envisioned. Patients and their families are suing over physicians' decisions whether or not to use bypass surgery, as well as methods of treatment based on the results of imaging.

Malpractice insurance premiums for OB/GYNs average over $20,000 a year, so some obstetricians have quit delivering babies altogether to concentrate on the lower-risk side of their speciality, gynecology. But the financial liability doesn't end when they stop delivering babies. A person can sue the doctor who delivered him even 20 years later.

Pressure on hospitals

No other country allows the spread of state-of-the-art technology far beyond the need for it to the extent the U.S. does. Especially in health, nothing is too good, too expensive or too extravagant. A hospital that presumes to be a top-notch, full-service facility figures it must offer transplants, open-heart surgery, MRI machines (at $4 million each) and the latest in cancer treatment, lasers and other technologies to attract a skilled staff and win patient referrals. Prestige plays a big part. As a result, two hospitals within a block of each other may each have an MRI machine and be completely equipped and staffed for transplant surgery.

You can figure on this changing in the '90s, because of cost pressures. Hospital expenses are increasing faster than revenues. Revenues are being pinched because of reimbursement caps on medicare and medicaid, high levels of uncompensated care, and slower payments from insurance companies and others. The problem will worsen as managed-care programs take a larger share of the market. Hospitals can't shift the cost of uncompensated care to managed-care programs and remain competitive for contracts with employers. Inner-city hospitals will be hardest hit. They will lose managed-care business and patients to suburban facilities that have lower uncompensated care costs.

The trend will be to more hospital mergers, consolidations, conversions and downsizing. More hospitals will close, especially in rural areas, where over 200 have shut down since 1980, and another 600 will likely close by 1995. For most rural hospitals it's a case of economics—90% of them with fewer than 25 beds lose money. They simply don't have enough patients.

To stay busy, some hospitals will specialize in short-term care for patients recovering from heart attacks or surgery, much like a hotel but with nurses. Others will try long-term care and even day care. Many hospitals will move from double-occupancy rooms to more privacy, even luxury suites with cable TV, fresh-cut flowers, gourmet meals and extra bedrooms for the family.

To control the cost of high-tech equipment that is available elsewhere in the same community, there will be more specialization and fewer hospitals offering all things to all patients. In cities, five or six hospitals will get together to lower costs by splitting up the specialties, one handling obstetrics, another recovery care, a third cardiology, etc. The idea is to cut overhead, save through joint purchasing and perhaps swing more weight with the insurance companies. There will also be more regionalization. A hospital in Philadelphia, for example, may do most of the heart transplants in the mid Atlantic, with lodging arrangements made for families of patients. Other hospitals in the region will specialize in treating cancer, AIDS, kidney ailments, drug and alcohol abuse, or psychiatric conditions.

Care for the elderly

Life-care communities and shared housing will be popular for older people who are independent but want health facilities nearby. In these communities, residents will have their own apartments or houses, plus access to meals, recreation and medical treatment. Such developments will combine elements of nursing homes, home health care and hospices. For older people, they're worth checking out. (The same goes for investors.)

Hospitals will get into the elder-care act with day-care centers for the elderly: drop grandpa off on the way to work and pick him up on the way home. They'll schedule social events and provide meals and regular medical checkups for a set fee. Others will help fill the need for more moderately priced nursing home facilities, perhaps by establishing senior-citizen wards to make maximum use of their professional staffs.

There will be continuing improvement in the health and lives of older Americans. Life expectancy will increase by several years during the next few decades but, more importantly, older people will live healthier and richer lives. With the legislative abolition of mandatory retirement at 65, many Americans will choose to work longer than before. However, due to company-paid pensions, IRAs and deferred-compensation plans, a financially secure retirement at 65 (or even earlier) will still be the norm, although many elderly people will start second careers of full- or part-time work, postponing true retirement until well into their 70s. Thanks to advances in health, retirement will be the beginning of a new life, not a winding-down of the old.

8 Improving Our Schools

Elementary and secondary schools will get better.

Meatier subjects, more homework, longer school year.

Business will get more involved in education.

Computers will become important as teaching aids.

U.S. colleges will continue to lead the world.

Student aid will be based in part on community service.

Shaping up our schools will be one of our toughest tasks in the '90s. Improvement is essential to higher living standards and competing in the global economy. As technology sprints ahead and international competition intensifies, there will be a growing demand for skilled people and fewer openings for the unskilled. A solid education will be needed to compete. Convince your children and grandchildren of this. Talk it up with your business associates and your neighbors. Make sure your local school officials know how you feel. Hammer it home.

Graduates must learn to think, to solve problems and to assume responsibilities, not merely handle rote tasks. Schools must develop learning as a lifelong process "that will distinguish the movers and shakers from the losers and crawlers," according to Ronald Pilenzo, president of the American Society for Personnel Administration.

147

Our high schools and colleges aren't turning out enough graduates who are prepared for the present job market, let alone the advanced economy they will face in the '90s. "Employment in the modern world increasingly demands basic literacy in science and mathematics," says Erich Bloch, director of the National Science Foundation. "Thus we should be concerned that in this country one out of four individuals does not finish high school, and nearly 30% of the nation's high schools offer no physics, 17% offer no chemistry, and 70% offer neither earth nor space sciences."

The National Science Foundation says that 60,000 math and science teachers aren't up to their jobs, and estimates that by 1995 an additional 300,000 math and science teachers will be required in U.S. secondary schools.

With fewer Americans choosing science or engineering careers, we'll be more dependent on foreign-born engineers in important high-tech lines. That hasn't been a problem yet, but it will be if the flow of foreign graduate students slows.

The danger is real, but thousands *will* continue to come to American colleges for the same reasons they always have. America has a larger number of rigorous colleges than any other nation, and our best universities are still the leaders in science and engineering studies. And America has more good job opportunities in technical fields than any other country. By accepting more immigrants in the '90s, the U.S. will benefit from new workers with special education and skills that will be needed in a growing high-tech economy.

But educated immigrants won't offset the shortcomings of our school system. This sharp indictment from the U.S. Department of Education's report *A Nation at Risk* is enough to jar anyone out of complacency: "If an unfriendly foreign power had attempted to impose on America the mediocre education performance that exists today, we might well have viewed it as an act of war."

You've read the horror stories of American students being far behind their contemporaries in Asia and Europe in math and science, language, geography and other skills; of students being advanced from grade to grade without ever learning to read; of schools where violence and drugs make learning impossible. Unfortunately, the stories are true. As a result, the U.S. has millions of people who are functionally illiterate and who will be left behind in the competitive climate of the '90s.

Education starts at home

Better schools will require efforts that go beyond education, and the effort begins in how we raise our children and the expectations we set for them. Today's public schools are undermined by societal problems that the schools alone are largely powerless to correct: a lack of respect for authority; too much television and not enough reading; too little parental involvement in child-rearing; overemphasis on commercial entertainment, sports and possessions; drug and alcohol abuse by kids; sexual permissiveness and teen pregnancy. All of these problems of contemporary society complicate the task faced by teachers and school administrators.

Schools aren't day-care centers or churches or scout troops. Their *primary* mission isn't to teach our children to drive a car, play football, cook meals, avoid pregnancy, or prepare them for marriage. Their job is to teach academic skills that will enable our kids to earn a living and contribute to a vital nation. Schools can't take the place of parents and other social institutions in teaching personal responsibility, honesty, self-control, compassion, courtesy, respect for work, tolerance, cooperation and patriotism. The underpinning of values must come from the home.

But there is a growing demand that our schools not *exacerbate* society's problems either. A child from a caring, respectful home must not discover that violence, disrespect and laziness are tolerated at school. So in the 1990s we will see schools put more emphasis on classroom order and moral standards. Teachers will no longer have to take a value-neutral approach—bringing up moral issues for discussion without revealing their own views and the commonly accepted values of society. In the years ahead, they'll be encouraged to exercise more discipline, provide guidance and firmly state their views of what's right and what's wrong.

Improvement on the way

There is often a lag between the public perception of a crisis and a turnaround in the crisis itself. By the time people come to accept that something is severely wrong, the worst is past and improvement has already begun. We're now in the early stages of a trend toward higher standards and better performance, a process that began when our schools hit rock bottom sometime in the mid 1970s.

American society has both benefited and suffered from the relentless democratization of education. In one generation, America nearly doubled the percentage of youths who graduate from high school and go on to some kind of further education. Surging college enrollments resulted from more student aid, establishment of new community and state colleges, and most of all, the lowering of admissions standards.

In the process of encouraging more students to attend some sort of college, we intentionally debased our standards both for getting a high school diploma and qualifying for college. Today's average high school and college graduates are less educated—as measured by skills in a wide variety of subjects—than the American high school and college graduates of a generation ago, not to mention their counterparts in other nations.

On the positive side, this democratizing process has the potential of giving more youths a shot at higher education, keeping more of our youths involved in education longer, compared to other countries. In many nations, higher education is still reserved for the elite. Relatively few students are selected in adolescence for a fast-track education, and the rest are relegated to the back of the class. Yes, their average college students are more capable than ours, but there are far fewer of them compared with America's, both in absolute numbers and as a percentage of their college-age population. Having said that, we know it's foolish to boast of high college enrollments if the entering students are leaving high school with inadequate preparation for either college or the job market.

The best indication that improvement in elementary and secondary education is already under way is the national sense of urgency, the new commitment toward improving our schools, the fact that education is a hot topic at every level of government today and in business circles. We pick this up in our travels around the country, in talks with local school officials and business people.

The changes occurring today in most states will start to bring results in the next few years. All over America, expectations for educational performance are being raised. School systems are feeling the heat of accountability. Courses are being toughened. The teaching profession is beginning to attract people better qualified to teach math and science, without regard for whether they ever attended a teacher's college or passed standards that are now badly out of date.

In the decade ahead, there will be fewer frilly electives, more emphasis on writing, math and science, courses that kids will have to sweat over. The school year will be extended another month or *two*. Teachers will lay on more homework, require more from their students. There will be more attention to developing analytical skills—making sure that youngsters are comprehending what they read. For kids who can't keep up, there will be remedial instruction and special tutoring, including Saturday sessions, some of them paid for by local businesses.

Choose your own school

Public education is a government-run monopoly, and it exhibits the two main flaws of monopolies both public and private: high price and a lack of incentive to innovate for improved quality. A growing awareness of this will make school-of-choice arrangements, giving parents a choice of schools within a designated area, commonplace in the '90s.

Competition among schools is not a new concept. Vermont has a 100-year-old system where state and local governments combine to pay tuition, up to a limit, regardless of whether families choose private or public schools. A pick-your-school program is already available in Minnesota, and similar approaches are planned or under way in Seattle, San Jose, San Francisco, East Harlem, N.Y., and Boston. The purpose is to spark competition among schools. Those that lose students will also lose revenues ($2,800 per pupil in Minnesota), go through personnel shakeups or even close.

And look for more "magnet schools" for motivating students to reach their full potential in math, science and other specialties. Some will be open year-round. And universities will get involved in running school systems, as Boston University is beginning to do with the schools of the Chelsea neighborhood.

State governments will beat the drum for accountability. In New Jersey, school districts that fail to meet standards and don't remedy their problems quickly will be taken over and run by the state. That has already happened to the schools in Jersey City.

Pressure and rewards for teachers

Teaching careers will be more rewarding in the '90s because of higher pay, more prestige and better working conditions. This will be especially true for teachers of science and math, whose earnings will reflect the intense competition for these skills from the private sector.

The demand for teachers will grow fast in the decade ahead to accommodate the waves of youngsters now flooding into kindergarten and first grade—children of the Baby Boom "echo" of the '80s. Grade-school enrollments will increase from now through 1995, and there will be two million more high-school students by 2000. By the early '90s, there will be a need for 200,000 new teachers a year, twice the rate of the early '80s, many of them replacing retiring teachers.

In many districts, there will be sizable pay raises and special career ladders for those who pursue advanced study. These will be coupled with competence-testing of current teachers, beefed-up remedial training of teachers and changed certification requirements that focus on subject knowledge rather than teaching techniques. Look for more hiring of college graduates with majors other than education—math majors to teach math, biology majors to teach science and so on. They'll bone up on teaching methods at nearby colleges. Also, retirees will be encouraged to teach, either full-time or as substitutes or teacher's aides. A retired chemist, for example, might teach science, or a retired accountant might handle a small-business class.

Most school districts will start paying extra for top-notch teachers, even though teachers' unions initially tried to sandbag merit pay. Principals, their assistants and teacher peer groups will decide merit, but there will be pressure to base merit pay on objective standards of student performance. There will also be a strong push for sharper, more imaginative principals, because they set the tone for the whole school.

One of the biggest problems in public education today—which

mirrors similar problems in business and government—is the high proportion of managers relative to firing-line personnel. Bloated educational bureaucracies will be whittled down to improve student-teacher ratios in the classroom and reduce the number of paper shufflers in the superintendent's office. In large part due to the size of our educational establishment, America spends far more money per student than any other nation in the world, which makes the low performance of our graduates all the more appalling.

The hierarchial nature of public schools will be broken down, spreading authority that is now concentrated in powerful state and county bureaucracies. More power and discretion will go to school principals, teachers and even PTAs, working in management teams that will make decisions on everything from textbooks and curriculum to deployment of the faculty. It will be part of an effort to treat teachers with more dignity and to benefit from what they see happening in their own schools.

Learning by computer

Computer-aided education, or "intelligent tutoring systems," will explain subjects, monitor the student's work and provide remedial assistance, tailored to the needs of the individual student. But it won't be a matter of machines replacing teachers— the role of well-trained teachers will grow in importance. Computers will be used as education enhancers and multipliers, a sort of electronic teacher's aide. A number of companies and universities are now working on software, teaching techniques and hardware for such systems. Computer learning, self-paced instruction and interactive videos will become integral parts of the normal school day.

Most youngsters will develop computer skills before leaving the elementary grades, skills they'll need for future jobs, even for running basic business systems. And the flow of ideas and information will expand enormously as kids use computers at school and home. Through telephone hookups they'll tap into hundreds of data-bank resource centers, take exams, receive comments and corrections and prepare essays—all by computer. Schools and classrooms won't disappear, but the traditional dividing lines will give way to "education at large."

Sharing of resources

Look for more sharing of school libraries and data-base systems, thanks to computer linkups and the ease of moving information electronically. For example, several of the universities in the Washington, D.C., area have formed a library consortium that contains six million volumes, the third-largest in the U.S. after Harvard and Yale. It will serve as a model for similar efforts by high schools and colleges in metropolitan areas all over the country. The same concept of clustering and sharing will apply to research labs and other expensive facilities, aided by computer and video connections. Schools will benefit from better facilities at less cost.

Upgrading of vocational-education programs

In recent decades, we have probably overestimated the number of American youths who need and can benefit from a traditional college education, while simultaneously slighting the value of vocational education (voc-ed), which at its best gives many students solid skills for the job market.

Voc-ed will be upgraded and will no longer be treated as the stepchild of college preparatory education, the dumping ground for the failing student. Work-oriented education will be seen as a cost-effective priority that can reduce the high school drop-out rate, especially in inner-city school systems. Voc-ed will be restructured to emphasize technical skills that America will need to compete internationally, including training with computers and health care equipment. And voc-ed students will get a heavier dose of basic math, reading and writing, which will come in handy for future training and retraining. Businesses will get involved in vocational education to assure themselves of an ample supply of labor for the future.

The role of business

If you think labor markets are tight now, just wait a few years. For the first time ever, there are now fewer teenagers than people 65 and over. Between now and '95, the number of 17- to 22-year-olds will drop by two million. And a third of all new workers will be immigrants or minorities, many of whom will need special remedial education. Businesses will also face even stiffer competition for young workers from the military and colleges. They're already recruiting like mad.

Thus, for businesspeople, lending a hand to local schools is no longer just a civic duty or community goodwill project. It's a matter of self-interest, perhaps even self-preservation. At stake is the quality of future employees, the bread and butter of business, the need for people who can communicate and handle math and technical skills. Companies really have no choice. They must either improve local elementary and high schools now or spend billions in the years ahead to make the unemployable employable. There's growing recognition that schools are everybody's responsibility, and that money alone won't fix the system. It's not simply a matter of writing checks.

IBM spends $2 billion a year internally for education. The United Auto Workers and Ford are cooperating on math and other courses that enable assembly-line workers to earn college degrees; each hourly worker receives a $2,000 tuition voucher annually. Nationwide, ten million employees are already taking courses every year, at a cost of $40 billion. By 2000, business will invest $80 billion to $100 billion a year in worker training and development, and nearly 10% of the work force will be in some sort of job-training program.

How to get involved

If you decide to get involved, work *with* the schools. Don't go in and throw your weight around with the attitude that you're going to straighten out the whole shebang. Start by meeting with the local principal, superintendent or school board. Find out what they plan and what they need. Swap ideas and let them know what you'll be able to do. Or work through community groups that already have worthwhile programs to help the schools. You can pick up ideas by looking at what others are already doing:

A number of businesses are adopting local grade or high schools, working with principals to offer volunteer teachers or providing computers and other equipment. Some outfits have set up science labs for schools and picked up the tab for study aids. Others line up tutors (in some cases employees) for math, science and other courses, to help kids catch up. In some communities retailers and other businesses make a policy of hiring top students as interns after school and during the summer, to give them the flavor of the workplace and reward their scholastic achievements.

Presentations by role-model employees who have graduated from the school often go over well as a means of showing how education and effort pay off in desirable jobs—"You can do it, too; here's how." These are good opportunities for zeroing in on the importance of good study and work habits, reliability and punctuality. Some businesses sponsor booster clubs for academic achievement, recognizing and rewarding top students. They're modeled after sports booster clubs. Others sponsor "business weeks" at schools to help kids learn the ropes of how the market works and how to plan for a career in business. The aim is to show the relevance of education to the students' place in the future job market.

Local involvement—everyone pitching in—is the key, not federal programs and rules. Businesspeople are finally wising up to this. More are running for school boards and haggling over bond issues and legislation needed to upgrade the schools. Think about getting involved yourself.

Colleges of the future

Higher education in America is far more diverse in its structure and mission than in any other country on earth, and this diversity will grow in the Global '90s.

In most nations, college is a place that a tiny percentage of the brightest students go to for a rigorous academic training in the sciences, social studies and humanities. In America, college can mean anything from taking bookkeeping and computer keyboarding courses at an open-admissions community college to premed studies at a highly competitive private or state college.

In the '90s, America's community and junior colleges will play a valuable role in sharpening the academic skills of the average high school graduate, while serving as a feeder system for more challenging colleges. They will continue to concentrate on practical education that is strongly job-related.

Even among academically demanding colleges there is a big

difference in mission between small colleges that emphasize undergraduate teaching and enormous universities that combine teaching with an emphasis on high-level scientific research, much of it funded by the federal government and large corporations.

In the '90s, the cost of higher education will continue to exceed the rate of inflation, and this will intensify the current debate over productivity in higher education. At many colleges, faculty are being paid more and more to spend fewer and fewer hours in the classroom. If the nonclassroom time is being spent in productive research, the nation is getting good benefit from the higher pay, but this linkage is not always clear.

Look for an acceleration of the trend toward closer cooperation between American universities and corporations—a relationship that once raised suspicion among many academics. More and more colleges are developing research parks adjacent to their campuses. Some are starting business-incubator programs, under which small businesses in high-tech fields are launched with faculty participation and investment. Universities and faculty members are jointly applying for patents on new processes and licensing their discoveries to the private sector. Corporations are often funding basic research at top colleges, not with any promise of exclusive use of the results, but for the benefit they'll receive from early knowledge of significant discoveries.

America's role in a more interdependent world will require that colleges offer a core curriculum that puts courses and knowledge in a global context, regardless of the student's major. Humanities and social sciences will emerge anew as sought-after majors for young people headed into business, as employers discover the value of a broad education with strong verbal and written communication skills. And the study of western civilization will re-emerge, no longer criticized as irrelevant to the present and future. Virtually all professions will require some knowledge of languages, cultures, geography and economics.

The federal role

Education issues will rate higher in the political pecking order during the '90s. A dramatic sense of urgency was the greatest contribution of Ronald Reagan's provocative Secretary of Education, William Bennett (now head of the federal war against drug abuse). George Bush recognized the potency of the issue and capitalized on it throughout the 1988 campaign, lamenting the slippage in elementary and high schools, the poor test scores, high drop-out rates, drug use, high school grads who can't read or write or think straight.

Like it or not, every President will have to be an "education President" in the years ahead. Recognition of the problems and willingness to DO something will cut across the political spectrum. There will be differences, of course, over how to allocate money—split the melon—and over the federal government sticking its nose into local schools. But arguments are what politics is all about.

Basically education will still be run and funded locally, but with much more involvement by parents, business leaders and others. Washington will help set priorities and try to get things accomplished through tax incentives, public-private cooperative programs and direct assistance. And Uncle Sam will continue to play a big role in student aid for college. But less than 10% of funding for elementary and high school education will come from the federal government. We're not headed for a federalized school system.

Federal programs will focus on the youngest children, through Head Start and other approaches. Educators figure we can get the greatest reward for the smallest investment—the biggest bang for the buck—by concentrating on the very young. "Every additional increment of age," according to former Secretary of Education Shirley Hufstedler, "means doubling and redoubling the resources that must be invested to tap the treasures within those children."

Federal spending will increase, mostly for aid to the states. There will be special emphasis on kids who are falling behind, remedial programs for minorities and the poor, youngsters with language problems and handicaps. And more money will be sluiced into programs to make sure immigrant children understand our language and culture. (Teachers who know Spanish won't have any trouble finding work.) But the vogue for full bilingual education—in which most of the school day is conducted in Spanish—will fade as we come to realize that this method slows the development of English skills and is therefore a handicap, not a boost, however well intended.

Educational vouchers will be hotly debated—the idea of government paying part of the cost of sending children to private or parochial schools. Proponents see it as another way of injecting choice and competition into the education system. But vouchers won't fly in Congress because of concern that they would undermine the public school system and that payments to religiously affiliated schools would violate the Constitutional provisions for separation of church and state.

New ways to pay for college

Although college costs will rise faster than the general rate of inflation in the '90s, they probably won't increase as fast as they have during the '80s. Some of the upward pressure on costs will be relieved by the fact that there will be fewer college-age kids coming along—youngsters born during the "birth dearth" of the '70s. For students, it will be a buyers' market, a wider choice of colleges and smaller increases in tuition and other costs. Unfortunately, the drop in enrollment will be the last straw for some small independent colleges that are barely hanging on now.

Earlier predictions of declining college enrollments didn't foresee, however, a surge of adults returning to the college classroom, or entering for the first time. Adult education will be the growth market for all higher education over the next decade. Some colleges will survive by working closely with local companies on courses and retraining for employees. And that, in turn, may lure more workers into degree programs.

To help families pay for college, the federal government will sell education savings bonds with IRA-like provisions. And there will be new angles to tuition prepayment plans and "futures contracts" to pay for college ahead of time. Other states will follow Michigan's example in setting up guaranteed payment of future tuition for those who buy tax-free bonds or participate in state-backed savings plans.

Sometime in the '90s, a national public-service youth corps will probably be set up, replacing much of the present federal student-aid program. Youths who want generous federal aid for college will have to join the military, tutor or work in nursing homes, hospitals or some other kind of community service. They would earn vouchers that could be applied to college, technical training or, perhaps, a down payment on a house. In any event, the student-loan program is sure to be changed, and the emphasis will shift to encouraging parents to save for tuition, instead of borrowing federal money that must be repaid by parents and students after graduation. The government feels that the present system isn't working.

By graduation, youngsters can now be saddled with over $17,000 in guaranteed student loans for undergraduate study, or almost $55,000 if they go on to take graduate or professional courses. Most have to scratch around a while for jobs. Then they need a car and perhaps an apartment. And usually within a few years they want to get married. The marriage is often a merger of huge student-loan obligations. Not surprisingly, when you combine the size of this burden with a lower level of personal responsibility in today's youth, the result is a staggering rate of default on federal student loans. That's why the White House and Congress think that education chits-for-service or tuition prepayment incentives make sense for everyone concerned, government as well as borrowers.

The rewards of a college education

College pays—and probably more than you think. The cold figures show that people who invest in college education get their money back in spades through future earnings. College graduates earn almost *twice* as much per year as those who graduated only from high school. And the risk of unemployment declines the further you go in school. Tell your youngsters. In your own case, if you haven't finished college and have a chance to do so, it might be a good idea to go back. Of course, many young people aren't cut out for a traditional college education. Some are good with their hands and might do better learning a skilled trade, such as computer installation and repair, construction and auto repair.

A technical college education will beat liberal arts for getting that first job quickly, and starting pay might be higher. But the benefits of technical specialization can be oversold. Liberal-arts knowledge and skills are more portable, more useful to a broad variety of employers. Increasingly employers are looking for strong aptitudes for communicating, getting along with people and leading others. Students should consider two majors, the one in which they'll start out professionally, a second in which they can broaden their general knowledge and interests. Technicians are essential, but they usually don't run things at the top.

For details on the big shifts in employment in the years ahead and the best fields for future jobs, read on to the next chapter. But before you get engrossed in looking at the various lines of work, remember that most people who make a lot of money do it incidentally, while doing what they're good at and enjoy.

The spirit of innovation

Many of the changes described in this chapter will jar the education establishment. The basic structure of our system has been the same for many years: parents forced to send their kids to the school they're assigned to, whether it's any good or not; buildings divided into boxcar rooms by various grades and subjects; curriculum set by state and county authorities; students coming from and returning to their neighborhoods at fixed times; school days measured by buzzers and bells; two and a half months of summer vacation, plus another month or so scattered through the year; youths going off to college at 18 for four straight years, never to return.

Much of this is changing. Schools are now often used seven days a week for educational, social, recreational and even religious activities. And many academic functions are moving away from the school environment. School years are being lengthened. Adults are returning to college for as little as one course or a whole new degree. Vocational education is leading the way into the workplace.

Lifelong learning, training and retraining is essential to productivity, achieving individual potential and international competitiveness. With the volume of information doubling every two years and change taking place at a faster rate, periodic upgrading of education will become routine.

Great improvements are often born of necessity—the realization that the old ways are not working very well (or in the case of education, that many of the innovations of the '60s and '70s were worse than the traditions they replaced). The first steps toward improving American education were taken when we began to face up to the enormity of the problem.

Back in 1925, Calvin Coolidge said "the business of America is business." Today we have come to see that the business of America is *education,* and quality education is inseparable from achievement in the marketplace. Listen to John A. Gilmartin, chairman of Millipore Corporation, a Massachusetts-based international maker of equipment for biochemical research and pharmaceutical production, as he explains this linkage. "It does not matter if the market success occurs in Europe or Japan or the U.S.," he says. "The technology base of our company is rooted in the U.S. and her extraordinarily fertile system of higher education, particularly in scientific matters. As a result, we are more interested in U.S. educational policies than in U.S. export policies."

There is much that is good about American education—its openness, creativity, and especially the democratic premise that all citizens, whatever their native intelligence and start in life, deserve to have their potential developed to the fullest. But there is a lot of room for improvement, and that is one of the greatest challenges facing America in the Global '90s.

9 The Churning Job Market

Slower labor force growth from now to 2000.

Productivity gains will accelerate in most fields.

Immigration will relieve tight labor markets.

Fewer young workers, a more-seasoned work force.

More women, blacks, Hispanics and Asians at work.

The male/female earnings gap will narrow further.

Second, even third careers will be common for retirees.

Unions will adapt to changing worker needs.

How well America works in the Global '90s will depend on our work force—our people—more than on computers and other high-tech tools that will be at our disposal. It is educated human beings who create the machines that raise productivity, and it takes skilled labor to operate these machines effectively. That's why education and training are so important to our economic performance.

You should know, for your own good reasons, something about the big shifts in the job market and the way people will earn a living in the years ahead. The more you know about such things, the better off you'll be in your own career, in managing your company's personnel needs and in helping your children or grandchildren select a career.

Employment will keep growing, although at a slower rate than in recent years. Nearly 20 million new jobs will be created in the

'90s. That's quite a slowdown from the recent job-creation rates, but it poses no broad problem because there will be fewer job seekers, too.

The American labor force of tomorrow is going to look different from today's in many ways. There will be a larger share of women, blacks, Hispanics and Asians, and a smaller proportion of white males. The age makeup will also change. Younger and older workers will be a smaller part of the labor force.

In the late '80s, we added about 2.5 million jobs a year. Even with a healthy economy, that's probably an unsustainable rate because we won't have that many new workers available. As a result, unemployment will stay low, around 5%, except for recessions, keeping upward pressure on pay. There will be occasional increases in the federal minimum wage, but in many labor-short industries even unskilled jobs will pay well above the minimum wage, so any increases will be almost irrelevant.

Higher productivity growth coming

Slower growth in the labor force will help boost productivity—output per hour worked. It was sluggish in the '70s while we absorbed record numbers of new workers, including Baby Boomers, adult women who never held outside jobs before and a flood of immigrants. Productivity perked up a bit in the '80s. In fact, growth in manufacturing productivity has been stellar in recent years, among the best in the world. This was largely due to automation. The worst productivity problems are in services that don't adapt easily to automation. There have been notable productivity gains in financial and other services, but how do you automate a barber shop? In the decade ahead, we'll see stronger productivity gains, and the service sector will be put on a low-fat diet that will improve output per worker.

When young job seekers were plentiful and cheap, many businesses saw no need to buy labor-saving equipment. But that has changed. As we go into the '90s, we'll have a more mature work force in addition to the payoff from recent heavy investments in automation.

Productivity growth is the key to rising living standards, so real disposable personal incomes will grow faster in the next ten years than in the past ten. Wage increases that match the rise in productivity are not inflationary, so better productivity growth is also a reason for expecting inflation to average lower during the '90s—around 4% a year, compared with 7.4% in the '70s and 5.2% through most of the '80s.

Booming service sector

Most of the 20 million new jobs that will be created in the '90s will be in the service industries, including health care, computer operations, international trade, accounting, communications, banking, insurance, transportation and engineering. Employment in manufacturing will continue to decline as a share of total jobs.

This is nothing new, of course; it's been happening for decades, and there's nothing wrong with it. As productivity rises in American manufacturing and agriculture, fewer workers are producing more goods at higher value. As income grows, people spend proportionately less on goods and more on services, spurring job creation in services.

By 2000, almost 90% of workers will be in services, and half of all the service workers will be collecting, analyzing, storing or retrieving information. Over 80% of all management will be knowledge and information workers. Taking the global view, the U.S. will continue to be the major exporter of information and information technology.

The changing face of labor

After allowing for retirements, women, minorities and immigrants will account for almost all net additions to the work force between now and 2000. Nearly 65% of the growth will be women, because relatively fewer women will retire. Blacks will account for 17% of labor growth between now and the end of the century—significantly above their current share. By the end of the '90s, blacks will make up 12% of the total force, Hispanics about 10% and Asians another 4%. There will be more Hispanic men than black men in the work force. White males will account for only 45% of the labor force, compared with nearly 50% now.

By 2000, the share of workers ages 16 to 34 and over 55 will decline, while the 35- to 54-year-olds—a bulge of middle-management personnel—will increase. The number of first-time workers, those ages 16 to 24, will drop until the mid '90s, before reversing and heading upward through the end of the decade. The number of 25- to 34-year-olds will increase through the early '90s, then decline sharply. And the number of 55- to 64-year-olds will drop off through the mid '90s before increasing rapidly, as the oldest Baby Boomers hit that age level soon after the turn of the century.

Short supply of new workers

Youngsters coming out of school in search of their first jobs will find a healthy demand for their services, mainly because there will be fewer of them than there were in the '70s and '80s. The youngest of the Baby Boomers are now 25 years old. They will be followed into the job market by "birth dearth" youngsters, who were born from 1965 to 1978 when birth rates tumbled. The number of 18-year-olds, for example, will decline until 1994.

So high-school grads in the early '90s will have better pickings among employers, the military services and colleges than their parents did. In fact, the pool of young workers entering the job market will shrink to the lowest level since the '30s.

Businesses that rely on cheap, entry-level help will be in a pinch. They'll have to pay more and find alternative sources, such as immigrants, older people and disabled or handicapped individuals.

The looming tightness in labor supplies is underscored by the fact that the employment rate in America—the percentage of all adult Americans who work full- or part-time—has been rising for years, so there aren't as many untapped pools of new labor (such as at-home mothers) as there were before. As we go into the '90s, only 20% of the people between 20 and 65 remain out of the work force all year.

Moreover, as the Conference Board points out, a third of these nonworkers are too sick to work, institutionalized in prisons and mental-health hospitals, in school or have been job hunting for a full year without any luck. Drug testing by employers is further reducing the supply of available labor, as are rising numbers of functionally illiterate and marginally literate young people and others who are unprepared for work.

Thinning down to boost productivity

To hold down costs and run more efficiently, companies will get rid of layers of management. This streamlining will put bosses more in touch with what's going on in the sales territories and on the shop floor, giving them an opportunity to listen to the ideas of people with hands-on experience.

Computers are beginning to make a real contribution to productivity. For years, cash was poured into them without much to show for it, especially in services. Finally, companies are beginning to reap the benefits in efficiency and cost-cutting. Even old-line manufacturers are becoming high-tech companies, using computers to orchestrate what goes on where and when in their plants. Formerly, machines replaced brawn. Now they replace brains, too.

A General Electric dishwasher plant, for example, increased production 50% and reduced labor 30% through automation. National Steel raised tons shipped per employee 26% over a two-year period while reducing man-hours per ton 10%. A maker of printed circuit boards in Georgia increased output 500% and cut design time 400% through automation. A Motorola plant in Boynton Beach, Fla., uses robots to take orders and assemble radio pagers in 1/100 of the time of previous methods; pagers are now made within two hours of order time. Goodyear used to make 100 tires a day on one line, with 20% of the tires faulty. Now robots on the same line make 1,000 tires a day—with almost no defects.

What's behind all this? The need to invest for the long haul. Managers are realizing that they can't compete in world markets if they focus on short-term results, so now they're looking farther down the road for ways to increase productivity.

In the '80s, much of the automating and cost-cutting was done to catch up with Japan and other foreign competitors. In the '90s, it will be a matter of continuous improvement. As a result, there will be fewer binges and busts in capital spending. Plant and equipment investment will be on a steadier course.

In 1980, the average industrial machine was 20 years old.

That's now down to 15 years. By the mid '90s, the average will be less than ten years. It will be a period of aggressive change for U.S. companies. Those that don't change won't be around for the turn of the century.

Big demand for older workers

The average working life will become more elastic, extending well beyond today's typical retirement age, about 62 for men. Note that we said "typical," because mandatory retirement has been abolished. Today workers are free to work as long as they wish if their performance is up to snuff. A lot of them would work past 65 except for social security and pension restrictions.

Present trends toward early retirement will probably continue because of rising affluence, but increasingly this will mean retirement from your FIRST career. The broader trend is toward *more* years of work, albeit with different employers.

As the growth of the labor force slows and companies run short of skilled help, older persons will be aggressively recruited in a wide range of fields, for both full- and part-time work. For many, these will be jobs for which their experience or education already qualifies them. For others, company-sponsored training, both on the job and back to school, will be necessary. Whether in retail stores, offices or other workplaces, older workers usually rate high in performance, personal responsibility, attendance, punctuality, commitment to quality, practical knowledge and customer relations.

With the ranks of younger workers already thinning, many companies are scouting for well-qualified older employees—and encouraging their own retirees and soon-to-be retirees to consider pitching in at least a few days a week. From the employers' point of view, it's a way to retain the know-how of experienced hands and reduce turnover and training costs. From the older workers' viewpoint, phased retirement is a way to stay active, useful and still have enough leisure time.

Beyond the '90s, people may *have* to keep working for another reason—concern about fewer workers available to support each retiree and about strains on social security and medicare funding. The first wave of Baby Boomers will hit 65 in 2011. Before then, there will be proposals to raise the "normal" retirement age to

70 or higher by delaying the eligibility age of social security benefits.

Women give us an edge

America's working women will enrich our competitive position in the world. They're an integral part of our economy, providing talents and vitality that many of our competitor nations waste or ignore. By 2000, three-fifths of all working-age women will be in the labor force. Many of them will hold down technical and professional jobs.

Adjusting to the surge of adult women into the workplace in the 1970s and early '80s wasn't easy. It was an awkward transition at many companies. In many cases, the new employee was taking her first job after years of raising kids, so she was inexperienced. For a while, this was a factor in slower productivity growth. Also, many women were taking on jobs that had traditionally been held by males, and this often caused resentment and ridicule. And women are still occasionally subject to illegal discrimination and harassment in the workplace.

But things are settling down now. America has absorbed the big influx and has millions of experienced and well-educated women contributing mightily to our economy. Due to the higher legal and social status of females in our society, we're far ahead of the Japanese and Europeans in utilizing the talents of women.

Over half of our college grads are women, most of whom now go on to careers. The share of women in law, medicine and other professions will keep rising. (Between 1979 and 1986 the proportion of female lawyers rose from 10% to 15%, and the share of female computer programmers increased from 28% to 40%.) Although still underrepresented in the corporate suite, many more women will move into executive positions during the '90s because their talents will be needed, and they will have enough seniority to go up the ladder.

The average earnings of full-time female workers ran roughly 57% to 60% of men's earnings during most of the years between 1945 and the end of the '70s. But since 1979 the percentage has gone up to about 70%. The pay gap is narrowest—and shrinking most rapidly—among the youngest workers, reflecting the higher education level and equal access to all kinds of jobs enjoyed by young women today. In fact, on average, women age 20 to 24 earn 86% as much as men of the same age earn.

Most of the overall pay differential between men and women is related to differences in continuous length of time in the work force and the resulting differences in experience and seniority. The typical male worker today has been in the workplace far longer than the average female worker, with fewer career interruptions. With no legal barriers to women left in any kind of employment, their earnings relative to men will continue to rise. Meanwhile, earnings are rising rapidly in female-dominated fields, such as nursing and teaching, because of labor shortages. So we expect the overall male/female pay gap to narrow further in the '90s.

After making significant gains in equal-pay-for-equal-work, women's-rights activists are lobbying for the enactment of "comparable worth" or "pay equity" plans, under which pay is based not on the market demand for a given kind of labor but on an estimate of its worth to society and the amount of education and skill required to perform the task. It is their feeling that this approach would boost the pay of many traditionally female jobs, such as teaching and social work.

Comparable-worth plans have been adopted in Ontario, Canada, covering all employers (public and private) with more than ten employees, and in a few state and local governments around the U.S. We think their spread will be limited in the '90s by a growing free-market orientation and—more importantly—by the rising demand for, and compensation of, female workers in all lines of work.

Child care in the '90s

The effects of the changing age and sex structure of the work force will be positive for productivity. How positive depends partly on how well employers take into account child care and other family needs. The needs will be great, by 1995, three-quarters of all school-age kids will have working mothers.

As companies depend on women for basic skills, child care will become more than just a desirable benefit. It will be a necessary incentive for hiring and keeping good workers. About 80% of the women who join the work force in the '90s will be of childbearing age. Most will, at some point, combine mothering and careers. To ease the burden, reduce tardiness and absenteeism and attract the people they'll need, more companies will offer child-care assistance of some sort, ranging from employer-run day-care centers at the workplace to subsidies for outside arrangements, shared participation in facilities or simply referral assistance. Smaller firms will enter plans, similar to health maintenance organizations, where day care will be available as part of a larger group. Business and employees will bear the bulk of the costs.

Employers will find other ways of lightening the load for working mothers, such as flexible work schedules, job sharing, use of permanent part-timers and extended leaves. Some women will be able to work at home, staying in touch with the office via the telephone line—by voice, facsimile machines and computers.

Quotas in hiring will fade

A healthy economy and slower growth in the labor supply will mean plenty of job opportunities for everyone who wants to work, has good work habits and a skill or willingness to learn one. Hiring discrimination against qualified applicants on the basis of race or gender will not only be illegal (as it already is), it will be downright stupid. The same will be true for illegally impeding the advancement of employees for any reason but performance. In a tight labor market, employees who don't get a square deal from their employers will find it easy to improve their lot elsewhere.

America hasn't yet tried to create a truly color- and gender-blind society. In the 1960s it went from egregious discrimination AGAINST racial minorities and women directly into programs of preferential treatment FOR the same groups. However well-meaning these programs of remedial affirmative action seem, they sometimes end up as discrimination against fellow workers who are in no way responsible for the past injustices.

At its best, affirmative action means a voluntary tilting of the scales lightly toward a competent person of any background who has shown special spunk in overcoming some disadvantage—physical, economic, racial, psychological, whatever. At worst, affirmative action entails rigid racial and gender quotas in hiring and promotion that constitute a different but equally undesirable form of discrimination.

The contradictions inherent in quotas—especially those enacted without evidence of past discrimination—have made them vulnerable to judicial attack in recent years. The pendulum is now swinging, and in the 1990s America will have a shot, for the first time, at truly color-blind and gender-neutral practices in hiring, college admissions and contracting of government services. As we said, the equal treatment of all Americans—on their individual merits—will be not only good human relations but also an economic imperative in the competitive international markets of the Global '90s.

Labor-management relations

Following the Japanese example, there will be more cooperation between labor and management to help companies thrive and to strengthen long-term job security—seeking a better balance among jobs, wages, costs, benefits, productivity and profits. Family arrangements, including sick-child care, will be important. But such issues as parental leave won't be pushed to the detriment of job security.

Contrary to how it may seem now, there won't be a continuous round of congressionally mandated employee benefits in the '90s. Sure, there will be pressure to keep piling them on, but politicians are finally wising up to the fact that increasing the cost of doing business makes American companies less competitive in world markets.

The mandated-benefits issue will evolve into a debate over affordable fringes. Employees will have to make more trade-offs between medical and other benefits, such as child care and elder care. Cafeteria-style, flexible-benefit plans will become the rule. Redundant benefits, as in the case of working couples, will be weeded out. Pension plans will shift to defined contributions instead of defined benefits to control costs. And individual pensions will become more portable as workers change jobs and careers more often, due partly to faster vesting.

There will be broadening of stock options and other incentives, such as deferred pay and profit sharing, to keep valued employees, not just the higher-ups. These will also spur productivity.

The role of unions

Union membership will stay low—less than 20% of all workers, down from 25% at the start of the '80s. It has been slipping for years because of declining employment in traditional heavy manufacturing, much of which has moved to other countries. The growth fields of American manufacturing—whether mini-steel mills, computer-software factories or biotech laboratories—have not been fertile ground for union organizing.

But the percentage of union membership won't sink much lower before the turn of the century. Tight labor markets will give unions more bargaining power in a few fields. And labor will make further inroads among health care employees, government workers, retail clerks and office workers, to name a few. The share of women in organized labor will rise.

However, the economic and political clout of the unions will be diminished by pressures of global competition, because companies will buy labor—that is, do business—wherever they get the best deal. The United Auto Workers and its drive to keep jobs in America has hardly slowed the inexorable internationalization of the auto industry, with elaborate combinations of joint ventures, outsourcing of parts to foreign plants, and joint marketing of similar cars under different names. The UAW's idea that we should even try to quantify and fix a minimum for the "domestic content" of an "American" car—designed by Japanese and American engineers, with parts made all over the world—will seem quaint by the end of the '90s.

Changing with the times, some unions will be less useful to their members as collective bargaining agents than as providers of services. Union dues will pay for services such as monitoring an employer's compliance with labor laws, child care, counseling, financial planning, debt management and retraining. To stop membership erosion, unions will seek "associate" relationships with workers who are not covered by any union wage contract.

Where the jobs will be

Job growth will be strongest, not surprisingly, in the southern and western parts of the country, which have been dominating population growth in the U.S. for the last 30 years. But in the following list of high-job-growth metropolitan areas, note that there are several Frostbelt cities, too. Their RATE of growth will not be impressive, but in absolute numbers they'll add more new jobs to an already large base of employment than most small cities will.

These areas will add the most jobs from now to 2010, according to NPA Data Services in Washington, D.C.: Los Angeles/Long Beach; Anaheim/Santa Ana; Washington, D.C.; Houston; Atlanta; Dallas; San Diego; Phoenix; Boston; Seattle; Tampa/St. Petersburg; San Jose; Denver; Chicago; Orlando; Nassau/Suffolk, N.Y.; Riverside/San Bernardino; Minneapolis/St. Paul; Philadelphia; Sacramento; Fort Lauderdale; San Francisco and West Palm Beach.

Staying ahead of inflation

How much will you have to earn in 2000 to keep up with inflation? Here are the figures, based on various assumptions of inflation rates during the '90s. (We believe inflation will average about 4% a year.)

Bear in mind that this would merely keep you running in place. To improve your own situation, you will have to earn more than the figures below.

1989 Income	Equivalent Income in 2000 If Inflation Is		
	4%	5%	6%
$20,000	$30,800	$34,200	$38,000
30,000	46,200	51,300	57,000
50,000	77,000	85,500	95,000
70,000	107,800	119,700	132,900
90,000	138,500	153,900	170,800

The average worker's pay, when benefits are included, has gone up about 1% per year over the past 15 years, after allowing for inflation, according to Marvin H. Kosters, an economist at the American Enterprise Institute. Benefits, including social security, vacations, sick leave and employer-paid health and life insurance, account for over 30% of payrolls, as reported by an annual U.S. Chamber of Commerce survey. Most of the evidence points to solid, although not spectacular, improvement in real disposable pay in the years ahead. But the growth in benefits will slow down as employees are forced to chip in more for health insurance and other extras.

Strong-demand careers for the '90s

For employees, constant updating and retraining will be essential or their skills will become obsolete. The average person taking a first job will go through some form of retraining several times during his or her work years.

The increasingly global nature of business will create jobs in some specialized fields. For example, there will be growing demand for people who combine science, engineering and computer skills with knowledge of languages, especially Japanese, Chinese and Spanish. They will be needed to translate foreign technical journals and prepare bids and contracts for overseas jobs.

Job prospects will be especially good in the technical and service lines. The aging of America will create excellent opportunities for such health-service professionals as bioengineers, pharmacists, nurses and nurses' aides, emergency medical technicians and physical therapists. (And yes, we'll need more morticians, too.) The increasing affluence of older Americans will require more money-management professionals, including mutual fund managers, stockbrokers and annuity salespeople.

The boom in computer technology will keep the demand for electrical engineers, computer service specialists and mathematicians very strong. Strength in both business and leisure travel will benefit airline pilots, travel agents and managers in the hospitality businesses—hotels, caterers, restaurants, meeting planners and the like. The rejuvenation of American education will improve pay and working conditions for teachers at all levels.

As we get serious about protecting the environment, there will be plenty of jobs for individuals trained in water treatment, waste disposal, recycling and pollution control. And the "help-wanted" sign will be out for skilled construction workers—carpenters, bricklayers, electronic-security experts, as well as people skilled in plumbing, air conditioning and other trades.

Prospects are good, too, for the normal complement of workers whose fields grow with the economy: accountants, lawyers, paralegals, bankers, insurance agents, real estate specialists, advertising managers and wholesale and retail salespeople.

You can add government services, too—at all levels. Despite taxpayer resentment, government employment will keep growing, just as it did under Reagan, who vowed to cut government down to size.

Selling convenience

If you are looking around for a business to go into and you don't have a technical background, check out the various personal-service lines. Working couples, well-to-do older people and many others are willing and able to pay for convenience, especially chores they don't like to do. There will be opportunities galore for housecleaning and shopping services, lawn care, home-repair services, child care, catered meals, pet care and home assistance for the elderly. Note that sales of consumer-bought housecleaning supplies are down because fewer homeowners do their own chores. But housecleaning services are booming—and there's no end in sight.

Even if you go into a conventional business, look for ways to save time and hassle for customers. For example, drycleaners have seen their volume boom when they advertised pickup and delivery on evenings and Saturdays. The same idea is behind the move to delivery of restaurant meals as well as mobile auto-repair units that come to your house to replace tires and change the oil.

Finding a job you'll like

In choosing a career or deciding on a job change, people should consider work that they will enjoy, as well as their personal aptitude and preparation. Money is important, but it shouldn't be the only consideration. You're more apt to do well at something you like, and it's much easier to roll out of bed every workday for 40 to 50 years if you're going to a job you enjoy.

It's important to know oneself. Most people who mess up their careers do so because they don't know where they are going or what their real goals are, or they lack a clear idea of their strengths and shortcomings. They slip and slide and stumble through life, and it hurts.

The '80s has seen a rise in the amount of job changing within a given field, plus more people choosing to go into entirely different fields. This trend will accelerate in the '90s. The most basic reason will be jolting, rapid change in the fortunes of firms within an industry, not to mention changing circumstances affecting entire industries. A quicker pace of technological change, especially with greater pressure from international competition, will place more jobs in jeopardy—even as it is creating boundless opportunities for the nimble. People will jump ship from a company or industry in decline to another in ascendance.

Each occasion of forced or voluntary relocation will be an opportunity for workers to examine anew their reasons for doing what they're doing. And from that reexamination will come a rising degree of job and career changing. As a matter of fact, midcareer counseling—aptitude testing, probing of interests, etc.—will be a boom field in the '90s.

Advice for young people

For young people just starting out in selecting a career, parents should be the first source of guidance, because they know the youngster's talents and shortcomings best. Part-time jobs are a good way to test abilities and interest and get an idea of what work in various fields is like. School guidance counselors and testing services may also be helpful.

And young people should check with those who are already in the business. They can help weigh the pros and cons better than any book or video. College professors can also provide worthwhile insights and suggestions.

Should a youngster avoid fields that are likely to be more crowded in the future, such as medicine or law? No, not necessarily, because much will still depend on the abilities of the individual involved. There is a surplus of doctors, dentists and lawyers today, but most of them do quite well. Even with a surplus of physicians through the '90s, doctors will still earn more than most other occupations. In any field, there's always opportunity for top-notchers.

10 Outlook for Key Industries

<u>U.S. will go toe-to-toe with Japan in electronics.</u>

<u>Information will be as valuable as capital and labor.</u>

<u>Trillions of dollars a DAY in world financial dealings.</u>

<u>Stronger exports of food and agricultural equipment.</u>

<u>Space-age materials will boost U.S. competitiveness.</u>

<u>Higher energy prices but no '70s-style oil crisis.</u>

<u>More-affordable housing for first-time buyers.</u>

<u>A 25% rise in sales of new cars and light trucks.</u>

Now take a look at what's ahead for a number of key industries—food and agriculture, financial services, electronics, telecommunications, autos, housing, aerospace, energy, materials, transportation and retailing. We realize that every industry is "key," especially if it happens to be your own, but we think we're covering most bases with what's in this chapter.

Our aim is to get you thinking about lines that will do well or not so well—and why. Try to fit yourself into the picture, from the viewpoint of investment or career opportunities, or perhaps because you have customers in these lines.

To tip you off in advance, the hottest industries will be electronics and telecommunications, health care and equipment, food processing and exporting, financial services, travel, bioengineering, aerospace, waste disposal and recycling, and advanced materials, such as composites and ceramics.

Here's our size-up for individual lines, starting with the most basic of all.

FOOD AND AGRICULTURE

The U.S. will retain world leadership in agribusiness, our largest and most technologically advanced industry. It's also one of the few industries based on renewable resources and will be a linchpin of U.S. competitiveness in the Global '90s.

We'll face increased competition from other producing countries, but none has the farming, processing and marketing system that we enjoy. We will export more than a third of all the food and fiber that we produce.

The sheer size and richness of the Farmbelt itself is a huge advantage for the U.S. Together with the prairie provinces of Canada, it is the largest contiguous mass of prime farmland on earth. Russia and China have more acreage but far less land favored by good soil and weather conditions.

Competition and innovation

As you may have noticed by now, a common thread running through this book is the advantage that our flexibility, openness, competitive experience and free-enterprise system give us in the global marketplace, even though these same characteristics sometimes make us vulnerable in the short run.

Nowhere is this more evident than in our food industry. It is the epitome of competition—beating the other guy to the punch, constantly working to bring costs down, improving yields and quality. You can see it in our broiler business, for example, an industry that uses less than two pounds of feed to make a pound of chicken meat. And in seed laboratories, where scientists are now working on higher-yielding plants that won't need insecticides and will produce their own fertilizers. While most countries export through government-run agencies, thousands of U.S. companies scramble for markets on their own—faster on their feet and more aggressive and innovative than government traders ever dreamed possible.

As noted earlier, Gorbachev caught on to this in his dealing with Western grain merchandisers 15 years ago, leading to many of the economic changes under way in the Soviet Union today. State planners in China and the Eastern Bloc are also flirting with capitalistic concepts that may lead them far beyond agriculture.

Booming world production

As in the past, surplus production will be the most persistent problem that American agriculture—and the world—will have to deal with in the next 20 to 30 years.

Even on a global scale, there is no shortage of food. The problem is distribution, which hinges mostly on political and economic considerations of who can afford food and who can't. So hunger and malnutrition in the Third World won't disappear in the foreseeable future, despite worldwide abundance.

Meanwhile, some countries that have been importers of food, including China, India and the U.S.S.R., will make great strides toward self-sufficiency. In fact, India will be a net exporter when it gets normal harvests. And Argentina, Brazil, Thailand and South Africa will be competing intensely with the U.S., Canada, Australia and Europe for share of export markets for wheat, feed grains and oilseeds. There will be plenty of sellers ready to pounce on any new business that turns up.

Don't fall for forecasts that farm subsidies will be eliminated in Europe, the U.S. and Canada. It's very unlikely. Production supports have evolved into a way of life to protect a way of life. In West Germany they keep the politically potent small farmers going. In Ireland they cause mountains of butter, but keep marginal farmers quiet and off the dole. The situation is similar in the U.S., where government assistance to politically powerful dairy farmers works out to roughly $1,100 per cow, and everyone from tobacco growers to beekeepers gets some help from Washington. But there will be some chipping away at trade barriers (in Japan, for example) and export subsidies (in the European Economic Community), as well as a gradual reduction of U.S. subsidies. Why? Because of the staggering costs these benefits impose on the taxpayers of every nation.

Fewer U.S. farms

Sometime in the early '90s, the number of U.S. farms will slip below two million. That compares with 2.1 million now, three million in '69, four million in '59 and seven million in the mid '30s. But the number of acres farmed hasn't gone down much since the '30s, and yields have zoomed, thanks to tremendous breakthroughs in plant development, chemicals, equipment and farming practices.

In another 15 years, as few as 100,000 farms may produce 90% of our food and fiber. The rest will be grown by people who make most of their money on other jobs. Most farms will still be owned by individuals; we don't look for much of a shift to corporate ownership. Corporations will find more profitable ways to invest their money.

Is farmland a good investment for individuals? Yes, for those who don't have to rely on profits from the land that they are buying to meet the monthly payments. For example, buying land might make sense for a neighboring farmer who has plenty of equity in his or her own property, but not for someone with no equity and very little cash flow to rely on month after month. Many of the farmers who went broke in the late '70s and early '80s got in over their heads because they figured that the land they were purchasing would be a constantly producing money machine.

Designer genes

Bioengineering—transferring characteristics of one species to another species—will bring tremendous changes to the food industry. Yields will be increased through enhanced photosynthesis and controlled plant size. Crops resistant to disease, drought, bugs and even frost will be developed, reducing the amount of chemicals that will be needed. And genes will be manipulated to produce leaner meat and make cows give more milk.

There will also be new uses for present farm products, such as biodegradable plastic containers made from cornstarch, which will help ease trash-disposal problems and dependence on petroleum. Also look for new crops to be developed for specific purposes: guayule for rubber; euphorbia for gasoline; meadowfoam for industrial oils. All have potential, especially as oil prices go higher.

Consumer trends

There will be a stronger shift to fresh fruits and vegetables and away from processed. You'll be able to buy any type of fresh produce year-round because of imports and produce grown indoors in controlled environments (including hydroponic vegetables). Per-capita consumption of poultry and fish will increase 12% to 15% by the turn of the century, at the expense of red meat. The various species of fish will also be available anytime, thanks to imports and aquaculture, which will be a high-growth industry. In cereals, baked goods and other foods, the trend to high fiber and whole grains will continue, with more focus on complex carbohydrates and away from sugar, fat and calories.

Low-cholesterol convenience meals will be popular with shoppers in the '90s—soups, salads, entrees prepared from scratch in commercial kitchens. So will ethnic foods—Mexican dishes and Oriental meals featuring seafood or meat as garnishes rather than the main course.

And that ultimate convenience, eating out, will grow in popularity. Recently there has been overexpansion in the chain-restaurant business, and many Baby Boomers with young children are dining out less than they did when they were single. But this is a short-term sag. During the '90s, more than 50% of the food dollar will be spent for food away from home, and restaurants will get a boost from gains in disposable incomes and even more two-income households. By comparison, only 25% was spent for food away from home in 1960.

FINANCIAL SERVICES AND BANKING

The changes ahead in banking and financial services are hard to fathom for those of us who remember when deposits earned 2% and were lent at 5%, and an aggressive banker was someone who promoted Christmas-club accounts. In those days "fund transfers" meant sending transactions from one part of the bank to another by pneumatic tube.

But times have changed. In the '90s, telecommunications networks will lead to one huge international financial system, moving TRILLIONS of dollars a day across national borders at the speed of light. It will be easier for businesses and governments to raise money around the world and for individual investors to dabble in the currencies and arrangements of their choosing, regardless of where they happen to live. This freer movement of capital and credit will make the world even more interdependent.

The enormous political ramifications of financial globalization haven't been fully appreciated yet. Already there is a mounting surge of world interest in private ownership and free markets as a replacement for state control of economies. Globalization of capital will boost this interest, helping to popularize the free market. Donald Marron, chairman of PaineWebber Group, puts it well: "There are few ideas more compelling than that of buying a stock at ten and selling it at twenty."

Rate shopping around the world

Corporate treasurers will do their business with banks that are linked to international telecommunications networks, scouring the world for the best interest rates, the best currency deals, the best arrangements for their debt and equity needs. Such capabilities will be a must for companies in the '90s.

The internationalization of financial services will involve more foreign ownership. Citicorp, for example, will lock horns with the world's biggest bank, Tokyo's Dai-Ichi Kangyo for control of banks in Asia, Europe and Latin America—and in the U.S. Foreign banks already hold 20% of U.S. banking assets through their branches and agencies in the U.S. In California, five of the ten largest banks are Japanese-owned. And Japanese investors are shopping around for further acquisitions.

International stock trading

Stocks, bonds and other securities will be traded around the world, around the clock, seven days a week. The main hurdle up to now has been the lack of international rules for clearing, settling, disclosure and surveillance, but it's just a matter of time until they're in place, along with uniform accounting and reporting standards.

The New York and Tokyo stock exchanges are already preparing for billion-share days. And economic integration of the

European Community in '92 will enhance the importance of the London exchange. Markets in Hong Kong, Taipei, Singapore, Sidney, Frankfurt, Zurich, Paris, Toronto and Montreal will grow, too, but they won't rival New York, Tokyo or London in size or importance.

We believe increasing financial interdependence will be a generally stabilizing force in the world, but there is the possibility that the collapse of one market, exchange or major commercial bank could trigger a chain reaction—a worldwide liquidity crisis. The world got a glimpse of this risk on October 19, 1987, when panic selling rolled serially through markets in one time zone after another. That's why international standards, exchange of information and good surveillance will be essential.

Over the past 60 years or so, American stock prices have increased an average 8% to 10% per year. We think a 10% average is likely in the '90s, pushing the Dow Jones industrials above 6000. Some stock markets in other countries will outperform the U.S. (See chapter 11 on investing in the '90s.)

Look-alike financial institutions

By the early 2000s, the lines between banks, s&l's, credit unions, stockbrokers and insurance firms will be smudged beyond recognition. For example, the remaining barriers to interstate banking will tumble. Banks will be able to operate like Sears—one in every town.

And banks will move more deeply into mortgages and home-equity lines of credit. They will be encouraged to do so by new international capital requirements and ongoing problems of s&l's, a third of which will go under by the early '90s. Eventually, to avoid a raid on the Treasury, lawmakers will cave in to pressure from healthy thrifts for a unibank approach. There will be only one regulatory agency for financial institutions and one deposit-insurance fund. There will also be further concentration of bank ownership, with large bank holding companies offering securities, insurance and real estate through their subsidiaries.

New risk-based capital requirements and a streamlined industry will mean better profits for the surviving banks and s&l's. In fact, now's a good time to invest in solid financial institutions. Stock prices are depressed because of the problems in the industry, but firms that are healthy today will be VERY healthy as we move into the '90s.

Electronic banking

Electronic banking will expand, including bill paying by telephone (using the keys on the phone or a personal computer and modem). There will be small gains for debit cards that immediately switch money from the customer's to the seller's bank account. Customer acceptance of debit cards has been slow so far because the customer can't see any benefit in giving up the free float from using a credit card or check; merchants will have to offer a price incentive for debit use.

"Smart cards" will be big stuff in the '90s—cards embedded with microchips that store the cardholder's account balance and update it as the card is used. Through use of such cards, customers will build up "spending profiles" that the issuing companies will sell to direct marketers and others. (Similar smart cards will carry your medical history and will be revised every time you see a doctor.)

But even with these new gizmos, we won't have a checkless or cashless society. People still enjoy the float they get when paying by check. And ATM machines will encourage the wider use of cash.

HOUSING AND CONSTRUCTION

With fewer first-time home buyers (25- to 34-year-olds), fewer marriages and slower growth in households, the housing industry won't be quite as frothy in the '90s, especially for builders of starter houses and apartments. Industrial construction will be very strong, but there will be somewhat slower growth in retail and commercial space nationally.

Housing starts

Housing construction will calm down, but it won't be a sackcloth-and-ashes situation either. Annual housing starts will average 1.5 million during the first half of the '90s (about the same as in the '80s) and 1.4 million from 1995 to 2000. Multiunit starts will tumble from the current rate of about 400,000 to about 300,000 a year in the early '90s. Most of those will be condominiums.

It will be a buyer's market on the low end of the scale—fewer young people in the market for their first homes and a lot of older Baby Boomers ready to peddle their starter homes and trade up. That means housing will be more affordable for young people.

Expect brisk demand for trade-up housing, bigger and fancier homes with all the bells and whistles for that huge bulge in the population, the 35- to 55-year-olds, who will be in their peak earning and spending years. They'll be the backbone of the housing market. And there will be a growing number of older people, fueling demand for low-maintenance, single-story retirement housing.

Fix-up, remodeling and additions will keep a lot of builders busy. The surge in two-career families means fewer corporate relocations—but more people fixing up and making do with the homes they're in. And more retirees will stay put rather than head for Florida, Arizona or California.

Strong home prices

For most people, their home will still be their best investment, especially after considering the tax breaks for homeownership. Congress will probably trim the interest deduction for home mortgages a little more in the next few years—perhaps for second homes and super-expensive residences—but your home will still be a good tax shelter.

The broad direction of house prices will continue UP at a rate faster than overall inflation. As a rule of thumb, if a home is worth $100,000 today, it will be worth about $200,000 at the turn of the century—about a 7% gain per year, compounded. So don't ignore the urge to buy a house as an inflation hedge. The increase in home values has been a major influence in housing booms since World War II. Homeownership will continue to pay off in the '90s and beyond. You live in it. You enjoy it. You get a tax shelter and, if you buy smartly, it appreciates while you're using it. Sure, house prices may soften in a sagging market, but not by much and not for long. Besides, buying forces you to save, to pay off the mortgage.

Adjustable-rate mortgages will still be the preferred financing for most homes. Most will allow for conversion to fixed-rate financing after the first year or two, and some will allow it any time thereafter. There will also be new "traveling mortgages" that borrowers will take with them as they sell one house and buy another. And reverse-equity mortgages, narrowly available today, will become very popular for older homeowners who want to draw income from their homes without selling and moving out; the amount borrowed, either in a lump sum or in monthly payments, is paid back to the lender only after the house is sold.

Local "impact fees" will spread nationwide and go higher, up to $40,000 per new home in some areas. Developers will be required to pay up front for new streets, sewers, water, parks, schools, child-care centers and other improvements, some only indirectly connected to the impact of new developments. In the past, local governments would ask developers to donate land for a fire station. Now they require the land, a building and the fire engines (everything but a dalmatian). This runs up the cost of new homes but helps restrain property taxes, easing the load on existing homeowners in the area. Politicians like impact fees because they tax people who are not yet voters.

Homes of tomorrow

The house of 2000 will look about the same as the one you live in now, but it will be different under the skin. Light, cheap plastics and composites will replace wood and metal in floor trusses and other parts. New homes will feature natural lighting, skylights, recessed windows, open floor plans, atriums and porches, elongated windows and doors.

Most homes built after the mid '90s will be computer-ready—wired with fiber-optic or digital cable for computers, home-entertainment equipment, security systems that will pinpoint intruders and call the police, and monitoring gear for keeping track of kids or checking on the well-being of the elderly. The house itself will act as an antenna, and personal computers will be automatically tied into telephone lines. You'll be able to call home before you leave work to turn the lights on, change the thermostat or start a meal. The same system will automatically draw the drapes at nightfall, fill the tub and even feed the dog.

Commercial real estate

U.S. real estate will still be seen as a bargain by Asian and European investors because on a square-foot basis it's cheap by world standards, regardless of the level of the dollar. They'll continue to shop around for a piece of the U.S., giving them a bigger stake in our prosperity.

Industrial construction will be strong through most of the next ten to 15 years, due to good health in U.S. manufacturing. Plant automation, retooling and restructuring that helped make the U.S. more competitive in world markets will go on at an even faster rate. Warehouse and distribution facilities will be needed in high-growth areas and distribution hubs such as Nashville, Memphis, Chicago and Kansas City, and in port cities that will benefit from booming world trade.

Construction of new retail space and office buildings will be slow for a few years as gluts are worked off throughout America. And there's no reason to expect another nationwide office-building spree later on. For one thing, there will be slower growth in office-type jobs, plus a trend toward better use of existing office space—less square footage per employee, more working at home, multiple shifts and even 24-hour operations at some service firms (even law and accounting). Much of the office construction will be to replace buildings that are obsolete, too small or inefficient—some built as recently as the '70s.

For investors, the best opportunities will lie in less-speculative and more-selective office projects. Look for strong growth in business parks that provide a lot of common-tenant amenities, including telephone-answering, word-processing and facsimile services.

RETAILING

The outlook for retailers is reasonably bright despite a slower-growing population, fewer household formations, and a tilt toward higher savings and relatively less consumption. The fact is that HALF of the working-age population will reach their peak earning and spending years in the early '90s. The needs of Baby Boomers for all sorts of goods and services will intensify as they leave the child-rearing stage in their lives by the end of the decade. Their high incomes will accommodate both a higher savings rate and a strong level of consumption.

Globalizing of retailing

Look for foreign merchants to set up shop in the U.S. and buy out some American retailers, similar to the 1988 Japanese take-over of Talbot's. Others, such as Harrod's of London, won't move here but will promote toll-free phone ordering and other gimmicks to tap the huge U.S. consumer market.

At the same time, American chains such as Sears, JC Penney and K mart will test foreign markets, perhaps even opening stores in Japan and the Soviet Union. There will be dozens of merchandising hybrids, American and foreign retailers entering joint ventures with new marketing concepts. The Americanized hypermarket—an enormous all-products store imported from Europe to Texas and other areas—is an example of this cross-fertilization.

More specialization

Department stores will no longer try to sell all things to all shoppers. They'll focus on soft goods, clothing and housewares displayed in small boutiques within stores, much like a grouping of specialty stores. There will be more leasing out of individual departments and counters within those departments, such as cosmetics and jewelry.

Micromarketing—tailoring merchandise to people in the neighborhood—will flourish. A store in Boise will look much different from a store of the same chain in Boston. Micromarketing will extend to catalogs, videos and other forms of direct selling, targeting people by occupation, age, income and interests. And electronic retailing will expand through interactive systems that let customers shop in their own family rooms, "trying on" 20 different garments through computer simulation. But catalogs and electronic shopping will not replace stores. The plain fact is, shoppers will still want to FEEL the merchandise.

Successful retailers will sell convenience—ways to make life easier for all those two-income and retiree households. Supermarket chains are on to this already with their no-fuss, heat-and-eat meals, soup-and-salad bars and virtually everything for one-stop, around-the-clock, hassle-free shopping.

Life at the malls

Shopping-as-entertainment will be used to draw crowds. You will see live theater, bands and skating rinks in malls—even amusement parks as at the West Edmonton Mall in Alberta, Canada, and the new supermall outside Minneapolis, which will have Knott's Berry Farm as its centerpiece. Merchants will work harder on decor and themes for drawing customers.

There will be fewer regional shopping malls built in the '90s than in the '80s or '70s. Recent takeovers and mergers in retailing leave fewer potential anchor stores for shopping centers. Those remaining will be in a strong position to bargain with developers. The trend in the next ten to 15 years will be to spruce up and add to existing retail stores (partly because of runaway land costs) and build smaller shopping centers in new residential areas. On the design front, the no-windows inward look for shopping malls will be modified. Architects are working on ideas that will open stores to the outside.

ENERGY

Energy conservation has become so ingrained in American businesses and homes—in appliance design, car engines, home heating, architecture and construction, and plant operations—that America's total energy consumption hasn't risen since 1980, despite enormous economic growth.

We see the trend toward energy efficiency continuing, but the percentage gains will be more modest. Someday there will be gigantic energy savings from being able to transmit electricity long distances with a lower loss of power, due to superconductivity. But don't expect anything much until well after 2000.

Look for expansion of cogeneration—the simultaneous use of heat from industrial production for generating electricity. There will also be new and cleaner methods of converting garbage and municipal wastes into power.

Alternative energy sources won't make much headway in the '90s because they're still far too expensive compared with other fuels. Photovoltaic and other solar units will be used mainly in remote areas and in the Third World, where big power plants aren't affordable. Wind power and such ideas as ocean thermal conversion and geothermal power will see only limited application in the '90s. And while progress is being made in the research area, practical application of nuclear fusion is a long shot for the '90s.

In the meantime, world oil consumption is creeping up again, and by the early '90s it will be back to the high levels of the late '70s. The U.S., which produces about one-seventh of the world's oil and uses a third, is already approaching its consumption levels of ten years ago. In the '90s, the U.S. will use roughly as much oil as OPEC produces, enough to put upward pressure on prices.

Will other forms of energy relieve the pressure? Yes, mostly natural gas, which will remain relatively cheap and abundant. We'll import more gas from Canada. Nuclear power won't make much of a contribution in the '90s. It was set back further by the Chernobyl accident and the unwillingness of local governments to let utility firms recoup the cost of new plants from electric bills. And interest in coal is declining further because of the greenhouse effect. You'll hear more talk of solar heat and electric cars, but for the foreseeable future we'll stay hooked on oil and natural gas for our energy needs.

No oil crisis ahead

Does that mean we're setting ourselves up for another oil crisis in the '90s, similar to what we went through in 1973-74 and 1979-80? Probably not, because even at current prices, foreign oil producers have surplus capacity that is YEARS ahead of demand. Overproduction by individual OPEC members to gain their "fair share" will continue well into the '90s. And there is still a substantial amount of oil in the ground yet to be drilled and processed. So for your own long-range planning, figure on growing demand and $18 to $25 per barrel of oil over the next ten years.

Keep in mind that a vast spot market and oil-trading network have been set up since the '70s, replacing rigid long-term contract markets and providing a series of shock absorbers for prices. Also, non-OPEC production now accounts for two-thirds of the market. And by the late '90s, the U.S Strategic Petroleum

Reserve will hold 750 million barrels, enough to tide us over for at least six months.

New nuclear plants

Near the turn of the century, a new generation of nuclear plants will appear. They'll be smaller and simpler than current plants, relying more on standardized reactor design and less on operators to prevent accidents. Plant manufacturers will receive design certification from the Nuclear Regulatory Commission, a guarantee that the NRC will license plants built to those specifications without additional review.

These new plants will come along just as use of electricity will have grown to the point that nuclear power will be attractive again. By 2000, many existing nuclear plants will be 30 to 40 years old, and utilities will be facing the task of mothballing them or extending their useful lives through design changes.

We'll come to grips with the nuclear-waste disposal problem in the '90s. It's a political and psychological problem more than an engineering challenge. We already know of safe ways to surround radioactive wastes in impervious glass or ceramic casings. But getting a state or local area to accept the wastes is another matter.

TRANSPORTATION

Airlines, truckers and railroads—and the companies that make their equipment—will benefit from greater international trade and a generally robust economy through the '90s. Annual U.S. auto sales will average 25% higher than today, and the American share of world vehicle sales will stabilize and then rise at mid decade.

Aviation

U.S. aerospace manufacturers will see substantial declines in defense sales through at least the first half of the '90s, and they will face intense competition from the Europeans and Japanese on commercial aircraft.

But increases in commercial orders should more than offset

decreases in Pentagon contracts. The aerospace industry will contribute $40 billion to our trade balance by the turn of the century, more than doubling the current level.

The air travel and transport business will grow about 5% a year. By 2000 planes will be bigger, faster and more fuel efficient. Because the outlook is bleak for enough new airports in the next ten to 20 years, the airlines will pack more people and freight in each plane and lobby for more runways at current airports. And connecting or "hub" airports will be built in rural areas to help disperse air traffic.

New kinds of planes

Airport congestion will also be eased by using tilt-rotor planes that combine the speed of fixed-wing craft with vertical takeoff and landing capabilities. Tilt rotors are being built for the military but will also be used for ferrying commercial passengers between city centers—Dallas-Houston, St. Louis-Chicago and San Diego-Los Angeles, for example.

The Aerospace Industries Association sees the day when pilots will be assisted by robotic "pilot associates," very similar to having R2/D2 flying along as a co-pilot. Air-traffic controllers will have systems that can handle ten times today's traffic. Satellites will track the position of planes and feed the information instantly to a robotic air-traffic "controller associate" that will follow incoming and outgoing traffic. And airline passengers will be able to watch TV programs in flight, beamed in via satellite.

By the mid '90s, double-decked supersonic transports will whisk goods in three or four hours from the U.S. to freight hubs in Spain and Portugal for distribution throughout Europe and the Mideast. Much of the airplane maintenance work will also be done in those countries because of lower labor costs. Development will be far along on a hypersonic plane that could go to the Far East and back in a day, but it will probably be well into the next century before such a plane is even tested.

Less turbulence in trucking

The '90s will be more stable and profitable for trucking companies than the '80s, which were marked by deregulation, rate wars and bankruptcies. Increased foreign trade, a stronger manufacturing base in the U.S. and more specialization in the industry will help truckers achieve annual growth of 4% to 5% on average, after allowing for inflation. Trucking won't lose its share of the market to other modes of transportation.

Count on further consolidation as shippers reduce the number of carriers they use. But there will still be opportunities for smaller trucking operations that can provide fast, dependable service to specialized markets. One of the biggest problems the industry will face is finding enough drivers and mechanics. There's already a shortage.

Trucking firms will use satellite relays, similar to those developed for aircraft, for locating their vehicles and signaling drivers to pick up and deliver shipments.

Shape-up time for railroads

Freight has been moving away from rail and to trucks in recent years. This is unlikely to change unless the rail carriers improve their productivity and service. They'll buy new cars and other equipment for handling containerized cargo, hoping to take business away from trucks near congested ports such as Long Beach, Seattle, New York and Baltimore.

Rails will sharpen productivity through automation, computerized scheduling and abandonment of uneconomical services and lines. They will also sell off some of their prime real estate, such as unneeded rail yards in big cities.

As for passenger traffic, look for bullet trains between Boston and Washington, Miami and Orlando, and perhaps a "gamblers' special" between Los Angeles and Las Vegas. But most improvements will come in less-exotic commuter transportation, using existing tracks to bring people to work in and around the big cities.

Autos

Even with crowded roads and air pollution, America's love of cars won't diminish. In fact, it will probably grow as new styling and features are introduced—and as American incomes grow.

There's already one vehicle on the road for each adult in the

U.S., and the average family owns two. Americans could all get into their cars at the same time and not need the backseats. Ninety-seven percent of us drive a car or light truck to and from work. In fact, increasing congestion on suburban roads is caused more by affluence than population growth. Two-career families mean more cars per family, with teenagers doing much of the driving that Mom used to do.

Sales of new cars and light trucks will run about 19 million a year by the late '90s, compared with 15 million now. About 12 million will be autos and seven million will be trucks, up from 10.5 million cars and 4.5 million trucks currently. With fewer first-time car buyers coming along (18- to 24-year-olds), the market will be more mature and aimed at replacement sales. To spark interest, automakers will change models more often, about every three years instead of the current five.

A third of all sales will be imports, the same share as now, but more will come from places like South Korea, Taiwan, Brazil and Mexico and fewer from Japan. A fifth of our "domestic" vehicles will be made by Japanese-owned plants here. Aside from the jobs they create, such plants will help our trade balance by exporting a lot of cars to Europe and even Asia. Thus, the distinction between "foreign" and "U.S." models will get fuzzier. We see the U.S. auto companies, which enjoy strong worldwide sales, picking up a little more market share as their quality, marketing skills and price-competitiveness continue to improve.

Selling cars

Dealerships will be bigger but fewer, selling multiple lines of competing cars at lower average profits (partly because automakers will shift advertising and training costs their way). Twenty percent of the dealers will account for 80% of total car sales. There will be less dealer loyalty to the manufacturer; megadealers will add or drop franchises as circumstances dictate. Expect more standardization and uniformity within the same new-car franchises. This will be evident in showroom appearance and separate sales and service approaches for the new GM Saturn division and Toyota's Lexus and Nissan's Infiniti franchises.

Computer simulators will allow buyers to "create" their own

cars by testing different colors, body panels and other features. By the end of the century, automakers will offer the basic frames, engines and transmissions, and buyers will choose from a smorgasbord of bodies, sunroofs and other extras.

After you finish choosing and dickering with the dealer, you'll end up paying $24,000 for the average car in '00, without a maintenance agreement. Auto-finance companies will promote the idea of "guaranteed monthly operating costs," combining car payments with full maintenance on a guaranteed cost-per-mile basis. About 30% of truck leases already include such a feature.

Cars of tomorrow

Autos of the future will be low, sleek, rounded and packed with high-tech equipment. They'll also be roomier inside. Familiar parts such as rack and pinion steering, wiring harnesses and shock absorbers will disappear, replaced by electronically controlled steering, fiber optics and electronic suspension. You'll have an air bag stashed in the steering column. Cars will be unlocked and started with plastic cards. On-board navigation gear will tell drivers the best routes to their destinations and even recommend ways to get around traffic jams. Cars will have automatic collision-avoidance monitors and maintenance systems that will let the driver know when it's time to go in for service.

Tune-ups may even become a thing of the past—computers will keep cars in constant tune. The catch is, unless you're a computer hacker, you won't be able to repair your own car.

Expect further progress on fuel efficiency and engine performance through use of electronics and new materials such as graphites and ceramics. Antilock brakes will be on all cars. And no-hands voice-activated phones will be standard, too. Same for plastic bodies, which will allow faster design changes and cheaper retooling. Further ahead, there'll be dashboard microwave ovens and alerts to rouse drowsy drivers.

Efficient electric cars—long promised and always "just around the corner"—will finally arrive in the '90s, thanks to strides in battery technology. The cars will make a splash for commuting in Southern California and other spots with serious air-pollution problems.

ELECTRONICS AND COMPUTERS

If you're looking for companies to invest in or for a career opportunity, you'll find good pickings in electronics, computers and telecommunications. These companies will be among the fastest-growing, most-profitable and competitive in the U.S. over the next ten years or so. On average, they'll grow twice as fast as other lines.

There are no clear lines distinguishing electronics, computers and telecommunications. Computers communicate as part of their operation. And all digital communications devices—telephones and the switches that route speech and data to them—are actually computers. So look at them together.

Telecommunications will be revolutionized in the '90s by fiber optics—pulses of laser light moving through hair-thin glass rods at a speed of billions of pieces of information per second. Replacing copper wires in industry and eventually the home, fiber optics will speed the convergence of two powerful technologies—computers and telecommunications—and further elevate the importance of information in the global marketplace. Intense competition between the U.S. and Japan will continue, with the Japanese gaining in personal computers and certain kinds of microprocessors, but the U.S. still holding a clear lead in design and sales of mainframes, high-speed supercomputers and especially software. Telecommunications and information equipment and services will be one of our strongest industries and top export earners in the next 30 years. But we'll be playing catch-up in important areas of electronics such as high-definition TV and semiconductors.

The information available via computer and fiber-optics networks will be overwhelming. You'll have easy access to more data than you can possibly use. So management systems will have to hone in on what's important for decision making and what's mere clutter. More than ever, managers will need their information in simple, concise, to-the-point form. Companies that move and manage information effectively will earn a competitive advantage here and abroad.

Amazing microprocessors

Today microprocessor chips half the size of a postage stamp

have the same power as giant computers of the '60s. The latest chips developed by Motorola and Intel pack over a million transistors onto silicon wafers and can crunch data five times faster.

U.S. firms are already testing powerful four-megabit D-RAMs (dynamic random access memories) that hold up to four million bits of information on a chip. The next step will be 16-megabit D-RAMs. They will be the centerpiece of the information revolution in the next ten to 15 years.

And the Japanese are developing a "neural computer" that mimics the human brain and can repair itself when damaged. Advances in silicon and gallium-arsenide chips, electronic transmission and software systems will keep driving down the cost of processing, storing, managing and transporting information, while speed, reliability and capabilities will keep growing. By 2020, it may be possible to store the equivalent of a 500,000-book library for no more than a $4,000 investment. Of course, rapid advances in technology shorten product life. That's why it's so important to move your products to market faster—make a commitment, then plunge in.

Computer sales

Expect booming sales of all kinds of computers in the '90s. Remember, only a small portion of world business and industry is computerized to anything like the degree that we're accustomed to in the U.S., and even American business has a long way to go to achieve the full benefits of computerization.

Giant mainframes will be under sales pressure from smaller and less-expensive systems that match them in power and flexibility. Laptop computer sales will soar in the early '90s, grabbing a quarter of the personal-computer market. They'll get better, lighter and cheaper, with five-pound models going for less than $700 by the mid '90s. Along with portable facsimile machines, they'll be standard equipment for sales and marketing people, lawyers, real estate agents, journalists, engineers, architects, construction managers and others.

And notebook computers will hit the market in the early '90s. Weighing less than three pounds, they'll be used by students for taking notes and writing papers and will have the capabilities of today's desktops.

The used-computer market will be far more active five or ten years from now because many of the 20 million or so machines now in use will be sold into the used market. If you're looking for a new business, this might be worth checking out.

TELECOMMUNICATIONS

In the 1800s, rivers, harbors and railroads determined the location and success of many cities and industries. Interstate highways, airports and universities played a similar role in the 1900s. As we enter the 2000s, it's clear that telecommunications facilities are a new infrastructure that will influence how well communities do and where business will go.

The boom in telecommunications and data-processing markets around the world is a result of the globalization of industries— autos, computers, chemicals, machinery, food, finance, you name it. To work right, the components of these systems must be tied together with instant communications, access to common data bases and the use of common information systems. The openness, flexibility and profit motivation of U.S. companies will give them an advantage in the global competition of the new information age.

Information will emerge as the essential resource and agent of change in the world—replacing energy, and as important in its own way as capital and labor. In the '90s, it will no longer be possible to limit information or data flows within national borders. This is good news for an open society like the U.S.—and bad news for traditionally closed societies like the Soviet Union.

Fiber optics

Fiber-optic cables are rapidly replacing existing copper telephone cables, along railroad rights of way, under city streets, across oceans. In the late '90s they will begin coming into the American home.

Already, economic development groups in Minnesota are using fiber optics and digital switching as bait to attract data processing and printing contracts to small towns that need jobs. In Frederick, Md., office parks advertise the advantage of being located along a new interstate fiber-optic cable. States will promote their telecommunications networks, much as they did their highways, ports and rail systems in days gone by.

Superphones in the '90s

The 12 push buttons on your phone will function the same as keys on a computer terminal for providing a vast array of information—selecting and buying merchandise from a catalog, buying or selling stocks and bonds, or ordering up a current movie or sports event on your TV. You won't have to buy or learn to use computer equipment; you'll be able to tap into the system with your present phone.

As fiber optics replace copper wiring in phone systems and new switches allow information to be carried in digital form, voice, computer data and video transmissions will be made at the same time over a single phone line. We expect that the antitrust barriers that keep phone companies out of the home entertainment and information business will eventually loosen, creating intense competition between phone companies and cable TV firms. Further competition will come from satellites beaming programs directly to small, inexpensive receiving dishes.

The new superphones will enable you to do at home many of the tasks that you've had to do at the office, bank or shopping center. Much ballyhooed electronic meetings will become a reality, even to the point of passing documents around via fax attachments. The same superphones will monitor the security system in your home and let utility firms read your meters from miles away. Of course, there will be a price for all this—your phone bill may double or triple.

High-definition TV

One of the great commercial wars of the '90s will be fought over high-definition TV (HDTV), which will transmit more electronic detail to TV sets so that viewers will see a sharper, richer picture. The phase-in will be gradual, like the switch from black and white to color, but by 2000 at least 25% of all homes will have HDTV, even though the cost of jumbo flat-screen sets will run $2,500 to $3,000. As we noted in chapter four, the Japanese and Europeans are far ahead of us in developing HDTV, but U.S.

firms will get a boost from government assistance, including a different transmitting standard than used elsewhere. The Federal Communications Commission is giving U.S. companies an opportunity to reenter consumer electronics and to spur the development of sophisticated chips and other technology that will be needed for HDTV.

The stakes are huge. By 2000, HDTV will be a $25-billion to $40-billion business. And HDTV technology will have important applications in military hardware, telecommunications, semiconductors and personal computers.

SPACE-AGE MATERIALS

Figure on basic materials changing as rapidly as electronics and computers and remaining on the leading edge of technology. More than 100 new varieties, including high-strength, low-weight ceramics and plastic composites, will jockey for position against steel, copper and alloys of traditional materials, providing specific solutions to design problems. Work is under way on exotic metal-ceramic combinations, for example, to withstand temperatures up to 3,000 degrees—primarily for jet engines. The same technology will be applied to auto engines.

Custom-tailored materials will change the way companies manufacture, the equipment they use and the skills their workers will need. For example, composites, which combine two or more materials to enhance the characteristics of each, will show up in everything from cars and appliances to tennis racquets, golf clubs, furniture and the construction materials in your home.

A fundamental change in the materials business will be the way new products are brought to market. In the past, a company would come up with something and then try to develop a market for it, such as Dupont with Teflon and Kevlar. Now customers go to suppliers, describe the characteristics they want in a material and expect them to figure out how to make it. This is especially true in development of highly engineered parts for aerospace but will expand to housing, electronics and other lines.

Metals outlook

Many manufacturers will produce several competing materials. And metals firms will move into nonmetallic goods or materials that combine metals and other substances. Aluminum producers, for example, will also make thermoplastic composite skins for planes. They will face intense competition from foreign firms that are moving aggressively to develop evolving materials technologies. Japan and Europe are the main suppliers of technical-grade ceramic powders and fibrous reinforcements—the raw materials needed for ceramic-matrix composites used in aerospace.

Advanced composites will grab a lot of business away from traditional materials. Substituting for aluminum and titanium, they can reduce the weight of aircraft by 15 tons, meaning huge savings in fuel costs. Use of composites in aerospace will more than quadruple in the next ten years.

Sales of composites will increase from $2 billion a year now to $20 billion by 2000.

Steel: leaner, more profitable

Specialization will be the name of the game in the materials industries, and the amount of "value added" will be increasingly important as well. In steel, expect further shifts toward specialty, stainless and higher-strength products.

U.S. steel companies will run leaner and more profitably after shedding over 30% of their capacity and 60% of their employees and investing $15 billion in new manufacturing technology during the '80s. They now take a customer-focused instead of production-focused approach. Steelmakers are working with their customers to supply the precise quality and types of steel needed. If the Eiffel Tower were built with today's high-strength steel, only 3,000 tons would be needed instead of the 9,000 tons used in 1889.

Small, specialized minimills that serve regional markets will keep gaining a bigger piece of the pie. They now account for 20% of steel sales, and a larger share of profits. That will grow to 40% by 2000 as they take business away from big integrated mills and from imports. Many of the minimills use inexpensive carbon-steel imports as a raw material that they fashion into a higher-priced, value-added product.

There will also be more joint ventures with overseas partners, such as the state-of-the-art mill that will be built by Inland Steel and Nippon Steel near South Bend, Ind. It will reduce production time for cold-rolled sheet from 12 days to one HOUR.

TAKING ADVANTAGE OF CHANGE

In the Global '90s, change in one industry will ripple rapidly through many others, affecting the way business is done in America and throughout the world. Years ago, it may have been sufficient for a business manager to merely follow developments in his or her own field, through the specialized trade press of that field. Today that's not enough. The alert executive must be broadly aware of things happening in every industry—especially in the core technologies of computers, materials and telecommunications.

That's why you should broaden your business reading list to include journals of high-technology change. The things you learn will be invaluable not only to your business and your career, but also to your success as a personal investor. In the next chapter, we'll tell you about the investment opportunities and strategies that make sense in the decade ahead. As you read it, check back to this chapter and use it as background for weighing the prospects of stocks in various industries.

11 Investing for the '90s

Declining interest rates will boost bonds AND stocks.

Dow Jones average will reach 6000 by 2000.

U.S. companies with strong worldwide sales will excel.

Foreign securities will be a major part of U.S. portfolios.

Real estate values will rise strongly—for the pros.

Gold, silver, collectibles will lag behind financial assets.

Buying value and holding it will pay off best.

Successful investing for the '90s won't require radically new strategies or techniques—nothing much different from the methods that have always worked for smart investors, whether in the '60s, '70s or '80s.

Sure, the mix of your assets should vary from time to time, as one kind of asset—stocks, cash, real estate or bonds—heats up and another cools off. And the demographic and economic trends we see for the '90s will make some industries surge while others just mark time. For example, the graying of America will make strong markets for goods and services catering to the elderly—health care, investments, second-home construction, travel and so on.

But the fundamental principles of sound investing—diversification, a long-term orientation, investing regularly, buying value rather than the current fad—do not change from decade to decade. We'll show you how to apply time-honored principles to the special opportunities we see ahead.

THE BASIC ASSUMPTIONS

In every money-management decision you make, you're starting from a few fundamental assumptions about the general economic outlook. When you borrow money to buy a new home or car, for example, you're assuming a very small risk of an economic collapse that will jeopardize your job or sharply reduce future earnings. (Your lender is making the same judgment.)

The economic outlook

The investment guidance in this chapter proceeds naturally from the thesis of the entire book: The 1990s will be characterized by solid economic growth worldwide, in a climate of moderate inflation and generally falling interest rates, with increasing interdependence among world economies.

Inflation will average less in the next ten years than in the past ten because of better productivity, steadier monetary policy, progress on federal budget deficits and intense global competition. Look for less conspicuous consumption and more savings as the 75 million people born between 1946 and 1964 start pushing middle age. That will help hold down inflation and make more money available for borrowers. For your own long-range planning, figure on 4%-per-year inflation. That may not seem so bad, but 4% would lead to a DOUBLING of prices within the next 18 years.

Progress on budget deficits will lead to lower interest rates on average than we've had in the '80s. That's one reason we're partial to adjustable-rate borrowing, for both personal and business loans.

What it means for investors

This forecast is hospitable to bonds, but even more so to stocks, as companies find capital for expansion plentiful and well priced. The 500 stocks in the Standard & Poor's index on the New York Stock Exchange have produced an annual average return (price appreciation plus reinvested dividends) of about 10% for decades, and we see no reason to expect a lower return in the '90s. Projecting similar performance for the stocks of the Dow Jones industrial average would produce a Dow of about 6000 by the end of the decade.

The real estate market varies so much from place to place and by type of property (residential, commercial, industrial, agricultural) that it's hard to generalize, but we believe that America's real estate will appreciate in value faster than inflation, although not as strongly as carefully selected stocks.

Growing globalization will demand that you take a wider view of investment opportunities as you seek to own shares in both U.S. companies with strong overseas sales and fast-growing foreign-based firms.

Our forecast is not very favorable to precious metals, especially gold, which is a traditional haven from soaring inflation and financial crisis. World production of gold is booming, and commercial demand—-ranging from jewelry to industrial uses—is fairly flat.

TAKING STOCK AND SETTING GOALS

If you figure you don't have enough money to be an investor, you've got plenty of company. Most people feel that way. Even many of those you look upon as well-to-do often complain about how hard it is to make ends meet and stick to a plan of systematic investing.

But chances are you're already an investor—or on the way to becoming one. If you own a home, you're an investor in real estate, even if it's just the roof over your head. If you have an individual retirement account (IRA), you're a long-term investor. If all your money is parked in fixed-rate, insured deposits and you add money to them regularly, you're already a saver, and you're a candidate to become an investor. Investing differs from saving only in the degree of risk you're willing to accept in return for possibly greater reward.

Before proceeding, take a moment to figure out where you stand today. Add up your assets and subtract your liabilities. You may be surprised to find that you have more than you imagined.

Everyone should have a financial goal—or more likely, several goals. These goals, and the methods for achieving them, will vary according to your own special circumstances—your age, income, whether you're single or married, whether you have children, whether you work for someone else or are self-employed, whether you can expect some financial help from family members. These variables will have an enormous bearing on everything from your life insurance needs to the kinds of investments that are right for you.

What are your goals? What do you want your investments to do? In general, your plan should meet the following needs:

1. To build enough funds for future needs, such as sending your children to college, starting a business of your own or providing for a comfortable retirement.

2. To protect your wealth from inflation.

BEFORE YOU BEGIN INVESTING

Before you even consider building an investment portfolio of securities, mutual funds or real estate, check to see whether you have taken care of the basics of financial security:

Insurance. You should have enough insurance of the right kind for your particular needs: life, disability, health and personal liability. That means plenty of inexpensive term life insurance for the young family, enough to replace lost earnings with just the *income* on invested proceeds, without having to draw down the principal. For the older person, it means using whole life insurance as part of the estate planning process.

Savings. You should have a cushion of low-risk, liquid savings to carry you through an emergency, such as loss of your job or extended illness. Aim for the equivalent of at least six months' worth of earnings. Savings may make it unnecessary for you to sell any of your other assets, such as your home or stocks. Forced sales often result in a sacrifice, a financial loss.

Tax-deferred retirement plan. You should take advantage of tax-deferred savings opportunities for retirement. That means setting up an IRA or Keogh plan and adding each year the maximum amount allowed by law, even if your income level doesn't permit tax-deductibility of the IRA contribution. The deferral of income taxes—even on the interest alone—until retirement will make your money grow much faster. (Some tax-deferred annuities and life insurance policies work similarly, with no limit on what you may put in.)

Homeownership. Your own home—whether a single-family residence, condominium or co-op—will be an anchor to windward for most families, probably your biggest investment. First of all, it's a way to stabilize your housing costs, compared with renting. It's also still an excellent tax shelter. And it will be at least a decent store of value, and possibly a good investment, too. Even after allowing for inflation, we think the value of homes will keep rising over the next ten to 15 years and longer. And the payments on your mortgage will amount to a forced-saving program. It's about the only way that many families manage to save anything.

Assess your risk tolerance

Now consider your expectation for the long-term performance of your investments and the level of risk you are willing to accept. Obviously, you want to beat inflation by some comfortable margin. But what margin over inflation is a good performance? Three percentage points? Five? Ten?

The first question to ponder is whether to take any risks at all. If you can't afford any loss, can't abide anxiety or can't take time to investigate investment opportunities or track results, the answer should be an emphatic "no."

There are ways to save without risk and still get respectable though limited returns: federally insured savings accounts and certificates of deposit (CDs), U.S. savings bonds and short-term Treasury securities. All are backed by Uncle Sam. Money-market funds, although not similarly guaranteed, are nearly as safe. Longer-term Treasury issues and many federal-agency offerings come with the same protection, although their market prices fluctuate in the opposite direction of interest rates.

You've probably heard the argument that no savings or investment vehicle is totally risk free, because inflation erodes—and at times may wipe out—the buying power of investment earnings.

But as we were writing this book in early '89, federally insured deposits were beating inflation by several percentage points—not a bad return for zero risk. What's more, you get a measure of inflation protection from many safety-first investments, including money-market funds, savings bonds and some passbook savings accounts. That's because when prices rise, interest rates go up, too, boosting their payouts. Just remember that for inflation protection, keep maturities short—within a year, so you can roll them over quickly—and stagger maturities.

The pyramid of risk

Whatever your target annual return, there is a degree of risk associated with it. No one has found a way to unlink risk and reward. If you swing for the fences every time you're at bat, you're going to get an occasional homer, but you're going to strike out more often.

Think of your investments as a pyramid of risk, with a broad base of insured, low-return assets. As the pyramid tapers upward, you will want less and less of your wealth invested in increasingly risky kinds of assets. Here are the assets that comprise the pyramid:

On the bottom: Low-risk or no-risk federally insured investments, as described above.

Part way up: High-quality corporate bonds and bond mutual funds; stocks of substantial companies with a long history of solid (and rising) dividends; balanced mutual funds, which own both stocks and bonds. Your principal is at risk, but usually not to a great degree. You are, as a rule, rewarded with higher yields on corporate bonds than you would find with government-guaranteed issues. In the case of stocks with moderate to high dividends, you have current income to give you the patience to wait out a slump in price.

Near the top: Speculative stocks paying little or no dividends (such as those of small, fast-growing companies); junk bonds; futures; limited partnerships in real estate, gas and oil, equipment leasing and the like. The stocks and bonds are typically volatile in price. Limited partnerships sting you with high start-up costs—sometimes as much as 20% of your investment. Options are sometimes no more than crap shoots.

At the apex: Penny stocks and stock issued by start-up companies (the most speculative equities); commodity futures and stock-index futures; precious metals, gems and collectibles of almost every stripe. (We don't regard collectibles as investments at all, as we'll explain later.) At this level of risk you are either making bets on megaevents (inflation, the direction of stock prices, famine) or joining a game in which the deck may be stacked against you. As for commodity trading, surveys indicate that 75% to 90% of the people who try it end up losing money. Don't join them.

Historical returns

Historical rewards are generally commensurate with the risks you'll find as you climb the pyramid. Between 1926 and mid 1988, long-term government bonds produced total returns averaging about 4.3% a year. Corporate bonds averaged a total return of about 5%. Stocks in the Standard & Poor's 500-stock index came through at 10%, small-company stocks at 12.4%. Inflation ran a compounded annual rate of about 3%, so all of these beat inflation. (There's no comparable data for other kinds of investments, such as real estate.)

You probably aren't interested in such very long comparisons, since you remember times in the recent past when particular kinds of assets sprinted past the others. In the '70s, stocks didn't do so well in general, but high inflation sent real estate soaring. In the late '70s and early '80s, interest rates were so high that previously issued bonds went into the tank, and money-market funds produced double-digit annual returns (but beat inflation by only a couple of points). Between 1982 and 1987, falling interest rates made bonds into star performers and also helped send the stock market surging skyward.

We're partial to stocks because the record shows that acquiring quality stocks and holding them for long periods—through good times and bad—has paid off better than anything else. At a 5% return per year, the historical payoff from corporate bonds, $10,000 grows to $26,533 in 20 years. At 10%—the long-term return from blue-chip stocks—the same $10,000 becomes $67,275.

Strive for diversity

Because of the cyclical performance of every kind of asset, you ought to own a range of things, so that a sag in one will be offset by strong gains in another. That gets you into the game of asset allocation—finding the mix that's right for your income, age, life goals, risk tolerance and outlook for the economy. For example, if you're nearing retirement you'll want to emphasize income and reduce long-term risk by getting into high-yield stocks, CDs and short bonds. A younger investor can afford to take a chance on the long-term prospects of small, high-tech companies.

There's no pat formula everyone can adopt. It depends on your comfort level. A simple approach suggested by the *AAII Journal*, published by the American Association of Individual Investors, is to put a minimum of 25% each in stock mutual funds, bond mutual funds and money-market funds and apportion the rest according to your risk and return preferences.

Invest regularly

Some investors believe there are "good markets" and "bad markets." They try to time their investments precisely, pouring money into the early stages of hot stock markets and pulling out completely when things begin to sour.

We are not fans of market timing. We are not convinced that most people—even the so-called experts—can achieve good results with it. We think you will do better by buying quality stocks and mutual funds on a regular, periodic basis—in markets high, low and in between. The best way to do this is with the time-proven method of dollar-cost averaging (DCA). That means buying stocks at regular intervals—once a month is typical, or every quarter—regardless of the price. That lowers your cost, because you get more shares when prices are low and fewer when they are high. The only drawback of DCA is the high commission cost on direct purchases of small amounts of stock. That's why cost-averaging works best with a no-load mutual fund, in which you can make small deposits every month.

If you insist on trying to be a market timer, at least be a contrarian. Don't follow the stampede into fast-rising markets. Accumulate cash and wait for the inevitable sharp corrections that occur in every bull market. Buy when others are selling, adding shares of your favorite stocks every time they tick down a few points.

Take the long view

Invest for the long term and set achievable objectives. Your only solid benchmarks for setting objectives are the historical returns mentioned above. If the historical 10% rate of return for quality stocks seems unacceptably low, remember that it is twice the current inflation rate. Reaching for larger returns over an extended period could find you chasing every hot stock just as it tops out.

If you have confidence enough in the long-term performance of a stock or mutual fund to buy it in the first place, give it time to achieve the results you expect. Be an *investor*, not a *trader*. Traders generate enormous commission expenses, usually enriching their brokers more than themselves.

HOW TO BUY MUTUAL FUNDS

Mutual funds are not a *kind* of investment, but a *way* of investing. For most investors they are a very good way to get the benefits of professional stock-picking and diversity of holdings. There are more than 1,200 mutual funds in America, not including money-market funds. Some have dismal records of picking stocks for their investors, consistently under-performing the broad market averages. But some do consistently better than the averages.

There are mutual funds for every imaginable kind of financial investment—stocks, bonds, home mortgages, you name it. There are also mutual funds for real estate, ranging from shopping centers to office buildings. They are called real estate investment trusts, or REITs.

Mutual funds pool the money of their investors and buy a range of assets of one type or a mix, then they manage the basket of assets to maximize growth—buying and selling when they see fit. So a mutual fund gives custom portfolio management to investors who don't want to pick their own stocks and bonds or can't afford their own adviser. In the process, they offer the reduced risk of diversity by giving investors ownership of many stocks in numerous industries or in one narrow industry (so-called sector funds).

The cost of this management can range from an annual management fee of 1% or less (for a no-load fund, one with no sales commission) to a commission bite that can run as much as 8.5% of what you invest. There are some high-performing load funds, but they're like a racehorse handicapped with eight pounds of lead in its saddlebag. Their stock picks have to rise by at least the percentage of the sales commission before you have any gain at all. Given the wide range of successful no-load funds, you are generally better off sticking with them.

Choosing a fund

Don't buy any mutual fund—whether on the basis of a broker recommendation, a friend's advice or an advertisement—without checking its performance in one of the annual listings of mutual funds in financial magazines such as *Changing Times* and *Forbes*. Don't focus just on last year's return; the annual list of hot performers changes almost completely each year and it tends to be dominated by sector funds in whatever business category was hot—precious metals, health care, Asian stocks, airlines and so on. Look instead at which funds have finished in the top third of all funds over a period of five or ten years, in a variety of up and down markets. Presuming the same portfolio managers are still at the helm and haven't lost their touch completely, past performance over several years augurs well for future performance. There are many well-run funds that meet these standards, including Mutual Shares, Fidelity Magellan, Lindner, Alliance Balanced Shares and Vanguard Windsor, to name just a few.

Many investors make all of their asset allocation decisions—among stocks, bonds, money-market cash, etc.—by moving their money among the various no-load or low-load funds within a large family of funds, with no or negligible switching fees. This can be an effective way of occasionally shifting investment emphasis, but if it is done too often it can be as self-defeating (but not as expensive) as active trading in individual stocks.

Index funds: buying the market

If you want *really* broad diversity of holdings and you believe the general market trend will be up, consider an index fund.

These funds buy all the stocks in the popular stock indexes, such as the Standard & Poor's 500, the NASDAQ 100, the Wilshire 5000 or the Dow Jones industrial average. You take no chances on picking stocks that will outperform the averages, instead you hitch your star to the averages themselves and go along for the ride, however bumpy.

Index funds are perfect for those who think that random selection of stocks works as well in the long run as exhaustive study and elaborate theories. Look for a fund with no load, a low management fee (less than 1%) and no gimmicks that try to boost performance above the index. The Vanguard Index Trust 500 Portfolio, tied to the S&P 500, meets these standards very well.

PICKING YOUR OWN STOCKS

Creating your own stock portfolio is hard work, and most people don't have the skill, inclination or time to do it successfully. (This explains the boom in mutual funds.)

You need to study the past performance and future prospects of dozens of companies—both well-known and obscure—and you need to buy a range of stocks in numerous industries to spread your risk. Of course, there are many sources of help, especially business-news and personal-finance magazines, newspapers and stock-picking newsletters. There are also many sound books on investing, such as Louis Engel's classic *How to Buy Stocks* and Peter Lynch's *One Up on Wall Street.* You can get the lowdown on past performance of 1,700 publicly traded companies in *Value Line Investment Survey,* by subscription or at your local library. It's very valuable for the serious stock picker.

A traditional source of stock-picking guidance are the research departments of brokerage houses, which have varying degrees of success in helping their customers make money. (Brokers also have a natural tendency, as commissioned salespersons, to urge you to sell whatever you own now and stock up on the current hot pick.)

Strive for the same diversity of holdings that a stock mutual fund would have. Don't put all your eggs in one basket; create your own balanced portfolio. It might include 20 or more stocks—drugs, computers, airlines, retailers, utilities and regional banks, plus some cyclical stocks such as paper, chemicals or machinery. Then add a few smaller emerging growth stocks, either your own picks or a mutual fund.

Value investing

At *Changing Times* magazine and the *Kiplinger Letters* we've always urged our readers to devote most of their stock allocation to companies that meet the basic standards of value investing. That means companies that, compared with market averages, sell at a low multiple of earnings (usually less than ten) and a low ratio to book value (no more than 1.3 times book, or break-up, value), pay a decent dividend (say, 3% or 4%), reinvest at least 35% of their earnings and have relatively low debt (less than 35% of capitalization).

The list of publicly traded stocks that meet *all* these criteria is pretty small at any particular moment, and tends to be composed mainly of unloved, ignored stocks. The list is heavy in regional banks and insurance companies, with very few exciting industrial firms or small companies of any sort. So don't get hung up on meeting *every* standard. You should take enough liberties with these criteria to add some higher-growth companies to your buy list.

The P/E ratio

The true price of a stock is its multiple of earnings. A low price-earnings ratio means the market thinks the company's earnings will grow at a fairly slow rate. The market might be right. If you have good reason to believe otherwise, you should bet on the stock with a low P/E, especially if it's low compared with its industry and its own past P/E.

A stock with a high price-earnings multiple—say, twice the market average, or 20 to 25 times earnings—is not necessarily overpriced, but it is definitely riskier; only time will tell. The market is expecting its earnings to grow at the same dazzling rate they have in the past, and if they stumble for a quarter or two, disillusioned investors will probably bail out, sending the stock tumbling.

Over the long haul, stocks with a lower-than-average P/E have outperformed the general market, according to many studies.

Rising dividends

If you are interested in dividends, don't focus on the stocks that pay the highest dividend at a particular moment—a selection that tends to be dominated by utilities and banks (and a few companies that are in such precarious shape they must pay out a high percentage of earnings to attract investors). Instead focus on companies with a long record of rising dividends *and* price appreciation.

Remember, since Congress abolished the lower tax rate on capital gains, it makes no short-run difference to the investor whether a company pays in an annual distribution of earnings—a dividend—or through price appreciation from reinvestment of earnings.

In 1988, *Changing Times* went looking for a group of strong-growth companies that met all the following criteria: a doubling of dividends over the past ten years; a dividend yield of at least 3%; reinvestment of at least 35% of earnings; debt of no more than 25% of capitalization; and a 1988 price of no more than their mean P/E for the past decade. Surprisingly few stocks met all tests; the ones that did include a number of strong companies in many industries, among them were Coca-Cola, K mart, Chubb, 3M, Eli Lilly, McGraw-Hill, Dun & Bradstreet, GE, Pfizer, Florida National Bank, and Rockwell International.

Minimizing risk

If you want to invest in stocks but are fairly risk averse, look at the *Value Line* risk ratings of stocks—a 1-to-5 scale of risk that measures share-price stability and the company's financial strength. Among the 137 companies that received the lowest-risk rating of 1 in early '89 included IBM, General Motors, Eastman Kodak, Philip Morris, Boeing, Northern States Power and Crown Cork & Seal.

Growth stocks

If your resources permit, you have a fairly high tolerance for risk and you're willing to hold on for the long haul, your greatest reward in percentage gain will come from successfully identifying the stars of tomorrow—small and medium-size companies whose growth in earnings will greatly outpace the general market. Over the past six decades, publicly traded companies with lower-than-average total values (loosely defined as market capitalizations under $100 million) have outperformed the large-company S&P 500 by two percentage points. But because of their greater volatility, devote a relatively small portion of your total investment pie to small-company growth stocks.

Most likely you will not be the first person to find these companies, so you can expect them to sell for a high multiple of current earnings—often 20 to 30 times earnings or higher, anywhere from 50% to 300% above the market-average P/E. You should try to find the best growth potential for the lowest possible P/E.

These companies will be distinguished by market prominence in a fast-growing field, due to patents or just research leadership, so you will find them in such industries as computer software and biotechnology. Such companies tend to invest heavily in research and development. Their capital spending is high from constant updating of equipment to stay ahead of competitors and improve productivity. They prefer to finance their growth with the cheapest capital there is—reinvested earnings—so you can expect no dividend at all, or at most a low one. They expect to reward you with price appreciation on your stock.

Emerging-growth companies invest heavily in the talent of their managers and scientists, luring the best people and paying them plenty in salaries and stock options. (On the risk side, if the top people in a small company leave, things can fall apart fast.) They may be barely profitable today, but their managers expect strong profits ahead, when a new technology begins to pay off.

Remember, more emerging-growth companies will bomb than succeed. Your strong gain on one or two will have to carry the burden of the others that fail. If you don't have a lot of time and expertise to identify growth stocks, especially the smaller companies, you are better off buying shares in mutual funds that invest in small emerging-growth companies, spreading the risk over many companies in several key technologies. Over the last several years, the better-performing funds that specialize in small-capitalization stocks have included Acorn Fund, Pennsylvania Mutual and Janus Venture.

Another point to remember: The oldest and largest companies in many fields—whether computers, biotechnology or composite materials—are doing R&D work that is often at least as good as what the small firms are doing. For example, all the large chemical and pharmaceutical firms are heavily involved in genetic engineering. You can participate in the growth of this field by investing in the giants, not just in the little firms. Since biotech divisions are only a small part of the big companies' total sales, they won't boost earnings dramatically when they begin to pay off, but the risk is much lower.

TAKING A GLOBAL VIEW

If there will be anything distinctively different about investing in the '90s compared with past decades, it will be the advisability of considering the international aspect of everything you do. The American economy today is just one part—albeit the biggest part—of an intertwined world economy. World affairs—trade relations, movements of capital, political shifts, currency fluctuations—will play a major role in investment decisions, even for the small investor.

You should look for U.S. companies that enjoy strong sales and market leadership around the world. (Their overseas earnings may exceed their American profits in a given year.) You will want to own strong American firms in such fields as health care and equipment, pharmaceuticals, chemicals, food, aerospace, construction machinery, financial services, computers, telecommunications, entertainment, waste disposal and pollution control. The choice of stocks that fill this bill is wide, including PepsiCo, McDonald's, American Express, Ford, Boeing, IBM, Merck, Caterpillar, Corning Glass, Dow Chemical and Johnson & Johnson. Pay close attention to leading consumer brands—firms known for world-class drugs, foods, cleansers, beer, soft drinks, carpets.

Investing in foreign stocks

Several foreign stock markets, especially in the Far East, have strongly outperformed the U.S. market in recent years, reflecting the rapid growth of the newly industrialized nations. A barrier-free European Common Market in '92—and an expected boom in cross-border mergers, corporate reorganizations and capital investment—will do wonders for European stocks. In fact, they will probably show better gains in the early '90s than the Japanese market, which may be overpriced today.

So you should at least take a look at the possibilities overseas, especially shares of major export-oriented companies, such as Siemens, Alcatel, Unilever, ICI, NEC, Honda, Sony, Philips, Daimler-Benz, and Hoechst. Some market advisers suggest that clients keep at least 10% to 15% of their equities in foreign stocks, spreading them around by country and industry.

Investing in foreign stocks can be tricky. Currency swings can wipe out your gains. Overseas reporting requirements are not be as stringent as in the U.S. And insider trading is rampant in many countries. Unless you have some expertise in sizing up foreign companies, you're probably wise to invest through international mutual funds. There is a wide variety to choose from, including those that specialize in specific countries, regions and industries. Ask your broker about them. Or you can invest in individual foreign companies through ADRs, American Depository Receipts, available through local stockbrokers.

THE ROLE OF BONDS

Bonds—fixed-interest loans that rise and fall in value before they are paid back at term—have a place in your investment mix. Why? Because they'll give good steady returns in a stable economy and generally entail less risk than stocks.

Fifteen years ago, bonds were dull as dishwater and ignored by most warm-blooded investors. Then came the inflation and interest rate zigzags of the late '70s and early '80s, followed by lower rates, a fairly steady economy, the stock bust of '87 and rising rates the following year. Bonds became a lot more exciting and looked like a good way to make solid gains—if you could guess the general direction of rates, which wasn't easy. As we were writing this in early 1989, with interest rates high and good prospects for a gradual decline, bonds—especially Treasuries and tax-free municipals—were the first choice of many investors for short-term gains, say, over the next two years.

Assuming lower inflation and interest rates, marketable bonds make sense for the '90s, especially for investors who are more interested in steady income than appreciation and have enough liquidity so that they won't have to cash in before maturity. In that way, you know what you'll earn and need not worry about bond prices declining when rates tick up.

As with stocks, buy bonds on a regular basis, without trying to time the peaks and valleys of interest rates precisely. Stagger the maturities so that you have bonds coming due at various times in interest rate cycles.

Types of bonds

Consider 30-year Treasuries first because you don't have to worry about defaults, and most can't be redeemed against your will. Besides, you don't pay any state or local taxes on the interest you earn. Why 30 years? Because you usually get a higher yield on longer-term bonds, and the longer the maturity the bigger your total return.

Tax-free municipal bonds are one of the few remaining tax shelters. Anyone with reasonably high income should look into them. The interest paid is exempt from federal income taxes and usually from income taxes of the state in which they are issued. So municipals may pay less interest than corporate bonds of comparable quality but still deliver the same after-tax yield. Buy local municipal bonds if you know your state, county or city is financially sound. Otherwise, check out municipal-bond funds.

If you opt for corporate bonds, stick to high-grade bonds of large, solvent, well-run companies such as IBM, 3M or DuPont that won't go broke or be the target of a leveraged buyout, leaving them with piles of debt. Or buy shares of a high-grade corporate-bond fund with a good track record and low operating expenses. For safety's sake, avoid high-yield bonds. They're high yield because they're high risk. Some of the heavily leveraged firms that issued them will have trouble paying off in the next recession. If you can't resist owning some high-yield junk bonds, do it only through a mutual fund that owns enough different issues to keep the default rate low on the whole portfolio.

Zero-coupon bonds are sold in all three categories—Treasuries, municipals and corporates. Zeros are issued at a substantial discount from their face value and don't pay interest until maturity, when you get both principal and interest back. You can buy them at 10 cents to 20 cents on the dollar for a bond of 20 years or so, but you are taxed each year on the phantom interest you're not receiving. That's a major drawback, unless you're purchasing zeros for an IRA, a 401(k) or Keogh plan, or buying them for a child whose investment earnings under $1,000 are taxed at a low rate until age 14.

You can sometimes earn better returns on foreign government or corporate bonds than you can on U.S. bonds. But unless they're denominated in dollars, such as Eurodollar bonds, you may be whipsawed by interest rates AND currency swings. If you want to try foreign bonds, go through a fund or a dealer you have faith in.

REAL ESTATE INVESTING

For most investors, their first real estate investment—their own home and subsequent trade-ups—will probably be their last. Investing in real estate—whether income properties or raw land—is hard work, requiring a clear sense of market conditions, economic trends, tax laws, and many other skills. There is a lot of money to be made in it by those who know what they're doing, but it's not for amateurs.

In most regions of the U.S., investment property remains hung over from binges of construction during the '70s and '80s, when developers attracted billions because of incentives in the tax law. Tax reform and high vacancies sobered up the industry. The worst imbalances of supply and demand are in downtown office buildings, hotels and apartment buildings—especially in areas where the economy is still soft from energy and agricultural woes, such as Oklahoma, Texas, Louisiana and parts of the Midwest.

For the very well-heeled investor whose deep pockets will permit him or her to hang on with little current income, today's bargain-basement prices in distressed areas will spell strong appreciation in the '90s. Other areas that look promising for commercial and industrial investment include the usually robust Baltimore-Washington corridor, Southern California between Los Angeles and San Diego, and parts of the Midwest—such as

Columbus, Cincinnati and Chicago—which are benefiting from solid growth in U.S. manufacturing.

One way for small investors to earn money in real estate is through publicly traded real estate investment trusts (REITs), which pass profits along to investors untaxed. There are more than 100 of these real estate mutual funds; some have excellent records, while others have been dogs. Before you invest in a REIT, find out what kinds of properties it owns and where they are. It's fine if you want to be a contrarian and invest in a "vulture fund" with property in the Oil Patch, but you need to go in with your eyes open.

Residential real estate

Changes in the tax code—stretching out depreciation and limiting the offset of rental losses against other income—greatly diminished the appeal of investing in single-family homes and small apartment houses, even for the active property manager. In any event, it's hard work for an annual return that barely beats other less-grueling kinds of investing.

In the case of single-family homes, the premium prices buyers are willing to pay for their own residence makes it very difficult for the investor to buy the same house and turn a profit on rent, at least in the first several years. It's likely to run a loss until rent catches up, and that puts the investment burden on price appreciation. Over the next few years we expect the rise in home prices to exceed inflation, but not by more than 2% to 3%.

The trick for the small real estate investor is to find basic, average houses in solid but not flashy neighborhoods, especially houses that need a little cosmetic lift. If you can buy them for a low-enough price and fix them up, you have a sporting chance of turning an operating profit much sooner, and you should get better-than-average appreciation in the process.

When you decide to trade up to a bigger or better residence of your own, think of your current house as a possible real estate investment. Consider renting it out rather than selling it. It all depends on how hard you are willing to work at your investments and if you can swing the purchase of the new house without selling the old.

If you've owned the house for a number of years, chances are the rise in rents since you bought it will enable the house to run an operating profit immediately. Or if you want an operating loss for tax purposes, you can pull some equity out of the house in a refinancing deal and run up your interest expense.

Investing in raw land

Ah, land: They're not making any more of it. That's true, and it's the reason why raw land that is in the path of development has had an excellent record of long-term price appreciation. But that doesn't necessarily make every piece of land a good investment.

First, you have to figure out whether the land is likely to appreciate faster than the accrued interest, taxes and other costs involved in holding it. Then ask yourself if it is likely to beat other investments available to you, and whether you can afford to tie up your money for quite a while. Holding raw land has many of the disadvantages of investing in gold and silver, plus a few others.

Usually, you don't earn any current income to offset interest charges and local taxes and, possibly, special assessments. Unlike stocks and bonds or even gold, getting your money out of land often takes many months.

Nevertheless, land has made many investors wealthy over the years. When should you consider investing in land? After you've built up a comfortable equity in your home, a buffer of more-liquid assets to tide you over and a reasonable cash flow.

The trick is to find land that's in the path of future development before the rest of the world is on to it. Try to foresee who will buy it, for what use and when. You must know the area and its prospects. Once developers start bidding for the same acreage, you've missed the boat.

Even if you have found a good piece of land, is it priced right? Have you studied recent transactions on comparable sites? (Seems obvious to ask that, but many people think they've got a bargain, then plunge in and lose their shirts.)

Successful land investors usually take time to make a rough plan of how the property would be divided and used. For example, they calculate how many homesites the land would yield under present zoning regulations, or how many square feet of retail space it would accommodate. Then they pay no more than such utilization will justify. If through rezoning they can get higher densities, they've earned a bonus.

For these reasons, professionals who buy land usually ask for 60 to 90 days for feasibility studies before closing a deal. During this time, they determine whether the anticipated yield will materialize and whether construction permits would be granted. If not, they get their deposit back and walk away.

Be cautious about investing in a land syndicate. Up-front fees are high, and the organizers usually pay themselves well, taking their cut off the top. They often make more money from the syndication than from holding and selling the land, so they tend to favor quick turnover. The result is plenty of fees for the general partner and only modest returns to the limited partners, the investors.

PRECIOUS METALS

Many people feel naked unless they have some gold or other precious metals socked away as a hedge against runaway inflation or collapse of the financial markets. If you feel that way, go ahead and buy some, but only as a small part of your total investments, no more than 5%. You can own either bullion and coins directly—entailing storage and insurance charges—or you can buy shares in a gold or precious-metals mutual fund, which might own both bullion and shares in mining companies.

A better strategy would be to keep that portion of your money in a liquid, income-producing investment such as a money-market fund and switch to metals if storm clouds gather. The reason: Metals earn no income, and during stable periods prices can drop, as they have in recent years. Almost always, conditions that cause an upsurge in metals prices take time to develop. A watchful investor will have ample time to take a position in the metals market.

In any case, we believe precious metals will not outperform other investments unless inflation goes haywire or there's an international crisis. But as we noted earlier, we expect 4% inflation on average through the '90s. Foreign crises usually can't be seen in advance. There are bound to be some in the '90s, but probably nothing as long-lasting or severe as the oil crises of the

'70s. And the world is awash in gold, as mining and refining innovations have boosted production.

Silver is a similar situation. There will be an oversupply, partly because silver is being produced as a by-product of increased mining for copper and other industrial metals. Platinum is in a slightly better position on the demand side because of its rising use in catalytic converters and other commercial applications. But if you are not familiar with that market, don't sink your money into it.

The plain fact is that financial assets and real estate will probably beat precious metals by a wide margin in the next ten years.

COLLECTIBLES: NOT A TRUE INVESTMENT

Like many other people, we appreciate the beauty of antiques, fine art and gemstones, and we respect the rich history of rare stamps and coins. As a matter of fact, we are antiques collectors ourselves, and we consider ourselves pretty knowledgeable about these markets.

But we do not regard collectibles as legitimate investments, worthy of receiving a particular portion of your investment dollars. If you want to buy them for enjoyment, fine, but don't expect a return on your investment to equal what you can get from financial investments and real estate.

To us, an investment must meet most or all of a few basic criteria. It should be reasonably liquid, permitting a fairly quick sale through an organized market with many buyers and sellers. It should change hands at a low transaction cost—that is, sales commission or dealer mark-up. Ideally, it should pay some sort of current yield, or at least not cost the owner money to hold. It should have a long record of appreciation exceeding the rate of inflation.

While we know of lots of examples of dazzling price gains in particular collectibles—some superb paintings, antique chests, stamps and coins—we don't know of any whole category of collectible that meets most of these standards of an investment. The biggest problem is the uncertainty of resale markets and high sales costs.

Most collectibles are bought at a retail price, but are sold back to dealers at a wholesale price—often just 50% of retail. So something you own has to double its retail price for you just to get back what you paid, let alone any real gain. If you sell at auction, the sales commission might be only 10% to 15%, but you have the uncertainty of selling low or having to take the item back into your possession.

Be very wary of supposed price indexes for collectibles, which purport to show steady annual appreciation in value. They are quoted extensively and loudly by mail-order dealers in stamps and coins. But they are not true indexes, unlike records of stock and bond performance. Most are based not on actual sales transactions but are modeled on estimates of prices that would be fetched for exceptionally rare examples, which seldom come on the market and are beyond the financial reach of most collectors.

If you become a serious student in any area of collectibles, you will be able to collect with skill and taste, and there's a good chance that your collection will hold its value. You'll enjoy yourself immensely, and the collection might even grow in value over many years—if your kind of collectible continues to be fashionable. If that happens, it will be a pleasant surprise.

TRUST YOUR OWN INSTINCTS

Do not sell your own judgment short in making investment decisions. Of course, you don't want to be parochial, and it's increasingly important to widen your national and world investing vision. But don't neglect your own instincts, and don't kowtow to experts who recommend strategies you are not comfortable with.

Over the years, you've learned a lot by experience in your own company, industry and community. Put it to good use in your investing. Often the best investments are right under your nose—companies that make the goods and services that you and your family buy, companies that employ people you know, companies in your own industry or region.

Maybe your best bet is to put more money into your own business, through employee stock purchase plans, or into local companies you can follow through your acquaintances and the local papers.

Many people in our home area of Washington, D.C., have done this successfully with a variety of local companies, including

GEICO insurance, Giant Food stores, MCI telecommunications and others. Take, for example, a small D.C. restaurant chain and food-service firm that sold stock to the public for the first time in 1953, at $10.25 per share. Hundreds of small investors who lived or worked in the city and knew of the good food and service at J. Willard Marriott's coffee shops bought shares. They were hometown investors who could see how the restaurants were doing, eat some meals there and size up the management from across the counter. If they resisted the temptation to take profits over the years, they made a real killing. If you had invested $500 in Marriott in '53 and kept the stock, your investment would be worth well over $300,000 today.

You may not have a budding Marriott Corp. in your backyard, but you probably have some local or regional retailers, banks or manufacturing firms that would make excellent long-term investments. Look around, use your head. Buy companies, not just markets or abstract concepts of value.

In all your investing—whether in local, national or international firms—act on your confidence in the future. Whether as a shareholder or a lender buying bonds, you will be investing in human ingenuity and problem-solving. In the long run, we think you are bound to come out fine.

INDEX

J

K

ABOUT THE AUTHORS

AUSTIN H. KIPLINGER is editor in chief of *The Kiplinger Washington Letter.* His career has spanned five decades as a reporter, columnist, broadcast commentator and editor, specializing in business and political affairs. He has co-authored three best-selling books, *Boom and Inflation Ahead* (1958), *Washington Now* (1975) and *The Exciting '80s* (1979).

KNIGHT A. KIPLINGER is editor in chief of *Changing Times* magazine and associate editor of *The Kiplinger Washington Letter.* Before joining the Kiplinger organization in 1983, he spent 13 years covering Washington for newspapers throughout America. He is the co-author of *Washington Now* (1975) and *The New American Boom* (1986).

ABOUT THE KIPLINGER WASHINGTON EDITORS

Kiplinger Washington Editors, Inc. was founded in 1923 by W.M. Kiplinger, creator of the modern newsletter style. It publishes six business forecasting letters, with total circulations of 600,000, *Changing Times* magazine, with a circulation of one million, and books on a variety of business and personal-finance subjects.

The Kiplinger Letters include *The Kiplinger Washington Letter,* the most widely read business forecasting publication in the world, and letters on taxes, agriculture and the economies of California, Florida and Texas. The staff of the Kiplinger Letters keeps its readers ahead of trends in the broad economy, particular industries, personal investments, congressional activity, politics and world affairs.

The Kiplinger organization also publishes *Changing Times,* the first magazine of personal-finance guidance. Since its founding in 1947, *Changing Times* has advised its readers on investments, insurance, home ownership, cars, careers, retirement planning and much more. Recent titles from Kiplinger Books include *Make Your Money Grow, Buying and Selling a Home,* and *Sure Ways to Cut Your Taxes.*

For further information on Kiplinger publications, please write Subscriber Service, Kiplinger Washington Editors, Inc., 1729 H Street, N.W., Washington, D.C. 20006.